Between Us

Between Us

HEALING OURSELVES AND CHANGING THE
WORLD THROUGH SOCIOLOGY

*Edited by Marika Lindholm and
Elizabeth Anne Wood*

THE UNIVERSITY OF CHICAGO PRESS

CHICAGO AND LONDON

The University of Chicago Press, Chicago 60637

The University of Chicago Press, Ltd., London

© 2024 by The University of Chicago

Published 2024

Printed in the United States of America

33 32 31 30 29 28 27 26 25 24   1 2 3 4 5

ISBN-13: 978-0-226-82711-7 (cloth)
ISBN-13: 978-0-226-83387-3 (paper)
ISBN-13: 978-0-226-83386-6 (e-book)
DOI: https://doi.org/10.7208/chicago/9780226833866.001.0001

Library of Congress Cataloging-in-Publication Data

Names: Lindholm, Marika, editor. | Wood, Elizabeth Anne, editor.
Title: Between us : healing ourselves and changing the world through
    sociology / edited by Marika Lindholm and Elizabeth Anne Wood.
Description: Chicago : The University of Chicago Press, 2024. |
    Includes bibliographical references and index.
Identifiers: LCCN 2023049051 | ISBN 9780226827117 (cloth) |
    ISBN 9780226833873 (paperback) | ISBN 9780226833866 (ebook)
Subjects: LCSH: Sociology. | Social change. | Social justice. |
    Social problems. | Social structure. | BISAC: SOCIAL SCIENCE /
    Sociology / General | SOCIAL SCIENCE / Essays
Classification: LCC HM585 .B4844 2024 | DDC 301—dc23/eng/20231019
LC record available at https://lccn.loc.gov/2023049051

Contents

If You Want to Focus On . . .

Introduction

Dear Reader,

It's been hard lately. Climate change, wars, racist violence, political polarization, and the erosion of democracy have exposed the vulnerability of our individual and collective futures. Life has always been complicated, but now many of us are struggling just to maintain our mental health. We believe sociology provides the tools we need to find solace in our ability to make the world better and understand ourselves more fully. Sociology is powerful. By focusing on social interaction, social inequality, and social change, a sociological perspective offers insight into today's myriad of challenges.

In our search for guideposts, wisdom, and hope, we asked sociologists to write from the heart: to free powerful ideas from their academic trappings so that they resonate on an emotional level and show readers that thinking sociologically is useful and inspiring. We are confident that by connecting to the stories in *Between Us*, you will find a path toward healing. You will gain compassion for yourself and others while finding opportunities for working together to expand access to justice, peace, and happiness.

Sociology has helped both of us live more meaningful lives, and editing this collection revealed to us that other sociologists feel the same way. We are thrilled to introduce you to an eclectic group of contributors who were willing to step out of their academic comfort zone by sharing personal stories that, we believe, will promote empathy, understanding, and inspiration for change.

We each fell in love with sociology in college. Elizabeth remembers sitting in a Social Problems course and realizing there was a language and set of tools available to answer questions that had always puzzled her, especially about how unfair the world seemed. Mysterious injustices—her solo mom's constant financial struggles, painful wounds caused by bullying and sexual assault—suddenly made sense. She could see these were not solely personal experiences but part of larger social patterns, and that a sociological perspective offered insight into healing what could be healed while challenging what was fundamentally unjust. Indeed, Elizabeth is convinced that sociology saved her life as she's worked through clinical depression and anxiety. Medication and therapy have had their time and place, but it's sociology that gives her the framework she still uses to remind herself that she is not the problem: her depression and anxiety are connected to unreasonable role expectations, harmful cultural norms, and unjust social structures. That framework provides the tools needed to negotiate roles, challenge norms, and work to change the structures that cause injustice.

As a college junior, majoring in English, Marika took Intro to Sociology, and it blew her mind. Being given a framework for analyzing social problems like sexism, racism, and inequality was empowering and life changing. Instead of feeling hopeless and helpless, she found strength in understanding the social structures that constrain and cause pain. By launching a professional and personal life dedicated to learning about, teaching others about, and challenging inequality, sociology gave Marika a purpose. And although beliefs and institutions have been slow to shift toward a fairer society, she remains hopeful, determined, and ever so grateful to have discovered sociology many decades ago.

Sociology is often overlooked as a useful discipline for transforming lives. We know better. Sociology pulls back the curtain to reveal the communities, groups, and social structures that shape our lives. If we are unhappy, anxious, or wounded, we need to look for connections between our lives and the cultural forces and social systems that shape our experiences. Those systems are constructed and maintained by people and can be changed by people. But first, we have to see and understand. By sharing the personal stories of sociologists representing a wide array of experiences and backgrounds, we are excited to show you what's behind the curtain.

We've offered you two ways to navigate this book. The structure outlined below describes the way the book is organized from cover to cover. This is what you'll see reflected in the table of contents. At the same time, we recognize that there are many themes that transcend these chapters. For example, discussions related to race, class, and gender are woven throughout essays in each part of the book while other topics, like education, mental health, pop culture, and work, are common to several essays but don't have specific sections devoted to them. So, we've given you an alternative table of contents called "If You Want to Focus On . . ." to help you intentionally explore such additional topics in greater depth.

The first three parts of the book focus on foundational concepts to help you start thinking sociologically. Part one, **Discovering the Power of the Sociological Imagination**, introduces the value of thinking about the ways our individual lives are impacted by social expectations and norms. Whether it's Francesca Polletta coming to terms with blushing from embarrassment or Annette Lareau's description of grocery shopping with her adult son with autism, these essays demonstrate how social rules and expectations are acknowledged and challenged. In part two, **Navigating Social Structure, Culture, and Identity**, writers grapple with the day-to-day challenges of fitting in, expressing themselves, and navigating social structures that limit their agency. In essays that focus on Valentine's Day, YouTube videos, and more, we begin to understand the sociological wisdom of Harry Edwards's essay title "Dream with Your Eyes Open." Part three, **Facing Our Families and Communities**, recognizes that, for better or worse, we are embedded in families and communities, and that those ties and solidarities impact our well-being, identity, and place in the social structure. Amin Ghaziani's essay describes the comfort of finding a community where his coming out as queer and as an activist was valued. Together, these first three parts provide tools for thinking about the ways that norms, groups, and social structures impact how we think, feel, and react.

In parts four through seven, sociologists share their experiences of privilege and marginalization based on identity. We begin to see how class, race, ethnicity, gender, and sexual orientation shape opportunity and well-being. Our examination of life in a stratified society starts with part four, **Confronting Class and Status**. Whether it's Doug Massey remembering how his paternal grandmother looked down on his less economically privileged mother or Vivian Louie realizing that attending Harvard University wasn't a magic ticket to upper-class status, these essays expose the pain and challenge of unequal opportunity. Part five, **Crossing Borders and Ethnic Divides**, offers a behind-the-scenes perspective on immigrant legacies and ethnic identity. For example, Marta Tienda, a child of migrant workers, painfully reminisces about the scars that come with poverty and immigrant status. Each story poignantly offers a human connection to combat stereotypes and inflammatory headlines that obscure sociological truths. In part six, **Resisting Racism**, Black, white, and biracial contributors write openly about the impact of racial discrimination and racist legacies. Writers explore sociological concepts such as "double consciousness" and "white spaces" in their personal stories, offering insight into the structures and institutions that contribute to the daily psychological and physical onslaught of racism. For example, both Linsey Edwards and Heather Washington share their discomfort as Black women in "white spaces"—Washington in Appalachia where Confederate flags make her outsider status threateningly clear and Edwards in a fertility clinic where stereotypes about Black womanhood render her invisible. The essays in part seven, **Rewriting the Rules of Sex and Gender**, are personal and revelatory. Focusing on gender ideology and expectations around sexuality, each essay asks us to expand our ideas about what it means to be male or female or straight or gay. Whether it's Tey Meadow describing the psychologically liberating feeling of dressing in masculine clothes or C Ray Borck recognizing the harmful power of hegemonic masculinity in his experience as a trans man, these essays question the value of rigid sex and gender norms.

The essays in parts four through seven open a window onto experiences that might be all too familiar or completely foreign, based on your identity. Our hope is that they inspire you to be more compassionate about the pain of inequality and give you the courage to speak out against the injustices you witness. By sharing their truth, each sociologist offers awareness and inspiration for a kinder and more just society.

You may have noticed that this collection frames sociology as an active pursuit rather than something to be passively absorbed. This book provides readers a broader understanding of the world and suggests ways to advocate for social change. For those seeking an alternative to conventional self-help books, *Between Us* offers new ways to think and feel better. Thus, the essays in part eight, **Healing and Changing the World**, end on a transformative and inspirational note. These essays, such as "I Am Neo" by Michael Walker, remind us that once we've seen behind the curtain (or the computer code), we can't unsee! You will be able to imagine new futures while more clearly understanding the past and the present. You will see patterns where you previously felt pushed around by unpredictable forces. You will blame yourself less for your own problems when you see the social forces behind them. And you'll also see where your actions may contribute to the troubles of others, motivating you to work to make things better.

We hope reading these powerful real-life stories, all told by sociologists working for change, impacting lives, and healing themselves, provides a transformative experience. Our wish is that reading *Between Us* helps you become a more compassionate and powerful person, one who can heal yourself, inspire others, and work with others to create the kinds of communities and institutions that foster justice and peace.

Warmly,
Elizabeth and Marika

PART 1

Discovering the Power of the Sociological Imagination

Neither the life of an individual nor the history of a society can be understood without understanding both.

C. Wright Mills

1

My Son with Autism Breaks the Rules

Annette Lareau

Some sociologists have done "breaching experiments" where they break **social norms**—for example, by facing the wall in an elevator—as a way to reveal powerful, invisible social rules and sanctions shaping daily life. Our son with autism, now middle-aged, is a person whose interesting and valuable perspective on the world leads him to constantly perform breaching experiments. As someone frozen in time, developmentally, with many skills similar to those of three-year-old children, he often loudly comments on the world around him—both aware and unaware of key social norms.

Richard is mesmerized by death as well as the passage of time—which he only partially understands. "You won't be here in 2050!" he says. "No," I say, slightly somberly. He cheerfully smiles and says, "Nope!" (I use a pseudonym when writing about my son. He understands, in a very basic fashion, that I write stories about him, just as he draws pictures. But, of course, he cannot truly grasp the concepts of the social sciences, public sociology, or peer review.)

I bring him to my office, as I have to pick up something. I introduce him to my department chair, who is in her late fifties. "Richard, this is Sarah." Immediately and loudly, he says, "She is an *old* lady." I apologize. She takes it in good humor, saying, "Why yes, I *am* old."

Sometimes his breaches move into more socially charged territory. We two white people are in the grocery store. An African American clerk is rapidly scanning our chicken, canned tomatoes, and yogurts. I am getting out my wallet when I hear Richard loudly ask, "IS HE FROM AFRICA?" Flushing a bright red, and glancing with an embarrassed smile at the clerk, I say in an elevated voice, "No! He is American! He is African *American*. He was born here—just like you and me." I add,

"He is helping us with our groceries, and he is doing a super job." The clerk is smiling broadly. I say to him, more quietly, "Sorry." He waves me off and continues to chuckle as he scans the remaining groceries. Richard's social blunder, which suggested an exclusion of an African American employee from legitimate birthright and citizenship in the United States due to skin color, was worse because of its public nature—much worse, for example, than a young person asking their parents the same question quietly at the dinner table. Social rules vary by social context.

On good days, our son makes us laugh. He makes announcements, such as "Don't go to sleep underwater." He tells me, "Young over" on the day he turns forty.

He draws countless pictures of animals. He remembers the birthdays of people he met briefly two decades earlier. He is mesmerized that babies small enough to hold in one's arms grow up to be too big to be held. He charms us and others. But on bad days, he yells, says mean, racist things, throws items, and, from time to time, hits people. He also changes as he ages. Recently, he was kicked out of his job (a "sheltered workshop") and his group home due to his tendency to threaten to attack people. Longer interactions are harder for him now, and he declines invitations to go swimming or deliver Meals-on-Wheels. I no longer take him to work or the grocery store.

Nonetheless, Richard continues to pick up on topics that are taboo. "We don't talk about Dad's turkey neck," he says in a questioning voice. "No," I agree, "we don't." "We don't talk about Black people; it might hurt their feelings," he says excitedly. He seems to like to talk about race, since he also knows it makes some people uncomfortable. His words are yet another reminder of social stigmas surrounding bodily changes connected to aging and broader racial hierarchies.

In the past, when we had young white people helping us take care of Richard, they often looked visibly nervous when I mentioned his quirks about talking about race. A few refused to take him out, panicked he might say something offensive in public. His socially inappropriate pronouncements about wrinkles, turkey necks, and babies didn't rattle them in the same way. Of course, racism is ingrained in America. But for whites, along with others, having conversations on the topic is one of many paths forward.

Richard's life also teaches us about the **stigma** connected to disability. This stigma actually almost never surfaces in face-to-face interactions, as people are remarkably kind, cordial, and helpful with Richard. (The grocery clerk was not unusual in responding to our son's social breach with smiles and laughter.) Social policies are a different matter. And many fail to see the gifts people with disabilities bring to the world; instead, they envelop people with disabilities in a veil of silence, embarrassment, and social devaluation.

Our son teaches me the incredible speed of social interaction. It often takes people just a few seconds to grasp that our son is socially deviant, and virtually never longer than one minute. I am struck by how much information people process in mere seconds and, especially, how many social adjustments they are making. These rapid-fire social adjustments are difficult for sociologists to illuminate, but that doesn't make them unimportant. Indeed, we need more studies that capture these speedy social modifications that people make to one another as we recreate social life.

In the end, there are countless social rules that help form our social structure. Many of them are invisible, making them hard to grasp. Yet, social structure is particularly important to see in a society that overemphasizes individualism—where we tend to assume our outcomes are socially connected to our efforts. We tend to dismiss the impact of social forces such as class, race, and gender on our lives, despite powerful evidence to the contrary.

Richard, as with every person, is a human being and worthy of love and respect. Additionally, as someone who is autistic, one of his many gifts is that he creates social breaches that, paradoxically, reveal routine social norms. These norms range from which topics of conversation are appropriate when checking out at the grocery store to social expectations and perceptions of people of a different gender, race, age, or class.

Ultimately, our son and others who have neurologically diverse reactions to life help us see the world in new ways. They often reveal deeply embedded **social scripts** that structure and transform our daily lives. These social scripts matter, not only because they guide life, but also because they create advantages and unequal opportunities for members of different social groups. By studying these social scripts with nuance and clarity, we introduce the possibility of changing social life to create a more just and equitable world.

KEY CONCEPTS

Social norms — Rules of expected behavior shared by members of a given group or society. Social norms become all the more obvious when people defy expectations, such as wearing a bathing suit on an airplane.

Social scripts — A series of expected behaviors in a particular situation or environment. For example, parishioners at a Catholic Mass follow a social script with a familiar and elaborate set of rituals that are expected in that environment.

Stigma — A personal attribute that disqualifies someone from full social acceptance. Stigma also impacts treatment of a person and can alter a person's own identity and understanding of themselves. The stigma of mental illness and the stigma of poverty are just two examples of the negative and unfair beliefs that negatively impact how an individual is perceived.

DISCUSSION QUESTIONS

1. What is your experience with neurodiversity? Do you or others you know breach social scripts as a result of neurodiversity? What kinds of responses have you witnessed?
2. Discuss the potential value of studying social scripts from a sociological perspective.
3. Can you remember a time when you stepped outside of a social script, intentionally or unintentionally? What caused you to depart from the script? How did others respond, and how did you feel?

LEARN MORE

Becker, Howard S. *Outsiders: Studies in the Sociology of Deviance*. New York: Free Press, 1963.

Falk, Gerhard. *Stigma: How We Treat Outsiders*. New York: Prometheus, 2001.

Goffman, Irving. *Stigma: Notes on the Management of Spoiled Identity*. Saddle River, NJ: Prentice-Hall, 1963.

Snyder, Sharon L., and David T. Mitchell. *Cultural Locations of Disability*. Chicago: University of Chicago Press, 2006.

Solomon, Andrew. *Far from the Tree: Parents, Children, and the Search for Identity*. New York: Scribner, 2012.

Annette Lareau is a professor in the Department of Sociology at the University of Pennsylvania. She is the author of the award-winning books *Unequal Childhoods* and *Home Advantage*. She is the coauthor, with Blair Sackett, of *We Thought It Would Be Heaven: Refugees in an Unequal America* (University of California Press, 2023). Her book *Listening to People: A Practical Guide to Interviewing, Participant-Observation, Data Analysis, and Writing It All Up* was published by the University of Chicago Press. Funded by the National Science Foundation and the Russell Sage Foundation, she is currently doing a study of the blessings and challenges of wealth for families. Annette Lareau is a past president of the American Sociological Association.

2

Saving the World, One Blush at a Time

Francesca Polletta

I blush a lot. I blush when I speak up in a seminar and everyone turns to look at me. I blush when someone asks me a question that I don't have the answer to. I blush when I talk about sex in my lectures. Sometimes I blush for no reason. Not just two pink spots on my cheeks: my whole face and neck turn crimson. "Look, I'm making you blush," the person to whom I'm talking says. I blush harder.

I used to think that getting embarrassed so easily—and showing it in vivid color—was a sign of my social awkwardness. I yearned for the poise that would let me sail through interactions with sangfroid—cold blood. Now I know that my inability to do that is a sign of just how socially adjusted I am.

To explain why, let me tell you about a couple of the many, many times that I have been embarrassed. Once was at the annual meeting of the American Sociological Association. The ASA meeting, which is usually held in a few big hotels in a chosen city each year, is a chance for sociologists to present our new research, look for jobs or people to fill them, and catch up with old friends and mentors. So, I was delighted, this particular year, when I saw a friend from my days in New York strolling into the lobby. "Hey, you!" I called out happily and strode over to grab her in a tight bear hug.

It was then that I realized she was not, in fact, my friend. I had confused her with someone else. The person I was now hugging was an eminent sociologist, whom I had recently met when she visited my department to evaluate it. Departmental reviews every ten or so years are routine, but they matter—and my colleagues and I were still waiting to hear the results of our review when I flung myself on our reviewer.

For a split second, I considered brazening it out: pretending that this was the way I greeted everyone, whether I knew them intimately or not. But my red face made that impossible, and I stammered out an apology before slinking away.

"I *died* of embarrassment," I moaned to my sister later. Yeah, she agreed, pretty bad. It was like the time she met a famous actress and gushed about her latest movie—only to realize mid-sentence that the movie she was talking about starred a different famous actress. "What did you *do*?" I asked. "I pretended I knew I was talking about someone else," she said. "In fact, cool as a cucumber, I asked her if she had seen the movie. We talked about it—smooth as can be." My sister had had the right idea, I concluded gloomily. My own lack of composure had made my encounter that much worse.

Sociologist Erving Goffman would disagree. In fact, he would credit me—the one slinking off with face afire—for having saved the day.

Goffman opened his remarkable essay from 1956 on embarrassment by detailing symptoms that are as familiar today as they were when he wrote about them: blushing, fumbling, stammering, "a feeling of wobbliness, consciousness of strained and unnatural gestures, a dazed sensation, dryness of the mouth, and tense muscles." Equally familiar, he wrote, is what we do to try to conceal our embarrassment: "the fixed smile, the nervous hollow laugh, the busy hands, the downward glance." Why do we get embarrassed?

"Whatever else, embarrassment has to do with the figure the individual cuts before others," Goffman explained. We feel embarrassed when we realize we are presenting ourselves to others in ways that are different from who we really are. We are not that clumsy, that naïve, that clueless, that uncontrolled in our bodily functions. (When I ask my students about embarrassing experiences, passing gas comes up frequently.)

Of course, some people are more prone to embarrassment than others. But Goffman argued that features of modern life put all of us in potentially embarrassing situations. We moderns have dispensed with some of the older rituals of deference that used to govern our relations with people higher in the pecking order. We no longer curtsy to our social superiors; in fact, we often call them by their first names. But we still are expected to behave in ways that are appropriate to our **social role** and our place in the status hierarchy—and when we don't, the results can be mortifying.

Imagine, I say to my students, that you are celebrating your birthday with friends in a local restaurant. You are being joyfully loud and silly and having a wonderful time. Then, you look to the next table over and see—me.

My students agree that the situation would be embarrassing. Why? Because they usually present themselves to me as studious and responsible, and now they are presenting themselves as something else. The self they have "projected," Goffman wrote, "is somehow confronted with another self which, though valid in other contexts, cannot be here sustained in harmony with the first."

We like to believe that we have only one self, but Goffman recognized that in our different roles, we really are different selves. In fact, to perform each role well, we have to be. Luckily, most of the time, our roles are segregated. My students and I meet each other only in the classroom or perhaps in the hall, places that don't put our roles in conflict. Sometimes, though, "worlds collide," as George Costanza put it on *Seinfeld*. In such situations, embarrassment is not the result of having "lost" one's composure. In fact, embarrassment is not located in the individual at all, but rather "in the social system wherein he has his several selves," according to Goffman, who was writing at a time when masculine pronouns were still used to refer to everyone.

But here's the really interesting part. We *are* the social system. Every time we interact with people, we are, along with them, responsible for ensuring the interaction unfolds successfully—that is, without someone bursting into tears, punching someone in the face, or leaving with the feeling that their status has been questioned. But interactions are *difficult*. Things go wrong quite frequently. Someone says the wrong thing or misses a cue or laughs in the wrong place and suddenly it seems like the interaction might be going off the rails. This is why embarrassment, far from being a sign of social failure, is actually a means of **social repair**. When the student demonstrates their embarrassment in the restaurant—*performing* it by reddening, removing the breadbasket awkwardly from their head, shushing their friends—they demonstrate to me that they are aware of the breach they committed. They perform the deference that both they and I believe is my due as their professor and on which their grade and my self-esteem depend.

Let's go back to my encounter at the ASA meeting. What if I had *not* blushed and stammered an apology to my wrongly-identified-friend-who-was-in-fact-my-evaluator? What if I had instead shown the aplomb my sister did with the Hollywood actress? Perhaps the professor would have worried that I was feigning intimacy in a callous bid to secure a good departmental review. Alternatively, and perhaps worse, she might have assumed that I (and perhaps others in my department) didn't recognize the importance of departmental reviews. The professor might have wondered why she even bothered to do such reviews when they were so clearly unappreciated, treated by people like me as some kind of social bonding opportunity. And if this professor, and others, stopped doing reviews, then might departments stop striving to meet the standards to which they claimed to be committed? According to Goffman's standards, by sacrificing my composure in that moment, I rescued the whole system of academic excellence and the collegial work on which it depends.

A few weeks after I taught my class about Goffman and embarrassment, I was having dinner with my husband at a local restaurant when a young man I vaguely recognized from class came up to our table. "Professor Polletta," he announced gleefully, "I'm here. And I'm not embarrassed!" I laughed, but I also blushed. I wasn't sure what to do: Should I invite the student to join us? Try to explain why he might not be embarrassed? Was he suggesting Goffman was wrong? Was he showing me up? I felt that my authority had been undermined, and I could only laugh ruefully in recognition of that fact.

The episode made me realize that people without power have the capacity to unsettle those with power simply by failing to be embarrassed. Think about what protesters do. They sit down on streets or push their way into offices where they are not supposed to be. They chant, they yell. When they are asked to leave, they stay put. Protesters' refusal to perform the embarrassment typically associated with violating the status hierarchy shifts the responsibility for social repair to the authorities. The authorities may call the police, but if the protesters have not harmed anyone or destroyed anything, such a show of force risks looking inappropriate and even unjust. Bystanders may take the side of the protesters, which in turn may undermine the authority of those in charge.

In short, refusing to abide by **rituals of deference** exposes and unsettles the relations of power. If you have ever participated in a demonstration, you know that raising your voice in that first chant is difficult— and for people like me, who are embarrassed easily, it is excruciating.

But if you continue on, chanting and waving your banner, you may begin to feel a subtle shift in which the burden of social repair shifts away from you, and the power in the interaction shifts *to* you.

Social order is more fragile than we ordinarily think. This helps explain why we engage in elaborate performances of embarrassment if we have just slightly missed the mark in performing a role. By the same token, though, insofar as the social order is constraining, we also—all of us—have the power to transform it.

KEY CONCEPTS

Rituals of deference — Acts that convey appreciation and respect for an elder, stranger, or authority figure, such as shaking hands, holding open a door, or using formal speech. For instance, in a courtroom, a lawyer would say "Objection, your honor," rather than "Hey bruh, I object."

Social repair — Offering a clear sign of deference to make up for a social breach in which deference was inappropriately withheld or denied. For example, if a patient mistakenly calls her female doctor "Nurse," the patient may show embarrassment and overzealously call the physician "Doctor" to make up for her faux pas.

Social role — A set of attitudes and behaviors expected of an individual based on their status or position in a given setting. Students, for example, are expected to attend class, study, complete assignments, join clubs and organizations, and explore careers. They might also be employees, though, who are expected to be on the job forty hours a week. Some might be parents, too, and have children to care for. We often experience conflict as a result of the competing expectations of our many different roles.

DISCUSSION QUESTIONS

1. Think about a time when you were embarrassed. What social expectation was at the root of the embarrassment? Did you hide your embarrassment, or did it show, as Polletta's does? Having read Polletta's essay, would you be more or less inclined to show your embarrassment in the future? Why or why not?

2. Polletta links emotion to the tension between maintaining social order and pushing for social change. She refers to those who "re-

fuse to be embarrassed" as the ones who push for social change. Can you think of a time when feeling embarrassed might be a sign that we need to work for social change (rather than fixing our own behavior)?

3. Polletta refers to Goffman's ideas about how we perform different selves in different situations. This doesn't mean we're being false, but rather that different parts of ourselves are relevant in different situations. Goffman lived in a time before social media. In what ways might his ideas about embarrassment have been different if he'd been writing in an age of social media?

LEARN MORE

Caplow, Theodore. "Christmas Gifts and Kin Networks." *American Sociological Review* 47, no. 3 (1982): 383–392.

Effler, Erika Summers. *Laughing Saints and Righteous Heroes: Emotional Rhythms in Social Movement Groups.* Chicago: University of Chicago Press, 2010.

Goffman, Erving. "Embarrassment and Social Organization." *American Journal of Sociology* 62, no. 3 (1956): 264–271.

Hochschild, Arlie Russell. *The Managed Heart: Commercialization of Feeling, Updated with a New Preface,* 3rd ed. Oakland: University of California Press, 2012.

Francesca Polletta is Chancellor's Professor of Sociology at the University of California, Irvine. She studies politics, social movements, and civic life, and is the author of *Freedom Is an Endless Meeting: Democracy in American Social Movements* (University of Chicago Press, 2002), *It Was Like a Fever: Storytelling in Protest and Politics* (Chicago, 2006), and *Inventing the Ties That Bind: Imagined Relationships in Moral and Political Life* (Chicago, 2020). With Jeff Goodwin and James M. Jasper, she is the editor of *Passionate Politics: Emotions and Social Movements* (Chicago, 2001). She is currently studying when and how social movements change not just laws and policies but people's opinions, beliefs, values, and everyday practices.

3

Mediocre

Abigail Saguy

One day in 1981, when I was in the second semester of fifth grade, I walked into my father's office and proudly announced, "I am mediocre."

I was proud that I'd found the perfect context in which to use this new vocabulary word. You see, my English teacher, Ms. Lobelle, who was also my math, science, and social studies teacher, had told us to try to use all our weekly vocabulary words in a sentence. I'd decided that I was mediocre because I was in the middle academic track of my school and was getting straight Bs—a middle grade, neither excellent (an A) nor terrible (a C or below).

I'd spent the previous year in England, where my father—an academic sociologist—had been on sabbatical at Oxford University. That year, something had clicked, and I had excelled academically. The public school system in White Plains, New York, however, did not have access to my academic records from England. Instead, they had tracked me based on my standardized test scores from two years ago, before I had had my breakout moment.

I enjoyed the positive affirmation I received that year for my academic excellence and had been working diligently all year to receive the same sort of feedback from Ms. Lobelle. Yet, despite earning near-perfect scores on all individual assignments, when it came time to assign grades for the fall semester report card, Ms. Lobelle gave me straight Bs. Initially, I responded by working even harder, convinced that, if I could prove I belonged in the higher academic track, I would be "moved up." But on that fateful afternoon in my father's home office, I was coming to embrace Ms. Lobelle's definition of the situation. I was mediocre. I remember feeling a certain relief in giving in.

I was not expecting my words to upset my dad or spur him to action, but they did. "What?" he cried. "Mediocre? You aren't mediocre! What makes you say that?" I explained: the middle track, the middle grades, my powerlessness to change any of it.

My matter-of-fact proclamation of my own mediocrity was a red flag for my dad. He knew about the power of **self-fulfilling prophecies**. He had read the studies and understood that if I began to internalize a sense of myself as mediocre, I risked becoming mediocre. He was not going to let that happen.

He requested an appointment with Ms. Lobelle to discuss why she had assigned final grades that did not reflect the grades I had earned on individual assignments. I don't remember everything that was said, but I do remember a moment when my father stood up and raised his voice. My teacher stood up and yelled back at him. I felt afraid and confused. I think it was in this meeting that I first heard Ms. Lobelle call me an "overachiever." I didn't know what that meant, but she seemed to mean that I was performing above where I would naturally if my parents had not been pressuring me. This confused me, as my parents never asked about my grades or helped me with my homework. I felt an inner drive to excel and be recognized for my achievements. Whereas I felt grateful that my father was defending my right to be evaluated fairly for my work, Ms. Lobelle presented herself as defending me against parents who were pushing me too hard.

After that terrifying meeting, my father appealed to the principal. When the principal supported Ms. Lobelle, Dad went to the superintendent. Ultimately, the superintendent intervened, and I was moved into the highest track, where I promptly began to earn straight As. Later, I was also put into the "gifted and talented" program. Through my dad's intervention, the mediocre prophecy was halted, and another supplanted it: I was intelligent, capable, and had grit.

Self-fulfilling prophecies are part of a larger phenomenon of what sociologists call **labeling**. We know that, for good or bad, how a person is labeled has ramifications for what they do and who they become. When later I declared that I was "bad at math," my dad said, "Nonsense! You're excellent at math!" He then proceeded to make it so by insisting that I continue to take the most difficult math classes offered through high school, helping me when I struggled, and repeatedly telling me how good I was at math. After a while, it was easier just to accept the new label!

When my younger brother—who had a severe case of dyslexia—was struggling in school and beginning to think of himself as stupid, my father again intervened. My dad, who had himself struggled with dyslexia as a boy, provided an (admittedly gendered but extremely helpful) analogy that was both consistent with my brother's experiences and predicted a rosy future. My dad told my brother that my brother's classmates were riding mares. Mares are relatively easy to ride, so his classmates were moving along nicely at a comfortable trot. In contrast, my brother was riding a stallion. The stallion was not yet tamed; as a result, my brother was being tossed around and thrown into the mud. Still, my dad predicted my brother was going to tame that stallion and, when he did, he would be riding a more powerful beast than that of his classmates. At that point, he would shoot past them. That analogy—along with years of excellent private tutoring—helped my brother overcome his dyslexia without internalizing a sense of himself as stupid. Once he did, he excelled academically, ultimately becoming a head-and-neck surgeon and a patient tutor for his own young children.

My fifth-grade experience also taught me the importance of **cultural capital**—that is, social resources, such as education, mannerisms, and tastes, that are associated with higher social class. Money was tight growing up in my family. As a professor at Queens College in the City University of New York in the 1970s and early 1980s, my dad didn't earn a lot of money, and my mom was not employed outside the home at the time. As such, I couldn't have the designer jeans that many of my friends had, and I was embarrassed that our pantry was stocked with "no frills" peanut butter and toilet paper. In other words, my family did not have a lot of economic capital (although we always found money for things that were really important, such as my brother's tutoring). But my dad's PhD and family background, as the child of two physicians from a prominent Jewish family in Providence, Rhode Island, gave him valued cultural capital. Being better educated with more advanced degrees than my teachers, the principal, or even the superintendent, my dad was not easily intimidated. Indeed, his cultural capital gave him (and, by extension, me) real power.

It was that cultural capital that emboldened my father to challenge Ms. Lobelle, the school principal, and the superintendent of the entire district. A parent without a college degree, an immigrant, or someone who did not speak English would have had more difficulty challenging these authority figures. Their child might have never moved out of Ms. Lobelle's class and may have internalized a sense of themself as mediocre.

These early childhood experiences provided two insights that would later inform my sociological research. First, how people understand and define the world has far-reaching implications. Second, people are not equally able to impose their perceptions of reality. These dual insights led me to study the material effects of framing, as well as how oppressed groups are sometimes able to redefine the world in ways that give them greater autonomy. For instance, I studied how women have been able to reframe behavior that previously had no name as what we now label sexual harassment. I examined how fat-acceptance activists have reframed bigger bodies as a civil rights issue rather than as a sign of medical pathology. And I've studied how a wide range of groups have harnessed the notion of "coming out" as a certain kind of person to resist others' definitions of them as sinful, pathological, illegal, or unworthy.

These insights also inform my work as a teacher, faculty mentor, and department chair. Beyond what I teach my students in class, I remind them that they are capable and worthy, that they belong at UCLA, whether as an undergraduate or graduate student. The other day, I jokingly said to a graduate student, "Our graduate admissions committee never makes a mistake," but the underlying message was serious: "You were admitted; you can do it. You belong." The student, a first-generation college student, told me that he tells himself the same thing and that it helps him quell his own doubts about his capacity to succeed in academia. One of the most rewarding aspects of serving as department chair has been to be able to offer empowering and affirming frames for my colleagues—of themselves and their work (for example, in a letter making a case for promotion or a well-deserved raise) or more informally in my discussions with the dean or other administrators. Paying it forward, advocating for others as others advocated for you, or how you wish they had, can be extremely healing and empowering.

KEY CONCEPTS

Cultural capital — Pierre Bourdieu coined the term to describe symbolic resources and social assets that communicate one's social status, such as style of speech, knowledge of the arts, education, and even leisure activities that can be used to one's advantage. Saguy explains that although her family lacked economic capital, her father's PhD gave him valued cultural capital, including the power to successfully advocate on her behalf.

Labeling — The process of defining someone based on a behavior or characteristic they exhibit. For example, a child who likes to be the center of attention might be labeled by a teacher or their classmates as a "class clown." If a person accepts the label, it can influence their behavior and sense of self.

Self-fulfilling prophecy — A psychological phenomenon in which an originally false belief leads people to act in ways that make that belief true. For instance, Saguy's father didn't want her to internalize the label of "mediocre," so he advocated for her to ultimately be placed in a gifted and talented program, and Saguy excelled with this new definition of herself.

DISCUSSION QUESTIONS

1. Saguy's story touches on the power of labeling, especially in schools. Labels can stick to us and affect our educational outcomes. Where else do you see the power of labeling in action?
2. What cultural capital do you possess because of your home or school environment? Do you think you would benefit by acquiring different kinds of cultural capital? How would you go about doing so?
3. Saguy uses her position to create affirming frames for her students and colleagues. Do you see places in your own life where changing the way something is framed could help you improve the situation for yourself or for someone else?

LEARN MORE

Berger, Peter L., and Thomas Luckmann. *The Social Construction of Reality: A Treatise in the Sociology of Knowledge*. Garden City, NY: Doubleday, 1966.

Bourdieu, Pierre. "Cultural Reproduction and Social Reproduction." In *Knowledge, Education, and Cultural Change*, ed. Richard Brown. London: Tavistock Publications, 1973.

Goffman, Erving. *Frame Analysis: An Essay on the Organization of Experience*. Cambridge, MA: Harvard University Press, 1974.

McCloud, Jay. *Ain't No Makin' It: Aspiration and Attainment in a Low-Income Neighborhood*. Boulder: Westview Press, 1995.

Abigail Saguy is a UCLA professor and chair of sociology with a courtesy appointment in gender studies. She holds a PhD from Princeton University (2000) and from the Ecole des Hautes Etudes en Sciences Sociales (EHESS, Paris, France, 1999). Professor Saguy has been a Robert Wood Johnson Scholar in Health Policy Research at Yale University (2000–2002), a fellow at the Center for Advanced Studies in the Behavioral Sciences at Stanford University (2008–2009), and a visiting scholar at the Russell Sage Foundation (2023–2024). Professor Saguy's research has been funded by the National Science Foundation, the American Sociological Association, the French Government, and the Council for European Studies. She is the author of the books *What Is Sexual Harassment? From Capitol Hill to the Sorbonne* (University of California Press, 2003), *What's Wrong with Fat?* (Oxford University Press, 2013), and *Come Out, Come Out, Whoever You Are* (Oxford, 2020); over thirty scientific journal articles; and several op-eds published in leading news outlets. She is currently writing a book (under contract with Russell Sage) about how the concept of gender neutrality has been deployed in the law, in the news media, and by activists to advance (or resist) gender equality and diversity.

4

An Accidental Sociologist Learns the Power of Listening

Jessie Daniels

For some people, going to graduate school is inevitable. Like a plumber entering the family business, they go because their parents went, maybe even their grandparents. In academia, something like a *third* of all faculty have a parent with a PhD. For me, graduate school existed in a different universe from the one I'd been raised, in which a "PhD" was derisively referred to as an acronym for either "Post Hole Digger" or "Piled Higher and Deeper." Entering grad school for me meant that I was crossing a threshold into a world of ideas. This world was one that I was both poorly prepared for and desperate to enter because I wanted it to transform me.

It's surprising I crossed the threshold at all. I'd thought about maybe going to law school but didn't really know about this thing called "graduate school" until a sociology professor, Dr. Joy Reeves, invited me to her office and suggested I go. I don't know where I thought professors came from, but I'm certain I'd never heard of grad school before she talked to me about it. She wanted me to go to her alma mater, LSU, but I knew I wanted to live in Austin, not Baton Rouge. So, I moved to Austin, worked as a receptionist for a team of lawyers for a few months before realizing I had no love for the law, then applied to grad school.

I wrote a crappy entrance essay—more of a paragraph, really—about my desire to end world hunger. I had read every word in the textbooks assigned to me as an undergraduate, but I'd never read an academic journal article or an entire book by a sociologist or any scholar before I applied to the PhD program in sociology at the University of Texas. By some miracle of keeping enrollment numbers up, I got accepted, but without any sort of financial package. If I was going to get a PhD in sociology, I was going to have to pay for it myself.

For the first two years of grad school, I worked as a bookkeeper during the day and cleaned offices at night because I hadn't been savvy enough to apply for the tuition waivers, stipends, and research opportunities my classmates received. I took afternoon or early evening classes, read what was assigned, and understood little of what I read. My eyes scanned over entire pages as I gleaned meanings in phrases and clauses, but whole arguments eluded me. I couldn't have been the only one, but unlike some of my more blasé classmates, I felt I couldn't afford the luxury of a cool pose. I was desperate to understand my own existence.

I would have dropped out if it hadn't been for a seminar I took that first year called simply Gender. In it, I read articles and books that I could actually understand, like the landmark feminist anthology *All Women Are White, All Blacks Are Men, But Some of Us Are Brave*. Although I could grasp the readings for this seminar, I still struggled to make connections between them. Yet being able to understand the readings in this one class gave me the confidence to think I just might be able to figure out the rest.

I thought that if I could find a way to work for one of the professors, I might have a better shot at making it through grad school and at least quit the bookkeeping job, so I knocked on Dr. Joe Feagin's door early in my second year. I'd heard about his research on race and ethnicity. Reading about the intersection of race, gender, and class made me want to learn more, but there were no grad classes on this being offered. What I knew about race came mostly from reading *To Kill a Mockingbird*, growing up in south Texas, and having discussions with my father. In other words, I knew nothing.

"So, why me?" Dr. Feagin asked. "There are lots of other professors on this hallway." He didn't smile much.

"I'd like to learn more about race and ethnicity, especially Native Americans. My father says we're . . ."

"Wait, let me guess: Cherokee? And it's your grandmother?" He chuckled knowingly, yet still looked severe and serious.

"Well, yes. Why is that funny?"

"You need to read Vine Deloria. He has a book, let me see if I have a copy of it here . . ." He searched the walls of books that lined his office on every side, shelved in no easily discernible order, but managed to put his hand on a tattered paperback with a bright red cover. The black print read *Custer Died for Your Sins*.

"Here you go, read this. He worked at the National Congress of American Indians and says he would have a white person come into his office almost every day, claiming they had a Cherokee grandmother." He thumbed through the book. "Ah, here's the passage: 'I once did a project backward and discovered that evidently most tribes were entirely female for the first three hundred years of white occupation. No one, it seemed, wanted to claim a male Indian as a forebear.'" *Great, I'm such a cliché that I'm even in a book.* I felt humiliated but undaunted. Still, I asked to borrow the book.

"Sure, keep it. I think I have another copy." I couldn't believe he'd just met me and was giving me a book for free. Books were shelved and stacked and scattered everywhere in his office; he clearly lived and breathed them. I wanted exactly that—to be slathered in books and ideas and words, to have such an abundance of all these that I could casually give away books to people I'd just met. I couldn't imagine being any richer or happier than to have that, to be what he was to me in that moment.

I finished the book later that night, but the key passage was on one of the opening pages: "It doesn't take much insight into racial attitudes to understand the real meaning of the Indian-grandmother complex that plagues certain whites. A male ancestor has too much of the aura of the savage warrior, the unknown primitive, the instinctive animal, to make him a respectable member of the family tree. But a young Indian princess? Ah, there was royalty for the taking. Somehow the white was linked with a noble house of gentility and culture if his grandmother was an Indian princess who ran away with an intrepid pioneer."

I felt ashamed that I had ever believed my father's stories about our Indian ancestry. The moccasins? They were probably from a county fair. My desire to learn how to bead so I could be "like my Indian grandmother"? Based on a lie.

Dr. Feagin hired me as a research assistant who ran library errands for him: copying abstracts, clipping them into perfect squares, taping them onto paper, and presenting him with batches from which he'd select the ones he wanted. I'd then return to the library to copy the complete articles. Sometimes he would have me write letters directly to leading scholars in the field asking for their latest publications. Doing so made me nervous, but introducing myself as Dr. Feagin's research assistant felt like protection.

"You've got to drop the 'Dr. Feagin' and 'Sir' bit and call me *Joe*," he said to me one day. "You don't say 'ma'am' to Christine or call her 'Dr. Williams,' do you? That's a little bit sexist, don't you think?"

"Yes, sir." He had a point, but I found this lifelong habit a hard one to break. I clearly had more regard for male professors than I did for the handful of female sociology professors. I wasn't proud of it, but there it was: the patriarchy had seeped into me. I could only wonder where else it lurked in my assumptions.

"And the 'yes, sir' bit, especially! Was your father in the military?" he chuckled, trying to cajole me out of my salutational habit. "Those are the students who usually have the hardest time calling me 'Joe' and the only ones who say, 'yes sir' to me."

"Well, yes"—I caught myself before I "sir"-ed again—"my dad was in the military, but before I was born. A paratrooper, stationed in Japan, during the occupation." I wished I could stop talking. He didn't actually want to hear about my father's military service, I told myself. "I'll work on it."

Having proven my usefulness on research errands, Joe asked me to work on revising his textbook. Each chapter was about a different racial or ethnic group. For each one, my job was to find the latest research on that group at the library. Joe then transformed that research into paragraphs that I read and reviewed. Doing this, I learned about how Native Americans had been treated in the United States and how different immigrant groups, like the Irish, **assimilated** into dominant culture. I learned that sometimes people from one ethnic group filled almost an entire job category, only to be replaced by more recent immigrants from another country in a subsequent decade. Joe invited me to coauthor the chapter on Filipinos, which became my first publication.

*

"Have you ever done any transcribing?" Joe asked me one day. He had been recording conversations with urban planners in Houston and Aberdeen, Scotland, for his research comparing the two oil boomtowns.

"No, but I'm a pretty fast typist. I bet I could figure it out, Dr. Fay—Joe."

Very quickly, the transcription machine and I became one. I controlled the "play," "stop," and "rewind" features with a foot pedal, freeing both hands to type. When the audio was clear and loud, I could type at about the speed of someone talking in normal conversation;

when the audio was difficult to understand, I had to use the foot pedal to stop and back up the tape.

Along with mastering the mechanics, I began to learn that there is an extraordinary kind of listening that comes from doing this work. There is something about typing each word a person says that makes you hear it differently and more fully than simply talking with them face-to-face or even just listening to a recording. Typing each word helped me understand their importance as a whole.

*

"I have a new project that's going to keep you busy with transcribing for a while," Joe told me.

"Is it from Scotland?" Some of the accents had slowed me down before.

"No, lucky for you. This is a study with middle-class Black Americans, asking them about their experiences with racism."

"Oh, really? Is that an issue? I would think if they're middle class they wouldn't experience much discrimination."

I was skeptical that there would be anything in these interviews worth writing about. Maybe an article could come out of it, but I didn't really see this as a book project, as Joe did. The Civil Rights Act had made discrimination illegal, so I was sure I'd be typing complaints from Black people who were just being overly sensitive, looking for discrimination where there was none. I didn't say any of this aloud.

When I heard the set of questions being asked, I thought they might skew the answers in a particular direction. The first one was "What's it like being Black in white America today?" Other questions asked about different areas of discrimination: employment, housing, public accommodations. All the interviewers were African American—some of them graduate students, others undergraduates, some not in school but picking up some part-time work. This was part of the study's design, matching the race of those asking the questions and those being asked, to eliminate any bias that might be introduced by white interviewers.

As I started listening and typing each response word for word, it didn't take me long to see a pattern. The answer to the first question was almost always something like "Oh, it's fine," or "It's all good," followed by a slightly uncomfortable laugh. My first assumption was already proven wrong: these middle-class Black people weren't quick to claim racism or discrimination at all. In fact, quite the opposite. I was intrigued. What else had I gotten wrong about this research? Remembering the lie of my Cherokee heritage still made me cringe, as it reminded me how little I knew about race. The people being interviewed experienced racism every day and were experts in nuances of something that I had never spent much time thinking about.

As I typed each word spoken by these people I would never meet, I got to know them a little. This listening changed me. I was struck by how accomplished they were, far more than anyone in my family. To be included in the study, interviewees had to have middle-class incomes, which in the 1980s meant earning $50,000 a year or more. Most had much higher incomes, and nearly every person had several advanced degrees. I couldn't get over it. I was one of the few people in my family to finish college, and graduate school was a country none of us had visited. Yet here were all these Black people earning degree after degree. The evidence from their lives made me reevaluate everything I'd been told about Black people.

Even so, I remained skeptical about their stories of discrimination. Those set in restaurants were the hardest for me to believe, for some reason. The first time I transcribed a story from a woman who said she had gotten seated at a bad table—in the back, near the kitchen—I rolled my eyes. *Oh, come on*, I thought. *That could happen to anyone. How do you know that was discrimination?* I argued with her in my head as I typed. But she couldn't hear me, and I couldn't actually interrupt her, so I just kept typing. She went on, and at one point lowered her voice to hushed tones: "It could be discrimination, or it could not be, but now I've got to spend my energy to try and figure this out, because you know, I don't want to be one of those complaining types." She and the interviewer both laughed. "Then, if it is discrimination, I've got to decide if I want to do something about it, or just leave it be. This is constant. And it's an exhausting way to go through life."

Her account of this deliberation convinced me, as well as the fact that nearly every interview told an almost identical story of this kind of internal calculation in response to discrimination. Until I typed this woman's story, I never thought about the psychic energy it must take to assess each negative interaction with another person and have to decide whether or not it meets some standard for discrimination. I tried to imagine what it must be like to live in a social world that is energy-draining and disease-causing because it is so hostile to your very existence.

As this work led me toward a more empathetic understanding of the pain of racism, elsewhere I read about how such accounts are part of a larger system—a machine, really—that's designed to keep inflicting this pain over and over again. Sociologists call this **systemic racism**, which refers to the automatic way institutions structure daily life so that it ensures pain, suffering, and a rigged game for some, while for others, who look like me, the same machine reliably creates comfort, ease, and unfair advantage.

While I'd scoffed and felt superior to my father's outrageously racist language, I could see now that my own racism is much more common-place and just as damaging. Until I started listening to these interviews, I thought most Black people were underachievers who didn't value education and exaggerated claims of racism. These were **stereotypes** I'd inherited, in the same way some people inherit the family silver. In sociological terms, stereotypes like these lay the groundwork for preju-dice and bias, intellectual tricks the mind plays that make it harder to understand the world we live in. By listening to their words, I learned I was wrong. These unspoken assumptions, I came to understand, are one of the most insidious forms of racism.

The educational accomplishments of the African American people in the study also made me think about my own family's lackluster performance in this realm. No one in my family had ever earned an advanced degree. My father had gone to college but hadn't finished; my mother hadn't finished high school. Both my brothers had high school degrees but showed no interest in college and got little encour-agement and no financial support for it. When it came to education, we were solidly mediocre. Educational underachievers, even. It was *we* who were not valuing education.

I plowed through the interview tapes, eventually transcribing all 209 of them. By the time I was done, I saw the contours of broad patterns across the interviews. These were people who were remarkably driven, composed, eloquent, and deeply committed to American ideals, yet at every turn they confronted roadblocks, challenges, obstacles, and outright death threats. Mostly, these barriers were there because white people—people just like me and my family—saw them as less smart, less capable, and less deserving than everyone else. I felt implicated in the hardships these people described. And I felt compelled to change the path laid out for me by whiteness. By the end of transcribing those interviews, something fundamental in me had shifted. Instead of arguing or disagreeing with the Black people I'd spent months listening to, I was in solidarity with them.

*

Today, there are AI-enabled transcription services that will, almost instantly, produce an accurate transcript of in-depth interviews. However, I'm grateful for having had the chance to truly listen to Black Americans tell their truth in their own words. The work of transcribing, of being forced into listen-only mode, of paying attention at the level of each word, is a transformative research method. At the end of this project, I was different, bent ever so slightly away from an allegiance to whiteness. It was not enough, but it was a good beginning.

KEY CONCEPTS

Assimilation — The process by which racial and ethnic groups are absorbed into the dominant culture of society, often changing their beliefs, values, and behaviors to fit into a new culture.

Stereotype — An assumption, usually false or exaggerated and often negative, about a person or group of people based on a belief that all people in that group are the same. For example, a common stereotype is that infant girls are fragile and weak, while infant boys are tough and strong.

Systemic racism — Policies and practices that exist across society's institutions that unfairly disadvantage and harm people of color while favoring white people.

DISCUSSION QUESTIONS

1. Daniels learns a lot about the power of listening as she transcribes the research tapes. What lessons does she learn by doing that kind of listening? How is that kind of listening different from other kinds of listening? How often do you have the opportunity to listen to people whose experiences are significantly different from your own? How could you create more such opportunities if you wanted to?

2. Daniels describes the many reasons it is surprising she ever went to—or got through—graduate school. Luck, relationships, personal motivation, and hard work all play a role in helping her fit into an

environment that is different from what she knew growing up. How would you weigh the importance of each?

3. It can be difficult to account for and challenge our own assumptions about others and to face the biases and prejudices in our own families. What is the value of doing so? How does it help Daniels to do so? Has there been a time that you've had to confront biases and prejudices in your life?

LEARN MORE

Deloria, Vine, Jr. *Custer Died for Your Sins: An Indian Manifesto*. Norman: University of Oklahoma Press, 1988.

Feagin, Joe R., and Melvin P. Sikes. *Living with Racism: The Black Middle-Class Experience*. Boston: Beacon Press, 1995.

Hull, Akasha Gloria, Patricia Bell-Scott, and Barbara Smith, eds. *All Women Are White, All Blacks Are Men, But Some of Us Are Brave*. New York: Feminist Press, 1982.

Wilkerson, Isabel. *Caste: The Origins of Our Discontents*. New York: Random House, 2020.

Jessie Daniels is a writer and professor of sociology at Hunter College and the Graduate Center at the City University of New York (CUNY). She is an internationally recognized expert on internet manifestations of racism, and the author or editor of several books, including *White Lies* (Routledge,1997) and *Cyber Racism* (Rowman & Littlefield, 2009). In 2014, the magazine *Contexts* named her a "pioneer" in the field of digital sociology. Her latest book, *Nice White Ladies* (Seal Press, 2021), was named one of the best non-fiction books of the year by Kirkus Reviews, which gave the book a starred review. She is currently at work on several other books, including one about healing from the trauma of whiteness; another about the people combating the far right; and a memoir, *Out to the Blue Water: A Story of Love, Racism & Madness*.

5

From Hubris to Humility on the Softball Field

Edwin Amenta

It was late summer, and I had been put in charge of managing my mediocre team in New York City's Performing Arts Softball League. My teammates were part of New York's beautiful mosaic: Puerto Rican, Black, Jewish, Indian, Dominican, and a guy who could have been cast in *Jersey Shore*. They were stagehands, personal trainers, bartenders, musicians scraping by as bartenders, mainly from working-class or second-generation immigrant backgrounds, with a playwright and a filmmaker wedged in.

My ascendance to manager was probably due to my ability to front the league fees. But no matter—I was on a mission. A sociology professor who grew up in a predominantly white, upper-middle-class suburb, I wanted to turn our *Bad News Bears* team into winners. And I planned to use my baseball and social science theories to do it. Also, I had recently been passed over as chair of my department. It was humiliating and made me want to prove even more that I could run a small, if somewhat annoying, organization. Anyway, it was going to be tough, as we had never won even half of our games.

The time was the mid-2000s, and sabermetrics, or baseball analytics, was all the rage following the publication of Michael Lewis's *Moneyball*. He had documented how the low-budget Oakland Athletics beat teams like the big-money New York Yankees by rethinking ideas that had held sway in baseball since the turn of the previous century. They applied the voluminous data available on players and games to find diamond-in-the-rough stars and identify outside-the-box strategies to slay the baseball giants. Though adored by academics and stats enthusiasts, sabermetrics was controversial among baseball people, most of whom followed the so-called Book, an unwritten compendium of received baseball wisdom taught by coaches and reinforced in the news media.

I was all in on sabermetrics. I had looked at all the numbers and tried to sell my team on what I thought of as "Eddy Ball," a set of ideas that applied analytical and sociological thinking to Central Park softball. Some Eddy precepts were decidedly anti-macho. One was "Don't be afraid to take a walk." Though disdained by most softball players, walks often turn into free runs. Another dictum was "Don't try to hit home runs." In Central Park, trying to go deep almost always meant making an easy out because the New York softball is very soft, there are no fences, and catching a fly ball is the simplest play for fielders to make.

Like most followers of sabermetrics, I thought batting order was unimportant. I resisted naming starters to regular fielding positions, as players tend to regard the positions they're assigned to as their property and view any change as threatening. As social scientists know, people tend to react more negatively to loss than positively to gain. Also, George Herbert Mead, the only famous early sociologist to discuss baseball, thought that when children play its different fielding positions, they are called on to put themselves in others' shoes, which gives them an appreciation for the **social roles** played by others and a greater orientation to the group.

There was a ritual on my team that I particularly loathed. Before the game, players would often put their hands together, count to three, and then shout, "Win!" Like baseball, softball is a sport of concentration. Batting requires us to be relaxed. Most hitters are anxious—and I thought that ritual just made it worse. It was an Eddy Ball precept to remain calm and alert rather than getting worked up. I put a stop to it.

My teammates did not embrace Eddy Ball. Sociologists may view our clash of views as one between **rational** and **traditional authority**, two types of legitimate domination identified by the pioneering German sociologist Max Weber. I was applying science, logic, and evidence to efficiently achieve our common goal—winning. The players, by contrast, could be seen as traditionalists, suspicious of any deviation from the Book's conventional wisdom.

But it was not that simple, because my teammates also saw themselves as rational. They viewed the Book not so much as a Bible but as a textbook based on a century of baseball experience. A synonym for that way of thinking in the early twentieth century, around when Weber visited the 1904 St. Louis World's Fair—but, as far as I know, did not catch a Cardinals game—was "scientific baseball." My teammates thought *they* were playing "scientific baseball." They viewed sabermetric ideas as crackpot, like numerology or astrology.

I realized the only way to win them over was through Weber's third basis of authority—**charisma**. That doesn't mean having a magnetic personality or a great body so much as demonstrating magical, inexplicable powers. Although I was a Little League failure and the team's shortest player, I started the season on a fantastic streak. Past the midpoint of the summer, I was somehow leading the league in several offensive categories. Among these was "runs batted in," a stat disdained by sabermetrics types because it depends less on the batter's performance than his teammates' on-base skills, but they were impressed. More importantly, my teammates wanted to win, and we were in first place! Though they still liked to try for the occasional home runs and hated to walk, they went along with the program.

All season, I experimented. I did things like picking numbers out of a hat for the batting order. I rotated players to different positions between innings as if it were volleyball. But during the dog days of summer, the magical run started to stall. My numbers were falling earthward, and our team had dropped in the standings.

I realized I should not have been thinking so much about Weber's concepts of authority as about Pierre Bourdieu's ideas of **class**. For him, all cultural practices, including sports, serve to enhance class distinctions in social hierarchies. He contrasted mass sports—those played and followed by the working classes, including softball—with the distinction-enhancing athletic activities practiced by the upper middle classes to maintain their positions, such as tennis and golf. The latter tended to be health-promoting and required money, spare time, and **cultural capital**—a kind of class-based know-how unavailable to most. By all rights, someone of my class status should have been spending the summer riding bicycles through Scotland or enjoying ecotourism in Nepal, or maybe just playing golf—not softball.

According to Bourdieu, however, middle-class people can retain their status when engaging in mass cultural pursuits, as long as they practice them in a way that confers distinction. One might be able to maintain one's class status listening to popular music if one were able to compare it to classical music or opera. With mass sports, an upper-middle-class person can safely follow them in expert ways. In fantasy sports, all contestants gather information, stop rooting for their childhood teams, and imagine themselves as general managers—an upper-middle-class status.

That was pretty much all I was doing by way of leadership. I was lording it over my teammates with my theories and analyses and reproducing a social stratification order by shoving my expertise down their throats. It was silly: after all, when the season ended, I was still going to be a tenured professor teaching a class called Baseball and Society. Even worse, my Eddy Ball experiments were freaking out my teammates and throwing them off their games.

I realized my unintentional class war with my teammates had to end. I established everyone in regular fielding positions and constructed the batting order in a conventional manner. Fast on-base machines would be at the top of it, power hitters in the middle, and slumping players near the bottom. We started to pull out of the slump.

As the season was ending, we played our archrivals with the championship on the line. Before the first pitch, I drew my teammates together in a circle for some final words of wisdom. We put our hands together and, on three, shouted, "Win!"

KEY CONCEPTS

Authority — According to Max Weber, authority is a form of power that followers accept as legitimate. Weber focuses on three types of authority. **Charismatic authority** is based on personal attributes of a leader, such as a dynamic personality. **Traditional authority** relies on long-established cultural norms and practices for its legitimacy. **Rational-legal authority** is power legitimated by laws, written rules, and regulations.

Class — In this essay, Amenta focuses on Pierre Bourdieu's conception of class as determined by one's position in the system of stratification and by one's style of consumption and common cultural practices. Amenta notes that Bourdieu describes individual sports, such as tennis and golf, as associated with the upper and middle classes and team sports as associated with the working class.

Cultural capital — Pierre Bourdieu coined the term to describe symbolic resources and social assets that communicate one's social status, such as style of speech, knowledge of the arts, education, and even leisure activities that can be used to one's advantage.

DISCUSSION QUESTIONS

1. Amenta comes to realize that he was using his statistical approach to softball to "lord it over" his teammates and decides to stop doing that. How often have you witnessed people correct their mistakes in this way? What challenges do people face in doing so?
2. How do your interests or hobbies reflect your class status?
3. Amenta offers two ways of looking at what was going on in his management approach: one is grounded in Weber's ideas about different kinds of authority, and the other is grounded in Bourdieu's ideas about class and culture. Which did you find more convincing? Why?

LEARN MORE

Bourdieu, Pierre. *Forms of Capital: General Sociology, Volume 3: Lectures at the College de France 1983–84*. Cambridge: Polity Books, 2021.

Lewis, Michael. *Moneyball: The Art of Winning an Unfair Game*. New York: W. W. Norton & Company, 2004.

Mead, George Herbert. "Play, the Game, and the Generalized Other." Section 20 in *Mind, Self, and Society from the Standpoint of a Social Behaviorist*, ed. Charles W. Norris, 152–164. Chicago: University of Chicago Press, 1934.

Weber, Max. "The Three Types of Legitimate Rule." Translated by Hans Gerth in *Berkeley Publications in Society and Institutions* 4, no. 1 (1958): 1–11.

Edwin Amenta is a professor of sociology and political science at the University of California, Irvine. He has studied political sociology, comparative and historical sociology, social movements, sociology of sport, and American political development. He is the author of *Bold Relief: Institutional Politics and the Origins of Modern American Social Policy* (Princeton University Press, 1998), *When Movements Matter: The Townsend Plan and the Rise of Social Security* (Princeton, 2006), and *Professor Baseball: Searching for Redemption and the Perfect Lineup on the Softball Diamonds of Central Park* (University of Chicago Press, 2007). He is the coauthor (with Neal Caren) of *Rough Draft of History: A Century of US Social Movements in the News* (Princeton, 2022). (Read the preface to see how he helped a fellow undergraduate become a billionaire celebrity!) He is completing a book with Francesca Polletta tentatively titled *Changing the Narrative: The Cultural Consequences of Social Movements*. He is also working on a book about why US right-wing social movements have been so much more politically influential than left-wing ones. His work has been published in the *American Sociological Review*, *American Journal of Sociology*, and *Annual Review of Sociology*. He has written for the *Boston Globe*, the *San Francisco Chronicle*, *PBS NewsHour*, the *Chronicle of Higher Education*, and *Salon*. The piece for this volume was based on his experiences managing a team in New York City's Performing Arts Softball League in the post–September 11 period. In 2019, he returned to New York and played in the Broadway Show League for team *King Kong*.

6

How the World Works 101

Robin Rogers

I love norms.

Many sociologists come to the discipline through their involvement in social protest movements, which aim to disrupt social norms. I came to sociology to understand how to maintain social order.

I craved order when I was growing up. I still do. I was raised in a chaotic beatnik family living within the bohemian counterculture of mid-century downtown New York City, and I was unprepared for the wider world. I wanted to be normal, but I didn't know how to be normal. All I knew was how to be an outsider.

So, I was riveted in my first sociology class when I learned about norms, social cohesion, and institutions. Norms, I came to understand, are expected behaviors within a particular culture (or subculture). Broad agreement on a set of norms creates social cohesion. Institutions, such as schools and workplaces, are cohesive patterns of socially expected behaviors (norms) that educate workers and produce goods. Yes, I thought, yes, that's right! We need norms and social cohesion. We need order and functioning institutions.

The core insights of sociology, contained in three concepts—norms, social cohesion, and institutions—are simple and yet powerful in explaining social dynamics. Clearly, many of the norms that the countercultures of the 1960s and 1970s, in which I was raised, sought to destroy needed to be destroyed. I don't feel nostalgic for the racism, sexism, homophobia, and other ills that were so firmly entrenched in the 1950s and early 1960s. But trying to live a life without norms? I've seen it. I've done it. It doesn't end well.

BLEECKER STREET

My parents and my sister moved to Manhattan's Bleecker Street in 1964, before I was born. Our Greenwich Village apartment overlooked MacDougal Street, home to music venues where the folk music scene blossomed in the 1950s and 1960s. It must have been a thrilling time for young men and women to escape the stultifying conformity of mainstream small towns and suburbs, and enter a world that encouraged intellectual and artistic creativity. And there was sexual freedom in the Village, which is always a draw.

By the time I came of age, the party was over. The 1970s and 1980s were "hangover years." Swinging couples divorced, addiction was rampant, adults focused on "actualizing themselves" during the "me decade" of the 1970s. And the children? Well, no one really knew what we, the children of the counterculture, did. No one was watching.

Some mothers worked, but there was little to no daycare. We feral children, begotten from the "summer of love," roamed the streets. Latchkey kids, we would later be called. We parented our mothers and fathers at night, cleaning up the messes they'd made in the throes of addiction and failing marriages. Young children were given responsibilities far beyond their abilities; ten-year-old children babysat infants. I did, anyway. The lawlessness of it all frightened me.

In my child's soul, I yearned to know the social norms of the society outside Greenwich Village. I wanted to cast light on the shadow world around me. I wanted the comfort of knowing what behaviors were expected of me out there, where things were "normal," and what behaviors I could anticipate in return. I wanted to know the rules of the game that the broader culture was playing.

After school, I'd watch repeats of *The Munsters* on an old black-and-white TV with rabbit ears. In the show, the one normal cousin, Marilyn Munster, was pitied by the rest of the family for her conventional good looks and devotion to propriety. "Poor dear," Mrs. Munster would say. "She's so dreary looking and dull." I wanted to be Marilyn Munster. I wanted to fit into the world that surrounded me as a teen in the 1980s. Steeped in bohemia, I was utterly unprepared for the mainstream world of preppies and jocks that awaited me. I wanted to be normal, but I had no idea how. What were the norms? Bohemian was the only language I spoke.

By middle school, I was sliding etiquette books from the shelves of the Barnes and Noble on Eighth Street into my backpack. How did others do their graceful social dances while I stumbled along trying to imitate them?

I studied people. "You have the most intense stare," adults would say to me, unnerved. I watched everything—shoppers in the grocery store selecting their goods, old ladies waiting in the doctor's office, burnout hippies nodding off on the street corner—and I took notes. I considered myself to be something of a spy, like Harriet the Spy or Encyclopedia Brown. The old Italian ladies in my neighborhood would glance at me and say, "Little pitchers have big ears." It was true. I had a lot to figure out.

SOCIOLOGY 101

Oddly, this insider/outsider status gave me an advantage as a student of sociology. Since I had been raised in a subculture with unconventional norms, I was able to see that the norms around me were not "natural" but constructed and variable.

I learned that children, from birth, are taught by example through a system of rewards and punishments, which sociologists call sanctions. They learn what behaviors they are expected to display and under what circumstances. These expected behaviors—norms—vary by culture and subculture.

Formal norms, like laws, are written down, but most norms are informal. We learn them by watching people interact, by being instructed by parents or by other children on the playground. When we follow norms, our behavior is reinforced by a smile or a good grade—what sociologists call positive sanctions. When we violate norms, we receive negative sanctions, such as frowns or demotions at work. Such **socialization** teaches people how to behave in a given culture.

I respect the work of those in social movements who push the boundaries of society. Some boundaries need to be pushed, and violating some norms—deviance—is essential to social progress and justice. Still, my experience growing up in a subculture explicitly devoted to **normlessness** and boundary-breaking left me adrift through much of my childhood and adolescence.

The dark side of the utopian bohemian society in which everything is acceptable is that many behaviors that are unacceptable in the wider society must be endured in the name of freedom. And sometimes these behaviors are broadly considered to be unacceptable for good reasons.

In my experience, **subcultures** that value extreme personal freedom and eschew traditional social expectations (norms), like the one I was raised in, can leave the weak, especially children, vulnerable to exploitation, abuse, and neglect. In their manic dismantling of norms, those in the beatnik and hippie subcultures sometimes forgot to ask *why* those norms had arisen in the first place. What purpose had they served? How might they best be replaced?

Sociology gave form to my amorphous insight that there were rules in the world that helped hold together what we cherish. With its conceptual frameworks, including norms, sanctions, and institutions, sociology gave me the tools to understand the shadow forces around me. And that gave me power.

And so, today, when I give the first lecture of my Sociology 101 class, I will look out at 250 beaming freshman faces in the auditorium and say, "This is Sociology 101 or, as I like to call it, 'How the World Works 101.' Welcome."

KEY CONCEPTS

Normlessness — A state of being when norms are unclear, no longer exist, or no longer apply. Emile Durkheim coined the term **anomie** to describe normlessness that occurs when there is a blurring or breakdown of social norms that regulate individual behavior. In this essay, Rogers experiences normlessness because of her socialization in a subculture that valued rule-breaking.

Socialization — The lifelong learning process by which we learn the norms, values, and ideals of the groups, organizations, and societies to which we belong.

Subculture — A cultural group within a larger culture that has distinct cultural ideas and practices that differentiate the group from the dominant culture. Subcultures can be religious, professional, cultural, or simply based on common interests, such as sports fans, cosplayers, or goths.

DISCUSSION QUESTIONS

1. Do you think of yourself as a rule follower or a rule breaker? What social norms do you follow without even thinking about them as rules? How do you decide when to break a social rule (norm)?

2. Rogers asserts that social norms are necessary to protect the most vulnerable, but from a different sociological perspective, rules are there to protect the powerful. Which perspective most closely aligns with your own?

3. Rogers identifies some very specific ways that the subculture of the neighborhood where she grew up shaped her emotionally as a child. How did the specific norms of the time and place where you grew up affect your sense of security or your sense of self?

4. This essay and Francesca Polletta's essay both illustrate the importance of norms in maintaining social order, while acknowledging that sometimes it's important to work for social change. Are there aspects of social order that many of the people around you think are important to maintain but that you think need to be changed? How do you handle such situations?

LEARN MORE

Becker, Howard S. *Outsiders: Studies in the Sociology of Deviance*. New York: Free Press, 1963.

Coontz, Stephanie. *The Way We Never Were: American Families and the Nostalgia Trap*. Rev. and updated ed. New York: Basic Books, 2016.

Jenks, Chris. *Subculture: The Fragmentation of the Social*. Thousand Oaks, CA: Sage Publications, 2004.

Mills, C. Wright. *The Sociological Imagination*. 40th anniversary ed. Oxford: Oxford University Press, 2000.

Wade, Lisa. *Terrible Magnificent Sociology*. New York: W. W. Norton & Company, 2022.

Robin Rogers is an associate professor of sociology at Queens College and the CUNY Graduate Center. A former Robert Wood Johnson Health Policy Scholar at Yale University (1998–2000) and Congressional Fellow on Women and Public Policy (1995–1996), Robin's areas of expertise include poverty, policy, crime, and gender. She is the author of *The Welfare Experiments: Politics and Policy Evaluation* (Stanford University Press, 2004) and a recipient of Queens College's Presidential Award for Excellence in Teaching. In her off time, she enjoys immersive theater, live jazz, alternative music, and painting her apartment walls different colors.

PART 2

Navigating Social Structure, Culture, and Identity

It's not our differences that divide us. It is our inability to recognize, accept, and celebrate those differences.

Audre Lorde

7

The Valentine's Dilemma

Joshua Gamson

I first met Richard at the height of a sweaty New York summer. I swear that for the first few days of our relationship I could see my exhaled breath, as if some glitch had been triggered in the logic of seasons. Our honeymoon period was short, though. Within weeks, we were in a rhythmic cycle of arguing and making up, offending one another and then making out. It was exhausting, and by the time winter rolled in, I had decided to give it a rest. I am a cautious sort, and not always trusting of my own decisions, but I was nine-tenths certain about this one.

It was, however, nearly the ides of February, and Valentine's Day was nigh.

I do not believe in Valentine's Day even the least little bit. The name itself, even scrubbed of its patron saint, is so un-Jewy. Then there's the fact that Valentine's Day, the number two card-sending holiday of the year after Christmas, has the perfumed stench of a Hallmark sales campaign. If you get me going, I will probably opine that it is forced intimacy of the most noxious kind, aimed at selling flowers, candy, and greeting cards in the name of a scripted fantasy of love, aggressively valorizing monogamous heterosexual coupling on the backs of uncoupled, queer, and nonmonogamous people. You might hear me complain that Valentine's Day suppresses creative and spontaneous expressions of emotional connection in favor of a dull romanticism whose true love is capitalist **hetero-patriarchy**. Worst of all, it's boring.

And yet, as that Valentine's Day approached, I found myself in a Duane Reade contemplating a box of chocolates. I knew Richard well enough to know that if I got him nothing at all, that could be the final closing of the door. It would be saying, once and for all: our story is not a romance, scripted or otherwise. I was not ready for the door to be completely shut. If, on the other hand, I got him anything at all, I would be betraying both my stated beliefs and my intention to make some kind of change. I walked out of the drugstore, stuck.

A few minutes later, with characteristic mistrust of my own decision, I walked back in and purchased a box of Russell Stover chocolates. I didn't select the big heart-shaped box wrapped in red foil and ribbons but a small white square one, wrapped in clear plastic with a bright orange sticker that said "$3.99" in big black type. It contained four chocolates. It said: I am not sure I can love you as big as you want. It said: I am not sure about the future. It said: Valentine's Day is joke-worthy. It said: I am hurt and angry and childish. I left the chocolates outside the door to Richard's apartment. I may have gotten a Hallmark card to go with it.

This was not my finest moment, with its passive aggression posing as clever humor, its immaturity presented as principle, its bravado covering up fear and loss. But then it didn't exactly feel like a choice, or at least not one to be freely made. That ought not to have surprised me. I had been teaching and writing about culture for a few years by then, but apparently was unwilling or unable to see myself in my own words. A couple of years prior, for instance, writing about "**shallow culture**"—by which I meant cultural practices and products that some would call trivial, and most would agree are surface-level experiences—I had attempted to synthesize some of the sociological understandings of how "culture which is admittedly superficial can have deep social significance *without* being deeply felt, *without* requiring the internalization or even perception of deep meanings." I was mainly thinking about superficial popular culture, like celebrity gossip, game shows, and reality television, but I had raised a question that I might have been well advised to ask myself while purchasing those chocolates at Duane Reade: "How and why are people, not necessarily shallow or pathetic, engaged with and by culture they themselves see as shallow?" That is, what do people get from consuming things they know aren't particularly deep and meaningful?

One of the answers, I suggested, was that **cultural codes**—customs, established behavioral scripts, and the like—constrain us regardless of the depth of our belief in them. I referenced a point made by Ann Swidler in her discussion of Theodore Caplow's study of Christmas gift giving: not everyone "believes" in giving gifts, and many criticize the commercialization of Christmas, yet most nonetheless give gifts because they signal something to the recipient. The gifts are made not so much because of a deep commitment to giving stuff but because giving Christmas gifts has become an unavoidable cultural expectation and form of communication. Whether you believe in holiday gifts is beside the point. Swidler went on: "When florists and confectioners try to increase their business by announcing National Secretaries' Week, few are presumably moved by deep belief in the principles that lie behind the announcement. But if every newspaper in the country is for weeks blanketed with advertisements implying that bosses who appreciate their secretaries will give them flowers and take them out to lunch, both secretaries and their employers may be, at the least, uncomfortable about what signals their actions will send." One could easily have substituted lovers of Valentine's Day for the old-timey bosses and secretaries of National Secretaries' Week and reach the same conclusions.

My own weird gift-giving actions made an excellent illustration. It didn't much matter what I thought about Valentine's Day, whether I internalized or rejected its assumptions and messages about romance or congratulated myself for seeing through its manipulations; what mattered was that the code was in wide circulation. I did not need to find the Valentine's Day script meaningful to be affected by it—to be, "at the least, uncomfortable about what signals" my actions would send. Chocolates, roses, cards, dinners out: these elements of the "code" could not be sidestepped, any more than one could sidestep the cultural codes surrounding funerals by wearing a bathing suit or the cultural codes surrounding greetings by answering "Hi, how are you?" with a lengthy and revealing description of your actual state of being. Valentine's Day could not be ignored, at least not without consequences I was unwilling at that moment to risk. I could only play with the script—using it to communicate ambivalence, to maintain a thread of connection, to make a joke.

As it turned out, Richard didn't put much stock in Valentine's Day either, and he seemed to receive the gift with a sign of recognition, laughing at the small square box and annoyed at what it communicated. What bothered him was the holding back, the sense that I could not or would not fully close the door on other options, whether breaking up or staying together with a full commitment. Richard, who had willed himself over one hurdle after another, had long been an expert at committing. "Sometimes you have to say no to one thing," he liked to say, "in order to say yes to something else." I was full of maybe.

A few days later, still wandering in the land of maybe, Richard and I somehow wound up together at a super-gay Valentine's Day party. We grabbed mimosas and went our separate ways while the hosts circulated with party favors. If you had RSVP'd, upon arrival you received a necklace with your name spelled out in lettered beads. If you had not, you were invited to dig your hand into a bag filled with necklaces whose beaded messages reflected those of Valentine's Sweethearts candies— "BE MINE," "KISS ME," "CUTIE PIE," and the like.

I heard Richard's enormous laugh from the other room. Eventually, we made our way toward each other, softened by the champagne and the company. He asked me which necklace I had gotten, and we each held the beads out to show the other. We had pulled the same ones.

Neither of us believed in Valentine's necklaces, Sweethearts, or trite little love sayings. But as cultural scripts sometimes do, this one, despite or maybe because of its silliness, brought us back to something deeper.

"SAY YES," our twin necklaces said. And so we did.

KEY CONCEPTS

Cultural codes — Symbols and systems of meaning that are relevant to members of society, such as giving flowers and chocolate on Valentine's Day. One need not abide by cultural codes to be impacted by them: Gamson, for example, is unable to ignore Valentine's Day, despite his disdain for the holiday.

Hetero-patriarchy — A sociopolitical system that privileges heterosexual cisgender men (men who were assigned male at birth) over all others. This system privileges heterosexual marriage over other relationships and gives heterosexual cisgender men inordinate power to define dominant culture norms and values.

Shallow culture — Cultural practices and products that many would call trivial and superficial, such as popular culture's focus on celebrities and social media. Gamson asks us to consider the impact of shallow culture by moving beyond the surface-level experience toward a deeper understanding of its impact on our thoughts and actions—even when we try to avoid it.

DISCUSSION QUESTIONS

1. Can you identify a cultural code that you don't necessarily respect but still follow?
2. How might shallow culture impact you even if you are uninterested in it?
3. What cultural scripts or codes bother you? Why do they bother you? Which ones do you love? Why?
4. How do cultural codes differ for underrepresented or minority groups, such as the queer couple in the story? How are they the same?

LEARN MORE

Bergesen, Albert J. *The Depth of Shallow Culture: The High Art of Shoes, Movies, Novels, Monsters, and Toys.* Oxfordshire: Taylor & Francis, 2007.

Gamson, Joshua. "The Depths of Shallow Culture." *Newsletter of the Sociology of Culture* 12, no. 3 (1998): 3–4.

Swidler, Ann. "Cultural Power and Social Movements." In *Social Movements and Culture*, ed. H. Johnston and B. Klandermans, 33. Minneapolis: University of Minnesota Press, 1995.

Joshua Gamson is professor of sociology at the University of San Francisco. He is the author of *Modern Families: Stories of Extraordinary Journeys to Kinship* (NYU Press, 2017); *Claims to Fame: Celebrity in Contemporary America* (University of California Press, 1994); *Freaks Talk Back: Tabloid Talk Shows and Sexual Nonconformity* (University of Chicago Press, 1998, winner of book awards from the Speech Communication Association and the American Sociological Association); and *The Fabulous Sylvester* (Picador Press, 2005, Stonewall Book Award winner, Lambda Literary Award finalist, *Entertainment Weekly* "Must List" selection, and *San Francisco Chronicle* bestseller). In addition to many scholarly publications on popular culture, sexualities, and social movements, he has written for outlets such as *The Nation*, the *New York Times Magazine*, *The American Prospect*, and *Newsday*. He has been a Guggenheim Fellow (2009) and a Fellow at the Center for Advanced Study in the Behavioral Sciences at Stanford University (2015–2016). Gamson lives in Oakland, CA, with his husband and their two daughters. His website is www.joshuagamson.com.

8

Hair Play

Robyn Autry

Twirl. Flip. Toss. Repeat.

I've been watching white women play with their hair for as long as I can remember. As a child, I watched little white girls twirl theirs at their desks and on the playground. I watched their high ponytails flop, their eyelashes struggle to liberate themselves from their shaggy bangs, and their hair cascade down their backs as they lifted it from their coat collars at the end of the day. Recognizing it as a mark of difference between us, beyond the color of our skin, I knew there was great power in hair that billowed with the slightest breeze. These were markers not only between us, but also among white girls with differently textured hair and between them and brown girls with silky hair. There was a clear hair hierarchy—a *hairarchy*: those with the longest, thickest, closest-to-golden manes were perched atop, while dark girls with coarse hair like mine were firmly at the bottom.

As an adult, not that much has changed. I watch white women swing their hair back and forth at work and on the train, tucking strands behind their ears before untucking them only to re-tuck them again, even sniffing and mindlessly sucking on the ends. For years, I observed a colleague gather and pull her thick amber tresses into a messy bun at the crown of her head, only to immediately release it, before pulling it back up every time she spoke. During a workshop, I sat with a group of mostly white women for hours, ducking and dodging as they endlessly flipped, tossed, and twirled their hair.

I have no desire to chastise or police what women do with their hair, even as blonde strands detach and find their way onto me. But what can we make of a Black woman watching such performances? It's a rather humdrum display, as far as public spectacles go, but it captures my attention every time. Was it envy or resentment that caught my eye as a child? I have never longed for whiteness, not even as a young girl, but I did feel left out of all the flipping and tossing. I knew what it was to be watched closely with suspicion (mostly by white people), but mostly I felt unseen.

Hair is everywhere, but I've always known a lot about white women's hair, much more than they know about mine. And for a long time, I even knew more about theirs than my own! Mary C. Waters writes about these asymmetries between Black and white people: white people aren't generally knowledgeable about Black experiences, which can feed into an objectifying curiosity when they actually notice us, while we're compelled to know a lot about them, for survival as much as to participate in mainstream culture. Yet, this didn't fully explain my interest in the hair shows. It was not so much that I was seeking knowledge, but rather that I was surprised they were so openly doing something that I and other Black girls did behind closed doors: fixing our hair.

In other words, they were taking up space on what Erving Goffman calls the front stage, doing what the rest of us leave backstage. Goffman developed his **dramaturgical model** to explain everyday social interactions that feel something like the scenes of a play. We perform different roles, or scripted parts—student, teacher, colleague, and so on—for each other. We do so, he stressed, to improve our image or manage the impressions we leave on each other. Is a hair toss part of this dramatic action? Sure. But where does that leave those of us with hair that grows more out than down, hair that defies gravity and refuses to be tossed around? Well, we tend to do our hair backstage. As children, someone else typically takes care of it at home, and that's it. My mother would have been shocked if I went to school and undid the woolly ribbons and plastic barrettes she'd applied to let my hair free and attempted to run my fingers through it. No, my hair didn't have much to do with any front-stage performances, except when it was used as a weapon against me to tease or harass.

I'd barely even touched my hair until I was a teenager. Before that, I was my mother's experimental doll, and she treated my hair like a playground. But this closeness was short-lived, because one of the hallmarks of Black girlhood was on the horizon: the transition from unprocessed (or natural or coarse or kinky) to straightened hair. First, my mother pulled a heavy hot comb through it to press the shaft flat, then rolled it up with the plastic and foam curlers that I learned to sleep on every night, like she did. Eventually, I straightened my hair myself with at-home relaxer kits and curled it with my sister's thick wand curling iron. Turns out we wanted curls, just not the super coily ones we were born with. Or did I? No one had asked me, and I'd never thought about what I might want to do with my hair. Instead, I was following what felt like a **social script**, a different one than those girls at school who seemed to flip and toss their hair the exact same way.

I was a college senior when I decided to stop relaxing my hair. A sociology course, Self in Modern Society, got me thinking about instances when my values and actions were misaligned, and what I might do about that. My sister Angela had already stopped straightening her hair, opting for locs instead; the course nudged me to follow suit. I felt good about the decision, but I didn't know what to actually do with my hair once I stopped straightening and didn't have money to visit a salon. So, I just watched the relaxed hair shed, braided the front, and pulled the rest back with a ponytail holder. It didn't look great, but it didn't look terrible, either. It was the hair equivalent of a shrug.

It wasn't until graduate school and, later, during my first academic position that I took a deep dive into Black hair play. YouTube hair tutorials had me mesmerized. I watched at least fifty before finally trying any of the suggested techniques for tightly coiled hair. My favorite was "CurlyChronicles." The host had a retro flair and discussed her hair like a fashion choice that changed from one day to the next. "Naptural85" was another favorite: she gave detailed instructions on cleansing, conditioning, and styling, along with DIY hair treatments. Like other bloggers, both hosts presented themselves at various stages before, after, and during styling. They'd appear with their hands wet with product, gliding their fingers along the strands, smoothing it as they went before fluffing for volume, trying a deep part on one side and then the other, and then finally laying their edges flat or leaving them fuzzy.

I was surprised and charmed by this "out-there"-ness, considering the amount of scrutiny and mocking that Black bodies, especially Black women's bodies, endure in the public eye. It was as if these young women were unaware or unbothered by any such risk, showing themselves first thing in the morning or directly out of the shower with their hair big and puffy, short and matted, thinning and uneven, or with no makeup and dark blemishes visible. It was as if they didn't know they were supposed to be hiding or masking their unadorned bodies rather than standing boldly, as if "naked without shame," before experimenting with accessories of all manner, and sometimes makeup, too. Something inside me danced.

As an educator, I was impressed by their level of detail, the audiences they amassed across platforms, and their commitment to transparency, sometimes even filming themselves detangling and shampooing while *in the shower*, albeit with a swimsuit on or shot from the shoulders up. Surely, this was akin to Goffman's backstage, yet they were online talking to a camera, performing for strangers. It didn't feel like a managed performance most of the time; it felt more like they were trusting their viewers enough to invite us backstage. I think this is what happens when we do as bell hooks suggests and "choose the margin" as a location of community and resistance: the way we understand social spaces shifts when we occupy them in unexpected ways.

From YouTube to TikTok, I'd found a world of hair shows other than the ones I saw every day at school and work. These were more exciting because I wasn't just watching other people tend to their hair; I could also see myself in their play. Charles Horton Cooley's **looking-glass self** describes how we make appraisals of ourselves—Am I smart, popular, funny, attractive, or the opposite?—based on how we believe we come across to others. Sounds a bit like Goffman's **dramaturgical model**, where we await reviews for our latest performance and then use them to judge ourselves. And online those reviews can be harsh.

Hair feels like a power play because of the role it plays in desirability. From how we flirt, age, and discriminate, so much of social life gets acted out through hair. And whether yours is long and wavy, curly and bouncy, frizzy, combed-over, graying, dyed, or thinning at the edges, and whether we're talking the hair on our heads or anywhere else on our bodies, we're all subjected to norms about how we present ourselves to each other.

Still, there is a playful side to hair that I couldn't access until I saw other Black women with kinky hair and dark skin doing just that. I learned which products to buy, what styles to attempt, and which accessories I might add for a playful touch. I also learned that my efforts never quite matched the final looks on the screen. They were bloggers, after all, not playwrights, and they offered what worked for them. But there is enormous variety in Black hair, and I've learned to appreciate that, too.

I still don't toss, flip, and twirl my hair in public or at home. But I do stretch, wrap, and twist it at night or in the morning, and when I'm out, I notice how it shrinks, elongates, or bounces throughout the day. Other Black women smile and notice, too.

KEY CONCEPTS

Dramaturgical model — Developed by Erving Goffman, this approach views human interaction as a theatrical performance in which we try to control and manage our public image, especially when we are "front stage," aware of having an audience. "Backstage" is the more private space where we can drop our front, relax, and let our guard down.

Looking-glass self — Charles Horton Cooley's term for the self that emerges as a result of seeing ourselves as we think others see us. As people act, others react. In those reactions, people see themselves reflected, which gives rise to a particular self-image. For instance, firstborn daughters may perceive that others view them as responsible and goal oriented, and thus take on this self-image.

Social script — A pattern of expected behavior in a particular situation or environment. For example, when we greet a friend or acquaintance in passing and say, "How's it going?" we don't expect them to answer "Actually, things are really bad right now" and begin a long explanation of their troubles.

DISCUSSION QUESTIONS

1. In what ways have you witnessed the "hairarchy"? Why do you think hair is so socially significant?
2. Autry notes that YouTube and other social media outlets provide a way for people to invite others "backstage." What are the benefits of revealing one's backstage world?
3. This essay illustrates that personal choices extend beyond an individual's life to challenge or reinforce cultural restrictions. What choices do you make in your own life that challenge or reinforce social norms or aspects of inequality?

LEARN MORE

Cooley, Charles Horton. "The Social Self—The Meaning of 'I.'" Chapter 5 in *Human Nature and the Social Order*. New York: Scribner, 1922.

Goffman, Erving. *The Presentation of Self in Everyday Life*. Edinburgh: Double-day, 1956.

hooks, bell. "Choosing the Margin as a Space of Radical Openness." In *Yearnings: Race, Gender, and Cultural Politics*. Boston: South End Press, 1990.

———. "Naked Without Shame: A Counter-Hegemonic Body Politic." In *Talking Visions: Multicultural Feminism in a Transnational Age*. New York and Cambridge, MA: MIT Press, 1998.

Waters, Mary C. "Optional Ethnicities: For Whites Only?" In *Origins and Destinations: Immigration, Race, and Ethnicity*. Belmont, CA: Wadsworth Press, 1996.

Robyn Autry is a sociology professor at Wesleyan University in Connecticut. She has broad interests in racial identity, collective and personal memory, and beauty. Her academic writing on commemorative practices around racial violence in the United States and South Africa has appeared in several journals, including *Visual Studies* and *Theory & Society*. Her public writing has appeared in *The Atlantic*, *Black Perspectives*, NBC News, *Aeon*, *Public Seminar*, and *Psyche*. She is the author of *Desegregating the Past: The Public Life of Memory in the United States and South Africa* (Columbia University Press, 2017). She is the recipient of the Andrew W. Mellon Public Humanities Fellowship at the University of Toronto (2020–2021) and Wesleyan's Binswanger Prize for Excellence in Teaching. She received her PhD in sociology from the University of Wisconsin–Madison.

9

Being Black (and American) in Paris

Jean Beaman

I started learning French in middle school. In college, I had the opportunity to study abroad in France. I lived with a (white) French family, and through that deep immersion, which included taking courses at local universities, I became fluent in French. My world opened up. Something else happened, as well: living in Paris revealed that being Black was simultaneously the most important part and the least important part of my own **identity**. Let me explain. I have always understood my identity as African American or Black American, but being an African American outside the United States revealed how **socially constructed** and multifaceted Black identity really is.

One afternoon, while walking near the Palais Opéra, I stumbled upon an English-language bookstore, Brentano's, and came across historian Tyler Stovall's *Paris Noir: African Americans in the City of Light*. Reading the book, I began to appreciate that I was part of a long line of African Americans living in Paris, following such luminaries as James Baldwin, Duke Ellington, Josephine Baker, and Richard Wright. I was excited to see signs of African American expatriates throughout Paris. I found a plaque for writer Richard Wright in the 6th arrondissement, where he lived from 1948 to 1959, and his grave at the famous Père Lachaise Cemetery in the 20th arrondissement. Singer and dancer Josephine Baker is marked with a plaza, Place Josephine Baker, in the Montparnasse neighborhood; a plaque in the 9th arrondissement, near where she opened her first cabaret; and a public pool on Quai François Mauriac on the Seine.

The Paris I'd seen in postcards and my French language textbooks in high school failed to capture its racial and ethnic diversity. Paris is a multicultural and multiethnic city, one with a long-standing Black presence. I experienced the diversity of Parisians every day while taking the subway, browsing in outdoor markets, and drinking coffee in cafés. Yet, despite this diversity, I was racialized in ways similar to and different from my experiences growing up as a Black person in the United States. As in the States, I was followed around in stores due to a presumption of criminality, but when I spoke French with an obvious non-native accent, shopkeepers suddenly became more friendly. I was not "just" a Black person or a Black French citizen, they realized, but a Black American, an American tourist—someone just passing through. The relative privileges of being American and having a US passport interacted in complicated ways with the suspicion and disadvantages that accompanied my Blackness.

During this year abroad, I learned a lot about the relationship between race, citizenship, and societal belonging. If Parisians treated me better after discovering I was American, and not French, then what did that suggest about how France's own racial and ethnic minorities were treated? Race and belonging are contextual. People "read" our race differently depending on their different personal histories and cultural societal structures. It is not just about appearance or skin color. The presence of African Americans in Paris is often invoked to minimize charges of racism in France: How could France be racist when Josephine Baker chose to move here? Or Langston Hughes? Or James Baldwin? The conventional narrative is that African American expatriates fled to Paris to escape the racism they experienced in the United States, expecting openness and acceptance in Paris. In a 1984 *Paris Review* interview, James Baldwin said: "It wasn't so much a matter of choosing France—it was a matter of getting out of America. I didn't know what was going to happen to me in France but I knew what was going to happen to me in New York. If I had stayed there, I would have gone under." But reality is more complicated, as when Baldwin writes that his US passport suggested he was not "to be treated as one of Europe's uncivilized, black possessions." France could recognize racism in the United States and even welcome African Americans within her borders but could not acknowledge or recognize racism against its own Black populations.

Indeed, my day-to-day life as a Black American exchange student in Paris exposed many of the contradictions of France and its ideals of *liberté, égalité, fraternité*. France disavows the existence of race and racism entirely, and instead promotes a colorblind, republican ethos.

Identity-based communities and groups, or le *communautarisme*, are not recognized. The French deflect racism as an American phenomenon and the United States as the true racist society. Parisians regularly asked me why the United States was so racist, and failed to see racism in their own societies.

The idea that the French do not even notice race didn't match what I was seeing and experiencing in Paris. Much like the United States, Parisian neighborhoods were divided by race. I saw fewer Black people in the 6th arrondissement, where I was staying, near famed luxury department store Bon Marché, than in the neighborhood of Belleville or Château Rouge, also referred to as Quartier Africain (African Neighborhood). "Social housing" (the French version of public housing) was concentrated in poorer neighborhoods with more ethnoracial diversity. I began to understand how race and place intersect, such that places become **racialized** even in a society without official racial categorization. The French minimize and deny their racism, yet it was hard to ignore how racial designations structure everyday life as I walked through the city. Colorblind racism—the simultaneous acknowledgment and disavowal of race and racism—became quite real to me. By not talking about it, and denying its existence, the French reinforce a kind of racism that is hard to fight back against.

At the restaurants and cafés I visited, white workers worked the "front of the house" as hostesses or servers, while the kitchen workers were Arab or Black. Walking around Paris, I saw unmistakable signs of France's colonial empire (in the Maghreb, West Africa, Asia, and the Caribbean), including various streets and Metro stations named for former colonial officers. I was unnerved by these signs that France is not and never was the racially open society that the presence of African American expatriates suggested. It made me think about my own identity—as both Black and American, but not only that. Seeing that neither the United States nor France was actually colorblind in practice helped me recognize the myriad ways that racism, including anti-Black racism, exists. Despite the many differences between France and the United States, racism, and how people experience it, is quite similar. The patterns I noticed in Paris were strikingly similar to the patterns I noticed and knew of in the United States.

My junior year abroad and many subsequent experiences in France as a visitor and scholar taught me about being Black beyond being African American. It is related to being a member of a particular society, but it is not only that. And I learned that being Black, or African American, is an important facet of my identity, but not its totality.

KEY CONCEPTS

Identity — One's sense of self based on membership in certain groups. Race, ethnicity, socioeconomic status, sexual orientation, gender, and nationality can all influence our sense of identity. Beaman's essay speaks to the fact that identity is impacted by social expectations that may differ based on nationality and culture.

Racialization — A process by which race becomes salient as a marker of social difference and thus integral to power differences between socially constructed racial groups. For instance, members of the first wave of Irish immigrants were considered non-white and worked low-paying jobs that most white Americans wouldn't do. Later, the Irish became racialized as white by securing jobs as police officers and firefighters. Historically, Jewish people also have been racialized, and today we see the racialization of Muslim people and people from Mexico and South and Central America.

Social constructionism — A perspective that asserts that certain ideas about physical and social reality arise from a collaborative consensus. Beaman's experience in France supports the belief that race is defined in language, ideas, and culture rather than being simply a biological fact.

DISCUSSION QUESTIONS

1. Beaman writes that "living in Paris revealed that being Black was simultaneously the most important part and the least important part of my own identity." What does she mean? Are there parts of your identity that work this way, too? What features of the culture or society that you live in make that possible?
2. Beaman notes that "Race and belonging are contextual. People 'read' our race differently depending on their different personal histories and cultural societal structures." How did this work in her own story? How has it worked in your experience, whether related to race or to some other significant category to which you belong?
3. There are significant social and political debates about how much we should center specific aspects of our identity (race, gender, sexuality,

religion, etc.). Does Beaman's story offer any insight into how deeply identity should be centered in our lives or our politics?

4. If our culture is grounded on racial inequalities but at the same time tells us that race is not significant to identity (as in France), does this make it easier or harder to address those inequalities?

LEARN MORE

Clerge, Orly. *The New Noir: Race, Identity, and Diaspora in Black Suburbia*. Oakland: University of California Press, 2019.

"James Baldwin, The Art of Fiction No. 78." Interviewed by Jordan Elgrably. *The Paris Review* 91 (Spring 1984).

Stovall, Tyler E. *Paris Noir: African Americans in the City of Light*. New York: Houghton Mifflin, 1996.

Jean Beaman is an associate professor of sociology at the University of California, Santa Barbara, with affiliations in Black studies, feminist studies, global studies, political science, and the Center for Black Studies Research. Her research is ethnographic in nature and focuses on race/ethnicity, racism, international migration, and state violence in both France and the United States. She is the author of *Citizen Outsider: Children of North African Immigrants in France* (University of California Press, 2017). She was a co-principal investigator for the Mellon Foundation Sawyer Seminar grant "Race, Precarity, and Privilege: Migration in Global Context" for 2020–2022 and a 2022–2023 fellow at the Center for Advanced Study in Behavioral Sciences at Stanford University. She is on Twitter @jean23bean.

10

The Only Girl on the Loading Dock

Marika Lindholm

I found our wedding invitations stashed in the laundry room under his smelly sports gear. When confronted, my fiancé admitted to having cold feet, so I immediately canceled the caterer, the venue, the flowers, and the band. Although I was in the middle of grad school, I had to get away. I decided to flee to Sweden—the homeland I'd left at age four—where no one knew my sad story.

At the employment office in Stockholm, I learned that with my experience—a couple years of sociology grad school—there were only two jobs available to me: the factory floor at Pripps, a beer manufacturer, or Tomteboda, the national post office. I opted for the post office. The interview took place at the terminal, a monolithic building with offices, locker rooms, a cafeteria, and a massive loading dock. In a small, sterile room, a pasty man grilled me about drugs, alcohol, and honesty before informing me that I would be sorting envelopes with all the other women. "Isn't there any other work? I like to be active," I inquired, trying to soften the hard *r* that Swedes tease us Americans about. Jowls shaking, he chortled, "Only men work on the loading dock."

Apparently leaving everything behind makes you do the unexpected, because I kept pushing. Relenting, Pasty-face took me to a room filled with sorting equipment, giant mailbags, and some metal bins. If I could lift a bag and drop it in the bin, he said, the job was mine. I'm no weight lifter, and when I went to lift the bag, it barely budged. A few men in blue uniforms gathered to watch, presumably for a good laugh. Filled with the fury I'd felt since finding those wedding invitations, I shoved the bin against the nearby wall, crouched down, and used all my arm and leg strength to roll the bag up the side of the bin until, miraculously, it fell in. Everyone laughed except me.

"So, do I get the job?" I asked.

"Ya, Ya, you can try," said Pasty-face, "but you won't last a week with those animals."

The "animals," I learned, were immigrants from Turkey, Africa, Poland, Russia, and South America—men, many of them college-educated political refugees who now spent their days sorting packages. Just like high school lunchrooms across the United States, the racial and ethnic groups tended to hang in their own clusters without much crossover. Swedes also worked on the loading dock, but they were generally foremen or had easier jobs, such as working the scale or making sure there were enough labels. On the whole, the Swedes worked less and complained more. Every worker wore identical uniforms—baggy blue pants, boxy blue jackets, and gray steel-tipped clogs—and we never picked up giant mailbags. In fact, rarely was physical strength required. The job primarily consisted of meeting the trucks that delivered packages to our loading dock. We controlled the hydraulic cargo lifts that brought the packages up to the dock, checked their weight, and distributed packages into metal bins according to their labels: fragile, bulk, business, express, and priority.

I lasted nine months. The job wasn't physically or intellectually demanding, but it was the hardest job I ever had. It wasn't until I returned to sociology that I began to understand why.

Back in grad school, and relatively recovered from heartbreak and humiliation, I read the work of Rosabeth Kanter. Over a decade earlier, Kanter had introduced the concept of **tokenism** in her book *Men and Women of the Corporation*. Like most people, my concept of a token was an affirmative action hire, but Kanter offered a different perspective that helped me understand why my job on the loading dock was so stressful and why I felt like an incompetent failure. Kanter described tokens as being in a unique structural position of one among many. Being the only one—that is, a token—is a role filled with many contradictions and structural realities that make work more difficult, she explained. Her book helped me understand that I wasn't flawed or unintelligent, and that even though I left the postal terminal in a blaze of failure, it wasn't my fault. Indeed, my reaction to being the first woman on the loading dock made perfect sense when examined structurally and sociologically.

The most fundamental structural reality of being a token is that you stand out. Despite my unisex uniform, it was obvious that I was one woman among many men. This *visibility* put an enormous amount of pressure on me. I felt like everyone was watching my every move. Did she put the package in the right bin? How many packages did she move per hour? Did she get the numbers right? The scrutiny was intense and unrelenting—I never got used to it. With this visibility came resentment that I got more attention and perhaps more compliments for a job well done. The guys driving the trucks called me Greta Garbo because I wore sunglasses to block the setting sun. Resentful that the drivers joked with me, my coworkers could be mean-spirited. One Finnish foreman dedicated himself to making my days miserable, often giving me the hardest jobs in the worst conditions, such as lining up metal bins for hours in subzero temperatures while the others worked indoors. Visibility puts enormous pressure to perform on the token, while dominants see the token as having an unfair advantage.

In addition to having visibility, tokens also *contrast* with dominants, writes Kanter. Specifically, one's token status *challenges **dominant culture boundaries***. In my situation, the men at work resented that they had to adjust their behavior because a woman was nearby. In fact, when the boss told them to tone down their sexist behavior, they only amped up the harassment by showing me porn magazines, using offensive language, and making everything—and I mean *everything*—sexual, from pretending long, thin packages were penises to making lewd gestures with various types of machinery. I always laughed it off, but it was decidedly unnerving and uncomfortable. At the start of each shift, I steeled myself for the inevitable onslaught and told myself not to cry.

A young musician from Poland and a former veterinarian from Nigeria befriended me, and we hung out after work a few times. But even they joined the chorus of coworkers asking if I wanted to smoke, chew tobacco, or look at porn magazines with them. In the beginning, it was threatening, but as months passed, it became a big, boring joke that wouldn't go away. Every time I said no or no thank you, it drove home the point that I wasn't one of them.

The foreman forbade me from operating a forklift, even though every new male hire was taught how to do this immediately. Kanter describes the process by which dominants exaggerate the differences between them and the token as *boundary heightening*. Every day, these macho questions and the ban against using a forklift reminded me that I didn't belong.

Another problem identified by Kanter is assimilation—the tendency of dominants to distort the characteristics or behaviors of the token to fit their stereotypes. So when I was kind to someone, guys taunted, "Look who wants to be your girlfriend." If I was in a bad mood, they accused me of having my period. Trying to resist assimilation is exhausting, and Kanter writes that many tokens end up accepting a type of **role encapsulation** and conform to a gender stereotype. In her work on female managers in a male-dominated company, the roles were "pet," "seductress," "mother," and "iron maiden."

On the loading dock, I also felt like a walking stereotype. When we had our 3 p.m. coffee break, the guys would expect me to clean up afterward. If the foreman wanted something from the cafeteria, I was the first to be asked. Physical boundaries were nonexistent—they'd touch my butt, put their arm around me when we were talking, and lean into me when we worked side by side. No matter how I acted, I was teased for being too sexy, too motherly, too cute, too harsh. Over time, I felt an increasing sense of insecurity, discomfort, and, ultimately, failure.

By explaining why a job that didn't require much skill or acumen felt enormously difficult to me, Kanter restored my sense of self. I was especially struck by her succinct description of three contradictions that come with token status and negatively impact the work lives of those who stand out among many.

First, *tokens are viewed as exceptions when they succeed and representations if they fail*. If I messed up, I stood for all women and confirmed my male bosses' and coworkers' belief that women were too fragile for the loading dock. If I succeeded, it didn't mean that other women could do my job. Instead, they focused on my "unique" muscles and height, suggesting I was still doing a man's job.

The second contradiction is that I was *constantly made aware of differences* through catcalling, sexual innuendo, and sexist behavior, while still being *expected to behave as if these differences didn't exist*. When we had to move hundreds of boxes of floor tiles, the men mocked me for having the audacity to stop every so often to stretch out my aching back.

The final contradiction is that tokens *stand out as individuals, but no one sees their individuality*. I was noticed, but no one really knew me. I represented all women, but no one knew my story or bothered to find out. When our shift was over, a sea of blue uniforms would pour into the subway, except for one blue dot that separated from the rest. Away from the others, I'd stare at the gorgeous city of Stockholm, with its pristine architecture, and pledge that the next workday I'd be more secure in my ability to sort packages. Yet the stress and discomfort continued. I didn't make huge mistakes, but I was called out repeatedly for a wrong label, not noticing a package in the wrong bin, and misunderstanding directions.

In the face of such scrutiny, tokens often strive to become insiders, sometimes compromising their own integrity in the process, according to Kanter. One day, after nine months of being tokenized, I decided to throw my fear to the wind and attempt to fit in. This time, when the guys showed me a porn magazine, I took it and turned the pages in admiration. When they offered me a smoke, I went to the smoking area and laughed it up while choking inside. And, the worst of the worst, I accepted some chewing tobacco, which prompted such a flood of sickening sensations that I gagged and my head spun. I could do this. I would show them!

Back at my station at the hydraulic lift, I was giddy from my bold attempt to be one of the guys. Laughing and talking, I pressed the button to bring the packages up to the dock. What I failed to notice in my reverie was that the delivery truck's door was open over the lift. The screeching sound of ripping and crunching metal got my attention. By the time I pressed stop, the lift had ripped the door right off! For what seemed like an eternity, the Finnish foreman reamed me in front of everyone: "You stupid girl! Look what you did! This will cost you! Go home!" In all the shame and confusion, I'm not sure if I was officially fired, but I never came back.

I'd tried to hang tough to prove a point—to rise above the shame of a called-off wedding and push through the daily assault of a job that made me feel incompetent—but it was futile. I was done. I'm not sure if anyone on the loading dock missed me or if more women work the dock now, over twenty-five years later. But I do know that learning from Kanter about the consequences of being a structural token allowed me to replace my feelings of failure with a sliver of pride.

KEY CONCEPTS

Dominant culture — The culture of the group that wields more power than other groups and is therefore able to establish its own norms and values as the standard for a given society.

Role encapsulation — When a nondominant token, despite their best efforts, isn't accepted by the dominant group and is encapsulated in a stereotypical role. For example, on the male-dominated loading dock, Lindholm was assigned the role of temptress and housekeeper.

Tokenism — The popular use of the word *token* implies offering a job to a member of a minority group to give the impression that diversity matters to that organization. However, for Rosabeth Moss Kanter, tokenism is a structural reality—being one among many—that leads to unique and often daunting challenges in any setting.

DISCUSSION QUESTIONS

1. Have you ever been a structural token? Describe the setting and how visibility impacted your experience. If you haven't been a token, have you witnessed someone else in this position?
2. Kanter highlights contradictions that come with tokenism. Have you experienced or observed these contradictions at school or work? In what situations were these contradictions most obvious?
3. How might a better understanding of the added performance pressures structural tokens face make us more effective leaders? For instance, what can teachers, managers, and bosses do to relieve some of the extra pressure on structural tokens?
4. If there had been more women working on the loading dock with Lindholm, how might her experience have differed? How might more diverse environments change the difficult dynamics of visibility and scrutiny?

LEARN MORE

Ely, Robin J. "Celebrating 'The Men and Women of the Corporation' 40 Years Later." Interview with Rosabeth Moss Kanter. In *Working Knowledge, Business Research for Business Leaders*. Harvard Business School, September 10, 2018.

Kanter, Rosabeth Moss. *Men and Women of the Corporation*. New York: Basic Books, 1977.

Reskin, Barbara F., and Patricia A. Roos. *Job Queues, Gender Queues: Explaining Women's Inroads into Male Occupation*. Philadelphia: Temple University Press, 1990.

Marika Lindholm is the founder of ESME.com (Empowering Solo Moms Everywhere), a social platform dedicated to empowering a broad demographic of women, who despite differences in age, race, culture, and route to solo motherhood are bound together in a conscious coalition that is strong, proud, and dedicated to their children. After receiving her PhD in sociology at SUNY Stony Brook, Lindholm taught courses on inequality, diversity, and gender at Northwestern University for over a decade. She's published scholarly and popular press articles, essays, and short fiction in a variety of outlets, including *Theory & Society*, *Journal of Historical Sociology*, the *Harvard Business Review*, the *Daily News*, *The Hill*, *Ms.*, *Writer's Digest*, *Working Mother*, *Mutha*, *Mind Body-Green*, *Psychology Today*, *Silent Voices*, and *the Southern Indiana Review*. Lindholm is also a coeditor of the award-winning anthology *We Got This: Solo Mom Stories of Grit, Heart, and Humor* (She Writes Press, 2019), a poignant and unflinchingly honest collection—written by seventy-five Solo Mom writers, including Amy Poehler, Anne Lamott, Mary Karr, and Elizabeth Alexander—that celebrates Solo Moms.

11

Dream with Your Eyes Open

Harry Edwards

There is tremendous power in understanding how your life is shaped by the social forces around you while also seeing the ways you can use your power to shape that same society. This is the fundamental lesson of the sociological imagination, and it's a lesson that's never let me down. You can't change what you don't understand, so open your eyes and take a look at your life, your community, your society, your world, and then dream. Your dreams aren't diversions. They are the fuel you need to make the world a better place.

EARLY DAYS

I was shaped by my early life in East St. Louis, Illinois, which was basically organized as a segregated apartheid system. For the most part, I—and others like me—were shut out of mainstream society. My mother and father did not have many opportunities. The social structure, the framework upon which a society is established that determines the norms and patterns of relations between the various societal institutions, was cruel and unforgiving when it came to the Black community. Our agency, or independent ability to act on free will and make choices, was profoundly limited. My mother dropped out of school right after middle school, and my father had gotten most of his education at Joliet State Prison. They managed to have eight children—no small feat, given the challenges they faced—before their marriage broke up. I watched my father lose his health trying to prove that a formerly incarcerated Black man in a racist society could support a wife and eight children on $65 a week without returning to prison. It might have been easy to feel defeated by these circumstances if I hadn't understood the unjust system that created them and let that fuel my desire for change—personally and socially. You don't have to allow the scope or height of your dreams to be limited by your current circumstances, but you do have to learn to dream with your eyes open.

By the time I got to college at age seventeen, I was ready to meet the challenges of the journey I'd chosen. I knew I'd have to work harder than my white classmates, and I quickly became notorious for spending most of my free time in the library. I was an athlete but knew my academics needed to come first. After we won a basketball game, everybody else—students, fans, teammates—would head out to party, and I would pick up my books and go to the library. Every opportunity I got, I went to the library, because I wanted to be a great student, and I understood that meant behaving as if I already was a great student. I learned early on that one true, demonstrable, proven shortcut to educational achievement or any kind of success—being a great athlete, a great son, or a great worker—is HARD WORK. Hard work won't eliminate the barriers of racism, but it is the only thing that will allow you to climb over those you can surmount. Everything and anything else is a more difficult and less dependable path to achievement.

My hard work paid off, and I ended up graduating with high honors and a national discus record. I was scouted by the LA Lakers as a draft prospect, but instead I accepted a Woodrow Wilson and Cornell University fellowship, which would pay for all the costs of earning my PhD from an Ivy League university. Recognizing that academics were a more reliable path to success than athletics, I nonetheless found a way to combine my passions. My dissertation ultimately became the first textbook in a new sociology subdiscipline: the sociology of sport.

ATHLETES PRESS FOR EQUALITY

Applying a sociological lens to sport made sense, given the breadth and influence of sport in American society and around the world. I was interested in how athletes were at the forefront of **social movements** for change, especially athletes involved in the ongoing struggle for Black freedom and justice—the struggle to broaden the bases of democratic participation in America in our constitutionally mandated quest to form that more perfect union.

During Reconstruction, a Black baseball player named Octavius Valentine Catto protested the lack of voting rights for Black people. He was killed as a result. Fast-forward to the turn of the twentieth century, and Jack Johnson, Joe Louis, the Negro Leagues. Then Jesse Owens went to Munich to participate in Olympic track and field events that the Nazis staged and showcased to demonstrate Aryan racial superiority. Owens demonstrated on that global stage that Black people could compete at the highest level of international expertise and not only succeed but dominate! By extension, we most certainly should be able to compete in our own country. Yet back in the United States, no matter how fast Jesse Owens ran, his feats didn't translate to agency. Racist structures and institutions continued to oppress.

Building upon that struggle for legitimacy, Jackie Robinson and other post–World War II athletes engaged in a "Second Wave" of all-out "struggle for access": Larry Doby in baseball; Kenny Washington and Woody Strode in football; and Earl Lloyd, Chuck Cooper, and Nat "Sweetwater" Clifton in basketball all set the stage for the Third Wave of athlete vanguard resistance and activism. The Third Wave included such greats such as Tommie Smith, John Carlos, Arthur Ashe, Jim Brown, Bill Russell, Curt Flood, Kareem Abdul-Jabbar, Lucius Allen, Mike Warren, and the Wyoming University 14, the Syracuse University 8, along with the San Jose State University football players, who provoked the cancellation of their season-opening football game in 1967 over issues of racial injustice. And, of course, there's the Fourth Wave, including Colin Kaepernick, Malcolm Jenkins, and others. Now we're in the Fifth Wave of increased agency, where entire teams in the NBA and WNBA are saying, "No, we're not going to play until you address the issue of social justice. You must address systemic injustice, as it impacts *all* of us."

There's nothing new about LeBron James, Chris Paul, Carmelo Anthony, the women of the WNBA, the US Women's National Soccer Team, and the courageous stands taken by Naomi Osaka, Serena Williams, Maya Moore, and other world-class Black athletes. They are part of a long-standing tradition of athlete activism. And even when only a few had the courage, the vision, and the commitment to speak up and speak out, they had an impact, leaving their mark on history.

ATHLETES AND SOCIAL MOVEMENTS

As a collective, Black athletes have more agency than ever because they are supported by the Black Lives Matter movement and evolving institutions that are reducing structural and **ideological barriers** to change. Athletes can't and shouldn't shoulder the entire burden of social change and activism, but when they are mobilized and galvanized within the context of some broader ideological movement's "political scaffolding," they are able to help others understand why those goals are critically important and why sacrifices are necessary. With their high profiles and sports platform, they can articulate the concerns and demands of the masses loudly enough to be heard. In other words, movements such as BLM enhance the **collective agency** of athletes who choose to speak up.

Only with a scaffolding of a mass movement and ideological sentiment supporting athletes can they collaborate with the masses to move a particular agenda forward. The convergence of the BLM movement and collaborative activism by Black athletes is a ripe political moment that ideally will continue to persuade more Americans that police accountability, prison reform, and social justice are necessary and worthy goals.

As an activist and sport sociologist, I have the honor of mentoring athletes all the time. I talked to Carmelo Anthony and other athletes who were in the NBA's COVID-19 bubble in Orlando prior to the work stoppage. I spoke with the LA Clippers organization and Jerry West and his staff, as well as the Oklahoma City Thunder team and Chris Paul and his teammates. I was able to share what my more than half a century of scholar-activism has taught me, in terms of how wave after wave of athlete activists have managed similar situations. I have always pointed out that the distinction between a mob and a movement is follow-through. If you're going to have a work stoppage, for example, you're using your platform to send the message to owners, players, fans, advertisers, and stadium workers that the issue you're protesting is important and that everyone should pay attention. But you also need to have a strategic plan of follow-through. Based on advice from people like me, and even from Barack Obama, these athletes used their platform to organize and mobilize people to vote.

And clearly, that's what LeBron James, Chris Paul, and the athletes of the NBA, the WNBA, and the NFL have succeeded in doing. We can each contribute to the follow-through by demanding that elected officials make critical changes. To get the right people into the right position, masses of people are going to have to vote, and that means organizing and mobilizing people, making it easier for them to vote, and fighting against voting oppression and suppression. That was my advice to the players, and I'm so proud of them, because they are functioning within the context of the struggles of their era. As usual, they're in the vanguard of getting that kind of work done. An inspiring example is LeBron's organization, More Than a Vote, which mobilized Black voters and helped transform Georgia's political landscape from red to purple. When we dream with our eyes open, we really can change the world.

KEY CONCEPTS

Collective agency — The ability of a social group or a social movement to accomplish its goals. Without collective agency, activism can't succeed.

Ideological barriers — Shared beliefs that uphold the existing social order, making social change more challenging. Edwards points out that beyond structural barriers such as policies, practices, and institutions that systematically disadvantage a marginalized group, Black activist athletes have been historically hampered by racist ideologies in their quest for social justice.

Social movement — Activism by large segments of the population working to achieve what they believe is desirable social change or to undo social change believed to be harmful. Pro-life and pro-choice activism are examples of social movements that organize collectively around the same issue, abortion, but from opposing perspectives.

DISCUSSION QUESTIONS

1. What does Edwards mean when he says it's important to "dream with your eyes open"?
2. How did Edwards overcome structural barriers through agency? Have you faced a situation in which, despite your agency, structural barriers were too great to overcome?
3. Edwards believes that despite the ebb and flow of their collective agency, athletes can use their platforms as a force for change. What actions by athletes do you think are currently having a positive impact on society?

LEARN MORE

Arsenault, Raymond. *Arthur Ashe: A Life*. New York: Simon & Schuster, 2018.
Edwards, Harry. *The Revolt of the Black Athlete*. Champaign: University of
    Illinois Press, 2018.
———. *Sociology of Sport*. Homewood, IL: Dorsey Press, 1973.
Mills, C. Wright. *The Sociological Imagination*. Oxford: Oxford University Press,
    1959.
Rampersad, Arnold. *Jackie Robinson: A Biography*. New York: Ballantine Books,
    1998.

Harry Edwards was on the faculty of University of California at Berkeley from 1970 to 2001 and currently is professor emeritus in the Department of Sociology. Dr. Edwards, a scholar-activist who became a spokesperson for what amounted to a revolution in sports, is now considered the leading authority on developments at the interface of race, sport, and society, and was a pioneering scholar in the founding of the sociology of sport as an academic discipline. In 1968, he called for a Black athlete boycott of the US Olympic team to dramatize the racial inequities confronting Blacks in sport and society. Years later, Dr. Edwards became a consultant on issues of diversity for all three major sports. In 1987, he was hired by the commissioner of Major League Baseball to help increase front-office representation of minorities and women in baseball. He was with the NBA's Golden State Warriors from 1987 through 1995, specializing in player personnel recruitment and counseling. In 1986, he began work with the San Francisco 49ers in the area of player personnel counseling and programs. In 1992, the entire NFL adopted the programs he developed for handling player personnel issues, as well as the Minority Coaches' Internship Program he and Coach Bill Walsh developed to increase opportunities for minority coaches in the NFL. Edwards has received dozens of awards and honors, including several honorary doctorate degrees. He has written scores of articles and four books: *The Struggle That Must Be*, *Sociology of Sports*, *Black Students*, and *The Revolt of the Black Athlete*.

PART 3

Facing Our Families and Communities

The future which we hold in trust for our own children
will be shaped by our fairness to other people's children.

Marian Wright Edelman

12

Boy!

Tony N. Brown

Thought I would be killed before age seventeen. My childhood friends thought the same about themselves. So, none of us made long-term plans. We were mired too deeply in the social dislocations that defined inner-city blight—unemployment, interpersonal violence, fractured families, and the drug trade. We were victims of the synergistic relationship between benign neglect and white domination. For your information, I grew up in southeast Washington, DC. My neighborhood sat on the *wrong* side of the Anacostia River. It was gritty, soulful, go-go-music loving, impoverished, hyper-segregated, chicken wings with Mambo sauce–craving, dangerous, and isolated.

Today, it is totally different. Nowadays, the Green line Metro subway, gentrification, Starbucks, high-end grocery stores, white fluffy dogs, Pilates classes, and so on define my old neighborhood. *Sigh.*

My childhood friends used to say to me: "You are different. You'll make it out of here, professor!" The irony of being called *professor* because I was bookish and excelled in school—not the run-down, underfunded varieties in my actual neighborhood (the ones my childhood friends attended), but the over-performing Catholic versions, way on the other side of town—still hurts me because I wasn't smarter than any of them. Not more deserving or worthy. Facts of our biographies and history intersected to shape who among us would and wouldn't survive. I just wanted to *belong*, yet my academic success meant I would always feel guilty about those left behind in my old neighborhood.

After graduating from the University of Maryland, Eastern Shore (a validating HBCU space), I went straight to graduate school at the University of Michigan and endured multiple attempted **spirit murders** there. In the educational context, a spirit murder represents denying a student inclusion, protection, safety, nurturance, and acceptance because of norms grounded in racist and anti-Black paradigms. It involves humiliation and systemic devaluing of a student's authenticity. At Michigan, it was clear "one of these things was not like the others." And, frankly, since earning my PhD, I have been somewhat uncomfortable in my own skin. I share this biographical note to lead into a story from twenty-six years ago that still causes me to exhale and smile.

The story captures the sociological concept of **linked lives.** Linked lives originates within Glen Elder's **life course theory** but extends to any research topic where one's own accomplishments, failures, feelings, and beliefs are a function of being enmeshed with others. The concept reminds us that human lives are experienced interdependently and that social relationships provide crucial sources of coherence across biographical time and history. Other people help us find our place in society. Others allow us to make meaning of our experiences. Others remind us of connections with those who came before us. We are each embedded in networks of important and significant others, and others we might never meet directly or know personally. Connections forged across generations, within families, with in-laws, between neighbors, among church members or coworkers, and so on. These social relationships all matter because humans are fundamentally social creatures. This is the essence of sociology.

But I am not a typical sociologist. I am a critical race theorist. The core of critical race theory is that racism is not merely individual bias but is embedded in legal systems, policies, and institutions that maintain racial inequality. Hence, I can confirm that racism shapes how Black people understand their social relationships and connections to each other. Racism ensures Black people in the United States and Global South are enmeshed *forever*. Anti-Blackness shackles us. Consequently, not one of us is free until we all are.

The story begins like this. I drove home to southeast Washington, DC, for a short visit a couple months after successfully defending my dissertation. At the time, I worked as a research associate for a University of Michigan soft-money institute focused on youth drug use because I had had no success earning a tenure-track position. In my mind, not earning a tenure-track position meant I had failed.

I entered Matthews Memorial Baptist Church on MLK Jr. Avenue through a door near the pulpit. Sister Gladys always sat in the last seat on the outside aisle in the second pew from the front with the other deaconesses. Sister Gladys was not president of the deaconess board but, make no mistake, she was in charge.

She saw me before I saw her. Then I heard her voice. She exclaimed: *Boy!* Her utterance radiated love, affection, admiration, and kinship. Sister Gladys jumped up from her seat and threw her arms around me, her quickness surprising me, given her age. Like Jonah in the belly of the whale, I was engulfed.

Her face beamed with joy. "Look at you," she said. "I am so proud of you. Your momma told us you earned your PhD."

"Yes, ma'am, I did," I said. "It was very hard, but I made it."

"Your momma is so proud of you," she said. "We all knew you would make it." Then she asked, "How long were you studying for your PhD?"

"About seven years," I said.

She gasped. "Oh, my goodness! It's cold up there in Michigan, huh?"

Making an exaggerated sad face, I said, "Yes. And lonely!"

She chuckled, then said, "Your momma kept your name in the prayer basket. She shared how you were doing and how you went through some tough times, questioning whether you belonged there. You should know: you were out of sight but *never* out of mind."

I must have looked surprised by her comment because she continued: "Listen, I watched you grow up and watched your momma struggle to raise you. You were a good kid . . . most of the time." She laughed. "These youngsters 'round here need someone like you to be their role model."

"Sister Gladys, I have no idea how I made it this far in life," I said. "I am nobody's role model."

She rolled her eyes and reiterated, purposefully this time, "I said, we kept your name in the prayer basket."

Just then I glanced toward the pulpit. There, twenty-five feet above the choir stand, hung a larger-than-life portrait of a white, blond, blue-eyed Jesus. It had hung there for as long as I could recall. I contemplated the absurdity of a white, blond, blue-eyed Jesus surveilling and looking down on my Black church community.

I snapped back to reality when Sister Gladys swiveled around and shouted down the row to the other deaconesses: "Look who came back home!"

Like a row of bobblehead dolls, they started nodding with approval. Right then, Sister Gladys grabbed me by the face as if I were five years

old and said, "We are so proud of you." Then she hugged me again—
the type of hug that sticks with you because it warms your bones and
heals your spirit.

The pianist started playing a hymn, and you could tell church was
about to start.

The pastor entered through the same door I had and strode toward
the pulpit to place his belongings there.

"Pastor Kearney, look over here," Sister Gladys yelled at him. "Dr.
Brown is in da house." Doing a little happy dance, she sang, "Dr.
Brown! Dr. Brown! Dr. Brown!"

The pastor froze. He locked eyes with me and shouted in a deep
baritone voice, "Dr. Brown! Amen!"

I leaned close to Sister Gladys and whispered sheepishly, "Being
called Dr. Brown feels funny. Just call me Tony."

The joy drained from her face. The ends of her mouth curled down.
Her forehead wrinkled. Her hands moved to her hips. Her eyes widened. She stood up straight. In short, she went from 0 to 100 . . . real
quick.

"Do you know how important your PhD is?" she asked sternly. I was
smart enough to not answer.

"Your PhD means the world to so many people," she admonished.
"Your momma. These youngsters running 'round this church. Me. The
Black people who try to live with dignity in southeast Washington, DC.
Your momma's family in Paincourtville, Louisiana."

She went on. "Too much blood has been spilled in the streets of DC.
Young Black men like you cut down for no good reason. Sadness and
despair spreading everywhere like a plague. You feel their pain and
suffering, don't you? We need your success. We need you to rise up,
but not forget where you came from."

A response tried to escape my mouth. She interrupted me, angry
and disappointed that her message was not getting through to me.

Sister Gladys then inched closer and asked, "Do you know what the
white folk called your grandfather, his father, my father, my brothers,
your uncles, and your great-uncles?"

O-U-C-H. I knew not to speak. Not to utter a word.

Her stare intensified. Her brow furrowed. I think she grew a couple
inches taller.

I knew what was coming. Right then, *she understood that I understood.* Lesson learned. But she would not let me off the hook. She just

stared through me, letting the moment swell with intensity. I needed to apologize, though it was too late.

"Boy!" She blurted. This utterance was unlike the one at the start of this story. This one was soaking with disgust, disdain, disregard, and damnation. This one embodied the routine racial trauma of generations of Black men and their loved ones. This one cut like a knife. It hung in the air. It changed me.

She turned and moseyed back to her aisle seat.

I stood paralyzed. That word, spoken in that way, in that church, and under the surveilling blue eyes of that Jesus portrait, immobilized me like a straitjacket. I might have earned a PhD, but I'd just gotten schooled.

Sister Gladys sat down and immediately looked up at me. The joy returned to her face. She smiled broadly and earnestly at me. I nodded in appreciation and humility, then hurried to find a seat near my mother.

Here's what I learned from Sister Gladys: *I* did not earn a PhD. *We* earned a PhD. Too many Black people sacrificed too much for me to survive, let alone begin to thrive, in a world dependent upon anti-Blackness. I needed to get out of my own feelings. Doing so has been a long process. I cannot enjoy the privilege of feeling uncomfortable being called Dr. Brown when others depend upon me to fight white domination while leaving the ladder down.

I'm on it, Sister Gladys. I'm on it.

KEY CONCEPTS

Life course theory — A perspective that asserts that each life stage influences the next and that examining how lives unfold over the long term offers powerful information about the health of our communities.

Linked lives — All of us live our lives interdependently and are embedded in social relationships across our life span. Brown describes this network of shared relationships as inherently sociological.

Spirit murder — Racism goes beyond physical pain, robbing people of color of their humanity and dignity, which results in spiritual injuries and even spiritual death. This term is often used to describe the Black experience in schools that fail to protect students from humiliation and undeserved punishment, such as white staff members forcibly cutting Black children's hair.

DISCUSSION QUESTIONS

1. The idea of linked lives is a powerful one that is often neglected in a society focused on individual accomplishment. Whose lives are linked to yours in relation to your "accomplishments, failures, feelings, and beliefs"? How are the circumstances of your own life enmeshed with others?

2. How did you feel when you read that Brown was uncomfortable being called Dr. Brown? Where do you think that discomfort came from? Were you surprised by Sister Gladys's response?

3. How did racism affect Brown's experience of education from elementary school all the way through graduate school? How was his experience different from those of his friends? Why do you think he says that since earning his PhD he feels "somewhat uncomfortable" in his own skin?

LEARN MORE

Coates, Ta-Nehisi. *Between the World and Me*. New York: Random House, 2015.

Crenshaw, Kimberlé, Neil Gotanda, Gary Peller, and Kendall Thomas, eds. *Critical Race Theory: The Key Writings That Formed the Movement*. New York: New Press, 1995.

Elder, Glen. *Children of the Great Depression: Social Change in Life Experience*. 25th anniversary ed. Oxfordshire: Routledge, 1998.

Giele, Janet Z., and Glen H. Elder Jr. *Methods of Life Course Research: Qualitative & Quantitative Approaches*. Thousand Oaks, CA: Sage Publication, 1998.

Love, Bettina L. "Anti-Black State Violence, Classroom Edition: The Spirit Murdering of Black Children." *Journal of Curriculum and Pedagogy* 13, no. 1 (2016): 22–25. https://www.tandfonline.com/doi/abs/10.1080/15505170.2016 .1138258.

Williams, Patricia. "Spirit-Murdering the Messenger: The Discourse of Fingerpointing as the Law's Response to Racism." *University of Miami Law Review* 42, no. 1 (1987): 125–157.

Tony N. Brown is a distinguished professor and associate chair of sociology at Rice University in Houston, TX. He earned his PhD from the University of Michigan and completed postdoctoral training at Michigan's Institute for Social Research. Before joining the Rice University faculty in 2016, he was tenured in the Sociology Department at Vanderbilt University. While there, he coedited the *American Sociological Review*, served as the inaugural Faculty Head of Hank Ingram House in the

Martha Rivers Ingram Commons, and held appointments in several departments and programs across the main and medical campuses.

As a critical race theorist, Brown investigates how racism works, from the womb to the tomb, to disadvantage Blacks and privilege whites. Mechanisms of racism include interactions across interpersonal, institutional, and cultural levels, implicating the mundane and extraordinary in the maintenance of white supremacy. With survey data from community-based samples, he is presently investigating whites' perpetration of racial discrimination, changes in racial apathy, the epidemiology of racial trauma, the psychological wages of whiteness, and culturally specific conceptualizations of mental health. Brown practices anti-racism through graduate training. For example, he founded and currently directs the Racism and Racial Experiences (RARE) Workgroup (https://rare.rice.edu/) and the Statistical Training and Research Techniques at Rice University (STaRT@Rice) program (https://start.rice.edu/).

13

On Being a Marginal Woman

Kathleen Gerson

In 1926, Robert Park proposed the concept of the "marginal man" to refer to "one whom fate has condemned to live in two societies and in two not merely different but antagonistic cultures." As a person of his time and place, Park no doubt used "men" to refer to all of humanity, not just a group that contains slightly less than half of the human population. In any case, let me bring that concept into the twenty-first century by declaring myself a marginal woman. To be clear, I do not just mean that being a woman makes me marginal, though all women are in various ways members of a marginal group. In this instance, however, I am referring to experiences reaching deep into my childhood, where I participated in two cultural groups without fully identifying with either.

Born in the Deep South, I spent my first fifteen years as part of a close-knit yet highly assimilated Reform Jewish community in Montgomery, Alabama. We enjoyed eating shellfish and pork barbeque, attended religious services on Sunday instead of on the Jewish Sabbath, and put presents under a tree every Christmas season. Yet despite our **cultural assimilation** and economic prosperity, my parents' generation remained socially separate from their Christian peers.

As the Jewish community spread out to disparate neighborhoods, my generation joined the same (at the time, racially segregated) public schools and participated in the same after-school activities as our white Christian peers. For me, this created two social worlds. During the school week, I hung out with neighborhood friends and classmates, while on the weekend, my social life shifted to worshipping, playing, and dining with Jewish relatives and friends. Although it would be years before I learned the meaning of the term *marginality*, the experience of tacking between these two social worlds structured my life and seeped into my consciousness. The challenges it posed prepared me for the resonance and inspiration I ultimately found in the sociological imagination.

Unaware at first that there might be tension between these worlds, an early hint occurred on a spring day in the third grade. While my friend Susan and I were strolling around the playground during recess, she asked if I knew that Rachel, another girl in our grade, was Jewish. Puzzled, I wondered aloud why she had raised such a question. Because, she said, since "Jews don't believe in Jesus as their savior they are all going to hell." Surprised and taken aback, I blurted out that I was Jewish too. Amid our shared embarrassment and discomfort, we quickly changed the subject.

Despite our unspoken agreement to act as if nothing disturbing had happened, the exchange put an irrevocable distance between us. We continued to visit each other's homes and play together at school, but it never felt the same. Nothing could erase my realization that she considered me different in some fundamental way, and I could not help but wonder how many others agreed. Fear that an invisible **stigma** might reveal itself at any moment now tempered my sense of belonging.

If this schoolyard interchange served as a warning that danger lurked just below the surface of ordinary daily encounters, the arrival of early adolescence brought my position as both insider and outsider to center stage. By the time I reached middle school, my school friends had coalesced into a close-knit group that gathered every weekend for sleepovers, where we stayed up most of the night to share our hopes, anxieties, and teenage secrets. Others called us "the crowd," making it clear that membership in this group conveyed social status. To be sure, I enjoyed the popularity, but sharing close-knit bonds with my good friends mattered much more.

Along with the obvious benefits, however, the visibility that came with status also increased the chances of exposure. One afternoon in the summer following seventh grade, the perils of exposure became all too real when my girlfriends and I met up with a group of boys from another school. One of the boys began taunting another friend with insults, including "You're a dirty Jew!" My girlfriends immediately grew silent and cast their eyes downward, prompting another boy to wonder aloud if one of us might be Jewish. Searching the crowd, he then pointed to my best friend, Maria, whose dark hair and prominent nose made her the most likely candidate in his eyes. Without any hesitation, I quickly raised my hand to "out" myself, correct the misidentification, and rescue Maria. Then, struggling to hide my embarrassment and recover my dignity, I once again did my best to shrug off the episode and continue as if nothing noteworthy had happened. Yet any uncertainty I may have harbored about my status dissolved altogether. My fair coloring and assimilated ways might allow entry into a privileged social world, but I now understood that these traits would never be enough to confer full-fledged membership in the group.

In their efforts to reassure me, my friends would later proclaim, as my friend Jennifer put it, "You're not *really* Jewish." She meant this as a compliment and assumed I would hear it that way. To the extent that I wanted to be accepted, she was right. I did appreciate the mental gymnastics my friends were willing to perform to include me. Yet even if they made an exception in my case, reassurances that I did not belong to a group they considered distasteful only confirmed their prejudices. I knew their assumptions—about how members of my community looked and behaved—were not only wrong but also hurtful and dangerously harmful. As much as I wanted their acceptance, it would never be worth the price of renouncing my Jewish identity. If the mere mention of my religion could so easily become an occasion for emotional injury, then the price of inclusion would be to endure the inevitable moments when my true self was exposed and people laid bare their disapproval. Since I valued their friendship and believed they valued mine, I was willing to pay this price.

At fifteen, my experiences of marginality took on a very different cast when I moved to San Francisco with my single mother. It felt liberating to leave behind the insular world of a small Southern city and enter a cosmopolitan metropolis that offered countless new possibilities. Yet the move evoked mixed emotions. While the prospect of starting over offered me a chance to shed my **marginal status**, it also posed the challenge of finding a place for myself in another unfamiliar social world. After years of learning to navigate the two worlds of my childhood, the prospect of facing a new one with no friends to rely on was daunting. My anxieties only increased when, shortly after my arrival, a distant relative hosted a party to introduce me to some girls who would soon be my classmates at the large, ethnically and racially diverse public high school I had decided to attend. As we sat in our host's living room drinking soda and eating snacks, these girls were the opposite of welcoming. They laughed at my "funny" accent, commented on my dubious fashion choices, and fabricated silly "Southern" names to introduce themselves. This was an early clue that, in an ironic inversion, the telltale signs of my Southern roots had replaced my religion and progressive politics as sources of marginality.

At the time, this encounter seemed like nothing more than the boorish behavior of a small group of "mean girls" (who, in another ironic twist, were mostly Jewish). Yet the hope that this experience represented an isolated event disappeared a few weeks later when the school year began. In my new homeroom, our teacher, known as Mr. K., asked us to introduce ourselves. When my turn came and I began to speak, the students burst into sustained laughter. The Southern accent that had once helped me blend in now exposed my difference. While neither my religion nor my liberal political outlook were now cause for notice or concern, my identity as a Southerner evoked puzzlement, skepticism, and even mockery.

This reversal of fortune did not banish my marginal status, but it did give it a different form. Rather than being hidden, the attributes that now set me apart were evident for all to hear and see. I no longer had to walk on eggshells, never knowing when my stained identity would reveal itself. I could also draw on the lessons of my previous life to address the challenges of this new one. Relying on the emotional resources that weathering past social injuries had nurtured, I learned to take pride in my difference rather than try to hide it. In this more diverse world, where no single ethnic or racial group predominated, hyphenated identities were just part of the water in which we all swam.

It took time to forge friendships, but when I finally did, it was with people who claimed a wide array of backgrounds—from Jennie, whose parents had emigrated from China, to Nathan, whose Muslim grandparents came from Lebanon, to Sheena, whose African American relatives had settled in San Francisco decades ago. Most of my new classmates occupied some kind of marginal status, and it was exciting and liberating to form close bonds that reached across so many ethnic, racial, and religious boundaries. Our shared experience of marginality created opportunities to learn from each other, enjoy our differences, and recognize our commonalities. In this context, I learned how to take a stand without fearing that exposure would mean banishment. I even welcomed the chance to teach my classmates that a Southern accent did not automatically denote ignorance and racism. Rather than feeling condemned (to use Park's word), I found that moving among different social worlds in this freer, more fluid context became enriching.

By the time I arrived at college, I had learned by experience to view my social world from the inside out and the outside in, yet I lacked a language to place these insights in a larger framework. Then, wandering into a sociology class midway through my junior year, I found a perspective that linked my own experiences to a more general set of social patterns and processes. Tacking between two cultures as a child had attuned me to how easily any aspect of one's identity can provide cause for celebration in one situation and disdain in another. My subsequent shift in adolescence to another cultural milieu had shown me that, despite their apparent differences, dominant groups everywhere are prone to draw social and moral boundaries between those whom they believe deserve full-fledged inclusion and those they think do not belong. These lessons were hard won, but they were well worth the price. Moving among so many social worlds has taught me that distinctions between entitled and marginal groups may take different forms in different contexts, but they are all mechanisms that serve to create and enforce social inequality.

My early biography helped me look beyond the obvious to see the conflicts and contradictions that shape human experience. Sociology gave me the tools I needed to put my personal experiences to larger and more productive use. As a feminist who came of age just as women's fight for equality was regaining momentum, my work has focused on uncovering the sources, shape, and consequences of the gender revolution. I have interviewed hundreds of women, men, and gender-nonconforming individuals from a variety of backgrounds about their experiences contending with the intensifying clashes between paid work and private life. It has been revelatory to hear their stories, learn about their inner lives, and discover the ways their everyday struggles have contributed to collective efforts that are transforming the ways people work, form relationships, and care for others.

My experiences tacking among conflicting social worlds convinced me that uncovering the sources of unequal status is an essential first step toward creating more just, humane, and equal societies. It is thus no accident that my work as a sociologist has sought to understand how people experience the social conflicts they face and how, under the right circumstances, they are able to overcome the obstacles and change the direction of their lives and their societies. Uncovering the obstacles that block people's life paths and showing how to overcome them has confirmed my conviction that sociological insight is integral to empowering the marginalized and creating a more inclusive world. If my experiences of marginality have paved the way to seek answers to these "big" questions, then I can only be grateful. Navigating what Park viewed as "antagonistic cultures" no doubt posed difficult challenges, but it also offered the opportunity to bridge divisive social boundaries and find the common threads among diverse social worlds that can bring us together.

KEY CONCEPTS

Cultural assimilation — The process by which racial and ethnic groups change their cultural beliefs, values, and behaviors to fit into a new culture. For instance, Gerson's Jewish family attended religious services on Sunday instead of on the Jewish Sabbath, put up a Christmas tree, and ate pork.

Marginal status — Gerson uses this term in reference to Robert Ezra Park's marginal man theory, which focuses on the struggle of individuals suspended between two cultures. Biracial people sometimes grapple with this when they feel as if neither racial group fully accepts them because of their racially mixed identity.

Stigma — A personal attribute that disqualifies someone from full social acceptance. As a girl, Gerson learns about the stigma of being Jewish in her Southern community and realizes she would never be fully accepted because of her religion.

DISCUSSION QUESTIONS

1. Gerson describes being an outsider as a child and then as a teenager. How are these experiences of outsiderness different? Why do you think her teenage experience leads her to view outsiderness, or difference, as something to be proud of?
2. Gerson's parents, along with others in their Reform Jewish community, used assimilation, either consciously or not, to be accepted as Jewish people in predominantly Christian Montgomery, Alabama. This strategy is double-edged. In what ways did it help Gerson, and in what ways did it cause harm?
3. Many of the stories in this volume contain themes of difference or outsider status. Do you think it is coincidental that so many

sociologists share this experience, or do you think there is something about the experience that might make people more inclined to think sociologically?

LEARN MORE

Brekhus, Wayne H. *The Sociology of Identity: Authenticity, Multidimensionality, and Mobility*. New York: Polity, 2020.

Ferris, Marcie Cohen, and Mark I. Greenberg, eds. *Jewish Roots in Southern Soil: A New History*. Waltham, MA: Brandeis University Press, 2018.

Park, Robert E. "Human Migration and the Marginal Man." *American Journal of Sociology* 33, no. 6 (1926): 881–893.

Kathleen Gerson is Collegiate Professor of Arts & Science and professor of sociology at New York University. Her work focuses on the sources, shapes, and consequences of the intertwined revolutions in gender, work, and private life in the United States and across the globalizing world. To make sense of these connections, she combines the deep understandings afforded by in-depth interviewing with the large-scale overviews provided by quantitative analysis to uncover the ways unfolding individual biographies intersect with social institutions in flux to shape the contours of social and individual change. She is the author or coauthor of six books, including *The Science and Art of Interviewing* (with Sarah A. Damaske), *The Unfinished Revolution*, *The Time Divide* (with Jerry A. Jacobs), *No Man's Land*, and *Hard Choices*. Her work has been recognized by a number of awards, including a Guggenheim fellowship, and has been featured in a range of media outlets, including the *New York Times*, the *Washington Post*, *USA Today*, *PBS NewsHour*, National Public Radio, and CNN. She is currently writing a book, tentatively titled *Why No One Can Have It All*, that examines how the deepening and widening collision between earning a living and caring for others has generated new gender strategies for fashioning commitments to paid work and family life.

14

Ghost(s) of Detroit

Waverly Duck

In the summer of 1983, when I was about seven years old, the son of a neighbor and family friend, Percy, became the first crack dealer in my neighborhood, on the East Side of Detroit. Percy rose to the status of local folk hero, facilitated by the economic downturn of the previous year, which led to layoffs for my stepfather and many other men employed in manufacturing. Percy was among the new crop of Black men in their late twenties and early thirties who discovered they could replace their lost factory wages with money from selling drugs. He had the money, clothes, and a Mercedes—in contrast to the older generation, mainly our fathers and uncles, who preferred Cadillacs and Lincolns. Once, he hosted a big Fourth of July block party, purchasing most of the food and fireworks, and creating a much-needed celebration in our economically depressed community.

Although I was not aware of it at the time, the party signaled a fateful transformation then underway in my neighborhood. By October, a new phenomenon had made its appearance: crack addiction. The crack cocaine epidemic of the 1980s devastated many communities. Directly or indirectly, it touched everyone in Detroit. I witnessed its effects firsthand with several relatives. Close friends and family members became almost unrecognizable, ghostly representations of their former selves. Once they were out of work, formerly trusted men and women succumbed to the enticement of drugs, abandoned their children, stole to support their habit, and were caught up in waves of violence from competition among dealers and raids by the police.

When I was eight, my childlike distance from death was shattered. Growing up, I often watched my parents struggle, especially during periods when we barely had enough to eat. My parents and my sisters had their room, and the third-oldest child, my brother, had his own room because he worked and contributed to the household finances. Though I was supposed to sleep on a pallet in the basement, I claimed the couch in the front room, our living room, as my preferred sleeping place. The neighborhood was becoming so unpredictably violent that my mother feared I would get hit by a stray bullet. After all, the front room faced the street.

One night, I heard the screeching of a car and several men yelling, then gunshots. I heard a woman screaming for help, then more gunshots. My mother awoke and made me move from the couch to the basement. She called the police, but they didn't show up until the next day. *The next day.* We—mostly the kids in the neighborhood—all saw this woman's naked, burned, dust-covered, bloated body lying in the dead end of the street. We later learned that she had been raped and murdered, and her body set ablaze. It resembled a mannequin with burned, matted hair.

The following week, I was sent to Mississippi for the summer. When I returned, my mother paid for me to live with a family friend while she figured out a better place for us to live. Unbeknownst to my mother, this woman—who had three children of her own—was also a drug addict, floating between heroin and crack. As a child, I didn't understand that my mother was sending me away to keep me safe, and I know she was unaware of her friend's addiction. In my mind, I felt if I said something, I would be sent farther away, like many of my Southern relatives who were sent north to live. The following year, I returned home to my mother, and we moved to the eastern outskirts of Detroit, near Seven Mile and Outer Drive.

In my new neighborhood, there were maybe two years of peace. I thrived in school. Because my siblings were older than me, I was mature for my age. For a short period, my family called me Man-Man, a name for young boys who acted like adults and shared the name of their fathers. I was also criticized because I questioned everything, which my elders found disconcerting. Yet, I loved my life. My stepfather was a jazz musician, carpenter, painter, cook, and construction worker. He personified the Black American notion of a hustler, a person who worked any and every job to make ends meet. He had formerly worked in the foundry at the auto plant; the dirtiest and most physically strenuous jobs were *always* reserved for Black men. His stock emotion was happiness. My stepfather adored me and believed I could do anything. I was his sidekick on carpentry jobs, an errand-runner for jazz musicians, and his good-luck charm for dice games. Here was a man who had fought in the Korean War, was profoundly active in the Civil Rights movement in the South, and was heavily discriminated against throughout his life, yet was always kind and generous. He was laid off by Chrysler after he was injured at work. Though he received a $10,000 settlement, the money didn't last long. Once he realized that he was permanently unemployed, he had a nervous breakdown.

At that time, a "nervous breakdown" encompassed myriad reactions to extreme stress. In my stepfather's case, he would shut down for weeks, unable to participate in routine human interactions. During these bouts of depression, he would leave for weeks on end, always returning with gifts and money from a hustling job. Though he became pessimistic about his own prospects, he saw nothing but endless possibilities in and for me. According to the famous Black saying, "You can do anything you put your mind to," and my stepfather said it to me repeatedly. He taught me how to drive at eleven, used my left-handedness as a particular skill when teaching me how to box and play baseball, and protected me from other people's homophobic stereotypes about boys doing art when I started taking after-school art classes in elementary school. When I left home, my stepfather cosigned on my first apartment. I was lucky to have a man in my life who did his best in a world that was hostile to his existence.

My stepfather is the reason I love Elijah Anderson's *A Place on the Corner* so much: the men in this book are my father, uncles, cousins. *A Place on the Corner* and Joyce Ladner's *Tomorrow's Tomorrow* were two of the first books by Black ethnographers to challenge a widespread belief that poverty in general, and the poverty of Black communities specifically, was the result of a **culture of poverty** that featured learned helplessness, bad habits, and lowered expectations that kept people from getting ahead. Instead, these books contained accounts and people I recognized, capturing the joys and struggles of the human condition under extreme pressure and structural anti-Black racism. I discovered that, instead of blaming a culture of poverty for the problems in our neighborhoods, we need to use an **interaction-order approach**. This approach counters the dominant stories told about a place by people who have never inhabited it with alternative narratives grounded in members' own ways of sensemaking. These counternarratives center members' own practices rather than the categories and preconceptions of outsiders.

My career as a sociologist has been shaped by my need to understand what was happening all around me as I was growing up in Detroit. The people and places I grew up with seldom figured in academic texts. For all their erudition, these works are missing essential stories and relationships, resulting in distorted representations of the world as I knew it. My own first ethnographic study focused on a community that reminded me of the one I had grown up in before it was ravaged by the crack epidemic. Here was a community of families who had migrated to a northeastern city from small Southern towns, only to fall on hard times. It was also the setting for an often-overlooked type of social solidarity on the part of a group of young men—mostly members of the same extended family—who created an open-air drug market. These men, connected by strong kinship ties, shared their entrepreneurial sensibilities to sustain themselves and their families within an interaction order that created economic opportunities in the **underground economy**—drug dealing— where there were few other alternatives in the **formal economy**. Though this interaction order was dangerous, with life-and-death consequences, many older residents were quick to point out to me that the men participating in it were their sons, brothers, nephews, and kin. While these men's actions were not celebrated—and were often condemned—they nonetheless made sense under oppressive economic circumstances. Indeed, their motivation and behaviors were a rational adaptation to the multiple structural obstacles they faced on a daily basis.

While the neighborhood I studied still stands to this day, the one where I grew up no longer exists. I speculate that the types of drugs, decline of the automotive industry, typography of the space, proximity to a network of Southern relatives, and rise of mass incarceration all shaped the divergent trajectories of these two neighborhoods.

For me, becoming a sociologist has provided insight into the meanings and long-term consequences of economic inequality, structural racism, and endemic violence that so many children experience. My life as a sociologist has given me a deeper understanding of the social world and my place in it, a precious opportunity to give back to the communities that have given me so much over the years, and a chance to understand the origins of various forms of inequality. While my research has focused on diverse topics, including inequality, race, stratification, urban ethnography, autism, and food insecurity, the thread uniting them has always been an emphasis on local sensemaking practices and the value of each person's own story. The mission of my work is to demonstrate how an interaction-order approach to the study of communities and institutional settings can lead to a deeper understanding of everyday life from the perspectives of those experiencing them, which is indispensable if we aim to build something better.

KEY CONCEPTS

Culture of poverty — The idea that people in poverty develop certain habits that cause their families to remain poor from generation to generation. Most sociologists are critical of this perspective because it blames the victim and negates the myriad structural forces that promote intergenerational poverty.

Economy — Generally speaking, an economy is a system for producing and distributing goods and services in a country or region. For sociologists, an important distinction is drawn between the **formal economy**, or the part of the economy that the government is fully aware of and that is regulated by labor laws and taxation, and the **underground economy**, where the sale of goods and services is unreported and in some cases illegal, such as the drug trade.

Interaction-order approach — Sociological analysis that focuses on cooperative social actions and shared social expectations by groups trying to make sense of their world. According to Duck, this approach is especially useful in understanding actions that are deemed deviant by the dominant culture. For example, against a backdrop of poverty and discrimination in the formal economy, informal economic activity like selling drugs, which may seem irrational to outsiders, might actually be understood as rational responses to limited opportunity by members of the community.

DISCUSSION QUESTIONS

1. What were some of the structural barriers facing the community where Duck was raised? How is your community similar or different?
2. How does focusing on the interaction order in Duck's community support his critique of the culture-of-poverty argument, which focuses on the moral failings of poor, urban communities?
3. How does a culture-of-poverty approach limit social change and help maintain inequality?

LEARN MORE

Anderson, Elijah. *A Place on the Corner*. Chicago: University of Chicago Press, 1978.

Cashin, Sheryll. *White Space, Black Hood: Opportunity Hoarding and Segregation in the Age of Inequality*. Boston: Beacon Press, 2021.

Duck, Waverly. *No Way Out: Precarious Living in the Shadow of Poverty and Drug Dealing*. Chicago: University of Chicago Press, 2015.

Goffman, Erving. "The Interaction Order." *American Sociological Review* 48, no. 1 (1983): 1–17.

Ladner, Joyce. *Tomorrow's Tomorrow: The Black Woman*. Lincoln: University of Nebraska Press, 1971.

Rawls, Anne. "The Interaction Order Sui Generis: Goffman's Contribution to Sociological Theory." *Sociological Theory* 5, no. 2 (1987): 136–149.

Waverly Duck is an urban ethnographer and the North Hall Chair Endowed Professor of Sociology and Associate Director, Center for Black Studies Research at the University of California, Santa Barbara. He is the author of *No Way Out: Precarious Living in the Shadow of Poverty and Drug Dealing* (University of Chicago Press, 2015), a finalist for the Society for the Study of Social Problems's 2016 C. Wright Mills Book Award. His second book on unconscious racism, *Tacit Racism*, coauthored with Anne Rawls (also with the University of Chicago Press), was the 2021 winner of the Charles Horton Cooley Book Award from the Society for the Study of Symbolic Interaction; received an Honorable Mention from the 2021 Mary Douglas Book Prize, the American Sociological Association Culture Section; was the 2022 Book Award winner for the North Central Sociological Association; and was the 2022 Winner of the Oliver Cromwell Cox Book Award for the American Sociological Association Section on Racial and Ethnic Minorities. With Anne Rawls and Kevin Whitehead, he also coauthored and curated *Black Lives Matter: Ethnomethodological and Conversation Analytic Studies of Race and Systemic Racism in Everyday Interaction* (Taylor and Francis, 2020). Like his earlier work, his current research investigates the challenges faced by socially marginal groups. However, this work is more directly concerned with the interaction order of marginalized communities, how participants identify problems, and what they think are viable solutions.

15

Solidarity in Tunisia and Texas

Mounira M. Charrad

I first realized in my childhood how important solidarities based on extended family ties can be. As a child and then an adolescent, I would hop in the car with my father and our dog to drive to small towns in Central Tunisia. A physician in charge of a regional hospital, my father provided medical care at clinics in several surrounding towns once a week. Accompanying him on those short trips was a treat. It gave me a chance to discover life in a slice of Tunisian society different from the urban, professional, cosmopolitan world in which I lived.

In small towns, I met men and women whose lives were immersed in their extended family and broader kinship ties. People defined their identity in terms of the larger kin group to which they belonged; their communities were named "Sons of" X or Z. They viewed their commitment to that group as central to their lives. This was for good reason, since group solidarity represented a safety net in a place that lacked public assistance and offered few economic opportunities.

Solidarities, which are related to identities, refer to the connections we feel to others and to the social groups that are meaningful to us. While identity relates to who we think we are, solidarities have to do with forms of belonging. They represent our social space and our meaningful communities. They are part of our **social capital**—the set of relationships that frame and shape our lives. As Durkheim taught us, and recent research has claimed, as social animals, we need social interaction. A sense of belonging is key to both our emotional and physical well-being.

While growing up in Tunisia, I experienced the support of my own kinship network for things small and big, even though it was more fluid and less rigidly compelling than what I had observed in small towns. Representing valuable social capital, my kinship network constituted a convenient resource to "get things done." I could reach out to a relative, close or distant, who would know someone who would know someone who would connect me to the right person who could help me. Take renewing my passport. Given the notoriously slow Tunisian bureaucracy, this task could require repeated trips to a government office over several weeks. Going through a relative or a relative's contact saved time and effort. I remember going to a cousin's house to give him my filled-out forms for passport renewal. My cousin then delivered my passport to me at my parents' house a few days later without my having to go to any office.

Networks of this kind are particularly helpful during times of illness or other crisis, such as death. Following a sudden illness, my father was bedridden for close to a month. During that time, relatives of various ages and professions came to the house to help. One cousin, a physician, visited daily to try to figure out the medical complexities of my father's case. An aunt stayed with us for the whole month to contribute to my father's care and relieve my mother of daily responsibilities. Younger cousins ran errands, from food shopping to trips to the pharmacy. All offered comfort with their presence, along with their practical contributions. All made my father, mother, sister, and me feel that we were not alone. They made us feel safe.

These **networks of solidarity** exist with a similar logic across social classes in Tunisia—from the very wealthy to professionals, the middle class, the working class, and rural populations. They constitute a system of reciprocal obligations: you do things for members of your network, and you expect them to do the same for you. This is not a reflection of personal liking. Rather, it is a matter of belonging to a social unit whose boundaries are understood by all, though they may shift from time to time.

When I decided to stay in the United States after finishing graduate school and marrying my American, New York–born boyfriend, my excitement at starting a new life could not fully eradicate a lingering sense of loss. I was leaving behind something precious in Tunisia and also in France, where I lived for five years before coming to the States and where part of my Tunisian extended kinship network had settled. As the French social scientist Jacques Berque told me in numerous conversations, "One never feels alone" in those worlds, because their kinship networks represent a safety net. That was true for me. I had a safety net.

Losing the care, support, and protection I had experienced from my extended family led me to consider hard questions. Was I making a mistake in leaving that support system behind to face a world in which I had nothing that came close to it? How would I know whom to trust? Who would come visit me if I broke a leg? How do people deal with death in the United States? Friends and acquaintances told me that, in this country, you get help from professionals who provide information and advice. I was not fully convinced, though, that this was a safe or comforting way to handle life. For years, I lived with nostalgia about the solidarities and social capital from which I had separated myself.

As time went on, I slowly discovered new forms of enduring, powerful solidarities through several experiences, first in graduate school and then later. Some of my friends from my graduate student days at Harvard and I have maintained unwavering friendships. A friend from our days as beginning assistant professors and I have rejoiced and cried together. Two of my former students and I have shared our life sagas for a couple of decades. They are now family to me. A friend with whom I share an interest in the visual arts and I have developed a powerful attachment.

These friendships are a treasure that define my life in the United States. They are all individual friendships, in that we have a strong bond, despite belonging to different social and professional networks. They represent for me what the British social scientist Elizabeth Bott calls a *dispersed network*. They are each tied to me but do not know each other well, if they know each other at all. This is different from a *dense network*, in which people are connected to each other and not just to a central node. When I lived in Tunisia and France, I had a dense kinship network in which my relatives had ties not only to me but also to each other. A dispersed network of the kind I developed in the States still offers support and friendship, however, since each tie in the network can be very strong.

During the Texas freeze of 2021, and the COVID-19 pandemic, I realized that I had not only a dispersed but also a dense network in the United States. This realization transformed my sense of belonging in Austin, Texas, where I have now lived for twenty-two years. In February 2021, Texas froze over, making the national and international news. My husband and I were without power for three days without any idea when it might return. We could not leave our house for six days because of our ice-covered walkway and driveway. Icy streets surrounded us. In many neighborhoods in Austin, the power outage lasted from days to weeks.

Power returned to our neighborhood sooner than it did to many others. After our power was restored, I received a text message from a friend who lives one exit away from me on the freeway. She was calling on behalf of one of our mutual friends, who, with her husband, was still stranded at home without power or water. The pipes were frozen, and the ice kept them from driving their cars out of their steep driveway. For about eight years, the three of us have belonged to a group of five women who have been getting together to exercise, followed by a happy hour. I used to think of these gatherings merely as a pleasant social experience. The group exhibited a different side during the crisis of the freeze. The friend who texted me asked whether my husband and I could rescue our common friend and her husband from their house and give them shelter. We had to call upon yet another friend with a 4x4 vehicle to fetch them and drive them over to my house, which they did. My husband and I hosted our friends for a few days, until power and water were returned to their house.

This experience had a strong effect on me. The chain of communication needed to help a member of our group in crisis worked beautifully and efficiently. Six of us were involved, the couple needing shelter, the friend who texted me, the friend who drove the couple in her 4X4, and my husband and I who provided shelter. We all came together to play a part in taking care of our common friends in a moment of crisis. Giving help was enormously meaningful to me, as was discovering new forms of solidarity where I live. Instead of feeling nostalgic for the kinship network of my childhood, I had a sense of creating something new, important, and meaningful in a different way. These friends and I solidified our bonds further over the course of the pandemic by helping each other at every turn. When some members of our small network lost relatives to COVID-19, others rallied around them. We remained in touch regularly and check on each other at least once a week. We know we are there for each other.

As someone who has lived out of the Tunisia/France orbit for a long time by now, I no longer enjoy the extended kinship ties I had while growing up. I maintain communication with a few relatives, but many things have changed. Despite making trips to Paris and Tunis, I can't remain deeply embedded in my kinship network of origin in the way I was when I was growing up in the midst of it. I am somewhat of a stranger now.

Early experiences with solidarities in Tunisia have shaped my personal life and my intellectual work. My nostalgia for supportive ties like the ones I knew in childhood led me to be open to forming strong bonds with friends, to believing in friendship, and to sharing in a recently discovered dense, close-knit friendship network. Those early experiences also provided insights that later informed my sociological research. The insights have helped me better understand how people come together when they feel threatened or need support to reach an objective.

Friendship can be as meaningful and powerful as kinship. Both enrich our lives with precious social capital and a sense of belonging. Built rather than inherited, the solidarities of friendship are equally enveloping and make us feel part of a warm and caring community.

KEY CONCEPTS

Networks — A group of individuals who are connected to one another. Our networks are a blend of strong and weak ties that offer support and information. A strong tie is usually a close friend, neighbor, or family member who is embedded in a similar web of mutual support. A weak tie is someone who you know but with whom you don't have a lot of overlapping ties. Weak ties may provide useful information that you might not get from your strong ties, as for example about job openings.

Social capital — The value derived from positive connections between people. Charrad's experience during the unusual freeze in Texas, in which her friendship circle helped one another, shows the value of social capital.

Solidarity — Cohesive social bonds and a feeling of unity that holds a group together. Solidarity inspires us to take care of each other and strengthens communities. During the pandemic, we saw many acts of solidarity, such as volunteers delivering essentials, designated shopping hours for elders, applause for healthcare workers, and singing from apartment windows.

DISCUSSION QUESTIONS

1. What similarities and differences does Charrad describe between formal kinship networks and those networks of friends that we

consider "like family"? How does each kind of network work in your own life?

2. Experiencing a new culture allows us to get a fresh perspective on things we might take for granted as "natural," like family structure. While this can be jarring and unsettling, it can also have benefits. What important lessons did you learn reading about the experiences of someone born outside the United States?

3. Charrad describes the difference between dispersed networks and dense networks. What are the strengths and weaknesses of each? How does each contribute to the creation or strengthening of solidarity in communities? If there are problems in your own life or community, does one of these kinds of networks seem more useful to you than another?

LEARN MORE

Bott, Elizabeth. *Family and Social Network: Roles, Norms, and External Relationships in Ordinary Urban Families*. London: Tavistock Press, 1957.

Bourdieu, Pierre. *Forms of Capital: General Sociology, Volume 3: Lectures at the College de France, 1983–84*. New York: Polity Press, 2021.

Charrad, Mounira M. *States and Women's Rights: The Making of Postcolonial Tunisia, Algeria, and Morocco*. Berkeley: University of California Press, 2001.

Durkheim, Emile. *The Division of Labor in Society*. Edited with a new introduction by Steven Lukes. New York: Free Press, 2014.

Gellner, Ernest. "Jacques Berque, a Fighter for Arab Culture–Archive, 1995." *The Guardian*, July 11, 2017.

Putnam, Robert D. *Bowling Alone: The Collapse and Revival of American Community*. 20th anniversary ed. New York: Simon & Schuster, 2020.

Mounira M. (Maya) Charrad is an award-winning author; an associate professor of sociology at the University of Texas, Austin; and a nonresident fellow at Rice University's Baker Institute. Her book *States and Women's Rights: The Making of Postcolonial Tunisian, Algeria, and Morocco* (University of California Press, 2001) received six distinguished awards, including the Best Book in Sociology Award from the American Sociological Association and the Best Book on Politics and History Greenstone Award from the American Political Science Association. She has edited or coedited *Patrimonial Power in the Modern World* (Sage); *Patrimonial Capitalism and Empire* (Emerald, Political Power and Social Theory Book Series); *Women Rising: In and Beyond the Arab*

Spring (NYU Press); *Women's Agency: Silences and Voices* (Special Issue of Women's Studies International Forum); and *Femmes, Culture et Société au Maghreb* (Afrique Orient). Her book *Forging Feminism: From Autocracy to Revolution in Tunisia* is forthcoming with Columbia University Press. Her articles have appeared in major scholarly journals. Her research focuses on state formation, colonialism, law, citizenship, kinship, women's rights, and social movements. She pioneered the study of how strategies of state building in kin-based societies affect women's rights. Challenging explanations based on a textual approach to religion, she calls attention instead to how social solidarities (kinship, marginality, or associations) enter politics. Her work has been translated into French, Arabic, and Chinese and has been featured on academic websites and in the media. She holds a PhD from Harvard and an undergraduate degree from the Sorbonne in Paris.

16

I Joined a Cult Because I Didn't Fit In—and Then I Didn't Fit In!

Victoria Reyes

I am the product of rape.

My mother had me when she was fifteen years old, so my Filipina grandmother raised me alongside my uncles and aunts as their sibling. My grandma always worked two to three jobs to take care of us, including as a restaurant server, a fast-food employee, and a domestic worker.

At age fourteen, I started working "under the table" at a Chinese fast-food restaurant to help pay for necessities. That was also around the time that I learned the truth about my birth: my biological father was a rapist. I started acting out and doing drugs. First weed, then trying acid and crack, one time each. That summer, my aunt invited me to visit her, so I took a Greyhound bus from Cincinnati to Arizona to stay with her, her partner, and their two boys. My aunt and her partner were doing drugs and dealing. After multiple out-of-body experiences due to drug use that summer, I vowed to quit and change my life.

Back in Cincinnati, we were evicted from our apartment. My grandma's boyfriend and I moved into his ex-wife's house, and my grandma went to live with another family member. Months later, we moved into a small home across the street after my grandmother cashed in her 401(k) to pay for the down payment. Because I had stopped doing drugs, I lost my old friends. I was alone, lonely, and just sixteen—the perfect conditions for being recruited into a fundamentalist international Christian church (read: **cult**), the International Churches of Christ (ICOC).

I remember my very first church service. The lead evangelist, as he was called, was a Korean American man. His wife, a white woman, had the formal title of lead evangelist's wife, a title that reflected the second-class citizenship of women in the Church. Sitting a few rows from the stage, I listened to the evangelist talk about how "sold-out disciples" were going to hell, and I asked myself what the hell I had gotten myself into. But when the service was over, the white teen leaders (adults in charge of teens' spiritual wellness in the Church) and the white, Black, and Brown teens in the ministry surrounded me and introduced themselves. They asked me questions and seemed to genuinely want to get to know me. I felt a deep sense of acceptance, one that contrasted starkly with both my chaotic home life and the almost all-white school I attended. Here, in this space, with these people, I felt like I was wanted. I thought I might belong here.

This search for belonging drove my desire to closely observe the social worlds I was a part of, even if only at the periphery. If only I could understand the rules of the game, maybe I could fill the deep hole inside me: the loneliness and sense of worthlessness I felt because of who I was and where I came from. Reading Pierre Bourdieu's work on fields (arenas of social life where actors vie for resources), social capital (resources associated with who you know), cultural capital (resources associated with what you know), and habitus (the feel for "the game," or common understandings in social situations) helped me understand why and how, despite my desperate attempts, I could never quite fit into the worlds around me.

Eager to fit into the ICOC, I set my sights high, aiming to become a world evangelism women's leader (because, of course, in this patriarchy, women could only lead other women). In Cincinnati, I'd been discipled by the teen ministers, a sign of my spirituality and potential for leadership. However, when I went to college, the campus ministry assigned me to a lower-tier discipler (the person assigned to look over my spiritual well-being) because I was seen as not sufficiently important or spiritual. I didn't have the right cultural capital, or knowledge and experience related to the Church's broader network; social capital, or networks of Church leaders as family members or friends; or habitus gained from growing up in the Church. My dreams of rising in the ranks of the ICOC were quickly dashed. "Kingdom Kids"—those who had been born and raised in the Church—were generally seen as the next set of leaders, particularly if they were white. I was neither a Kingdom Kid nor white. Once again, I felt like I didn't belong. I could do nothing right and could never be good enough, though I tried to do everything that was expected of me.

In the ICOC, the rules of the game were clearly spelled out. Members use a set of ten "studies" to recruit and indoctrinate future members. The foundation of Church beliefs and rules, the studies are set up to convince people that they are not "true" Christians and that the only way to become a true disciple is to join the Church and follow its tenets. I did all ten Bible studies in about a week. I was baptized soon afterward and threw myself into this life wholeheartedly. That meant trying to recruit other teens into the Church. It meant confessing all my sins—almost every waking thought—to my discipler. And it meant throwing myself into all the activities of the teen ministry and the Church more generally, including Wednesday and Sunday services, Friday-night teen devotionals, and Saturday activities. If I did all this, I thought, it would be evidence that I belonged and was wanted, a part of the group. These very desires made me vulnerable to the four characteristics of authoritarian control that author and former Unification Church cult member Steven Hassan has identified: extreme control over behavior, information, thought, and emotions.

One year, I was selected for the elite Hope Worldwide Volunteer Corps, in which teens training to become Church leaders volunteered in another city. I was told I'd been chosen because a church leader thought too many kids who had grown up in the Church had been chosen, so they added more recent recruits, like me. The rumor served as a reminder that I was different. Not a Kingdom Kid, and thus not good enough to be chosen on my own merits. Chosen only to fulfill a quota.

Although I attended Ohio State with many other young members of the Church, my experiences in the Church were very different from those of the white friend and college roommate who recruited me in high school, whose parents had been long-active leaders in the Church. And those of other white freshmen who came to Ohio State specifically because of the Church and who had similar familial and leadership ties to the ICOC. These white friends were discipled by the campus ministers, marked for leadership in the Church. Despite performative rhetoric proclaiming the diversity of the Church's membership, my own second-class citizenship and that of others deemed less worthy was obvious—as was the fact that we were not white.

In my second year of college, at age nineteen, I left the ICOC. I'd begun to question its practices and theology: the hierarchies, hypocrisies, lack of compassion and care, weaponizing sin, and twisting of scripture. In response, I was gaslighted, told I was the one who lacked faith and that I needed to meditate on scripture and confess my own arrogance to my discipler and others. During a conversation with the campus minister and his wife, I was almost drawn in again after being offered a leadership position mentoring the teen girl group. While I'd longed for a leadership position for the status and sense of belonging it would bring, the offer rubbed me the wrong way. If I was "struggling" (code for questioning the Church's doctrine and authority), why would they want me to mentor others? Recognizing it as a tactic to keep me involved, I rejected their offer.

After I officially left the church, I met with the white married campus leaders for the last time at Ohio State's Mirror Lake Café. This time, they tried a different tactic to keep me in the Church: they threw my past in my face, bringing up my previous drug use and reminding me of the loneliness and lack of belonging I had felt before joining the Church. They told me that while I might not end up on drugs again, if I left the Church, I would be following a path of sin and going to hell. I felt scared and anxious that I would return to a place where I would try to fill the emptiness inside me with people and activities that would only hurt me.

But my decision was final, and that meant my whole support system was gone. Everyone in the Church dropped me. One day, I saw a campus leader walking at a distance from me and felt like I was drowning. I couldn't move or breathe; I had to sit down.

The three years I stayed in the Church remain difficult for me to talk about. There's a stigma associated with it that feels different than other types of stigmas. I'm ashamed and embarrassed to admit to this period of my life because of the popular misperception that "smart" people know better than to join **cults**. Certainly, academics know better. Though I was recruited when I was young and in a vulnerable state, I fear that being a former cult member is evidence that I couldn't think critically—the very trait that is the foundation of scholarship—which brings me shame.

Only after many years of therapy did I realize that the **subculture** of the Church provided something I desperately needed at the time: structure and a sense of acceptance, no matter how limited. Sociology, too, helped my healing process. After reading the work of Bourdieu, I realized that my **outsider status** would have prevented me from ever being able to be completely accepted in the Church. I look back on my younger self, so filled with self-doubt, desperately trying to find a place and community to belong, doing whatever it took to finally feel valued and worthy. I'm not sure anything I could say or do would convince the younger me that she had nothing to prove, that she was worthy of love just on her own. More than anything, I wish I could reach back into the past and give her a hug. She deserves it.

KEY CONCEPTS

Cult — A relatively small group that excessively controls its members and demands devotion, usually by a self-appointed, authoritarian leader.

Outsider status — The experience of not fitting in or being accepted in a group based on your identity or beliefs. Reyes realized that because she's not white, the Church would have permanently relegated her to outsider status.

Subculture — A group that has its own distinctive values, norms, and beliefs that fall outside of mainstream society. For instance, swingers are a subculture of couples in which the partners often have recreational sex with members of other couples. There are swinger websites, parties, and conferences.

DISCUSSION QUESTIONS

1. The desire to belong, to fit in, is a powerful one. What groups have you had to work to fit into? What did you have to learn or do in order to fit in?
2. Are there communities that you've wanted to belong to but which didn't accept you? What cultural capital, social capital, or habitus did you lack?
3. Why does Reyes refer to the International Churches of Christ as a cult? Do you agree with this description?
4. Reyes reminds us that groups—even groups that we ultimately feel we can't belong to—are essential sources of structure and support for us. What groups provide you with emotional, social, and practical support? How deeply connected do you feel to those groups?
5. In what ways does Reyes help us see the dark side of the kinds of dense networks described by Charrad in her story about the Texas ice storm?

LEARN MORE

Bourdieu, Pierre. *Outline of a Theory of Practice*. Cambridge: Cambridge University Press, 1977.
Dawson, Lorne L. *Comprehending Cults: The Sociology of New Religious Movements*. 2nd ed. Oxford: Oxford University Press, 2006.
Hassan, Steven. *Combatting Cult Mind Control*. South Paris, ME: Park Street Press, 1988.

Victoria Reyes is an associate professor in the Department of Gender and Sexuality Studies at the University of California, Riverside. She received her PhD from Princeton University and is the author of *Academic Outsider: Stories of Exclusion and Hope* (Stanford University Press, 2022) and *Global Borderlands: Fantasy, Violence, and Empire in Subic Bay, Philippines* (Stanford University Press, 2019).

17

The Room Feels Queer

Amin Ghaziani

Sitting alone in my room one day as a thirteen-year-old boy, I realized with a curious mixture of delight and dread that I was in love with my best friend, Adam. As a first-generation kid growing up in a working-class, highly religious, non-English-speaking immigrant household in the suburbs of Chicago, I was too overwhelmed by being bullied for the color of my skin to have any head space to figure out what it meant to feel this way about another boy. My parents had relocated from Karachi in the late 1970s as part of a wave of South Asian immigration to the United States. Migration cycles like the one I lived through often fuel xenophobic backlash. "Camel jockey!" "Sand nigger!" All these years later, I can still hear the slurs in my mind. No wonder I settled silently into the closet.

The young boy in that room could not have imagined that sociology, of all things, would define who he became later in life. My parents wanted me to be a doctor, a lawyer, or maybe an engineer. Growing up as the child of immigrants, as a person of color, *and* as queer made me see the world through a unique **intersectional lens.** The literary critic Eve Sedgwick captured in three words the restlessness I felt in those years: "People are different." The words leapt off the pages of her landmark book *Epistemology of the Closet*: "It's astonishing how few respectable conceptual tools we have for dealing with this self-evident fact."

Sociology helped me understand the significance of sexuality as at once a life force and a world-making project. That one word—say it out loud: "sexuality"—uniquely expresses the meanings we assign to our body, the symbols we use to represent it, the ways institutions attempt to govern what we can or cannot do with it, and entire disciplines of study and professional pursuits that our bodies inspire, from politics to art, activism to city planning, and, of course, sociology.

By the time I graduated high school, the closet had become insufferable. College couldn't come soon enough, and I found myself choosing between Northwestern and the University of Michigan. I took a road trip to Ann Arbor with Sharon, my former eighth-grade teacher, with whom I had formed a friendship. We stayed with people she knew whose kids attended Michigan. After dinner, as I was helping the mom wash and dry the dishes, she took a step toward me and whispered some advice: "Don't come to Michigan." I flinched at her words. "Why not?" I asked with surprise. "There are too many *weird* people here," she said with alarm in her voice. "Weird people?" I echoed back. After glancing nervously around the kitchen, she leaned in even closer. "There are too many *gay* people here. Go to Northwestern."

In those seconds, my decision was made: Michigan it was. The mom's **homophobia** didn't discourage me; if anything, it enticed me. A month after I moved into my dorm room in South Quad, on Tuesday, October 11, 1994, I walked nervously into my very first gay bar. The Nectarine (now the Necto) hosted a "gay night" every Tuesday. The poetry of the night was unknown to me then, but October 11 also happens to be National Coming Out Day. That night, as I leaned against a rail next to the dance floor, I met a man named Brent. We closed the bar talking about all manner of topics, from the monomers that make up proteins (Brent was a biologist) to Kant's categorical imperative (I was taking a philosophy class). That was how I met my first boyfriend.

A key insight of sociology is that our biographies are intertwined with the social, cultural, and political contexts in which we live. I came out in a milieu characterized by rising anti-gay hate crimes, including murders and attempted murders. Brandon Teena, the trans man featured in the 1999 film *Boys Don't Cry*, had been raped and killed the year before I started college. My first year on campus, I read one story after another in the student newspaper about gay men being attacked with baseball bats in broad daylight. Brent was kind and loving. All he wanted from me was to hold my hand as we walked down Main Street together—but I was too afraid.

My first year at Michigan, I took sociology classes that inspired me to convert my fear into a motivation for social change. I learned about the connective power of emotions for protest. The readings aligned seamlessly with Michigan's rich tradition of student activism. By the end of my first term, I proudly displayed pink triangles and rainbow flags on my backpack and spent weekends protesting for gay rights shoulder-to-shoulder with Michigan's vibrant LGBTQ+ community. This, I came to realize, was knowledge in action: what I was learning in the classroom inspired practices of social justice. Slowly, through sociology, I also found the freedom to finally hold Brent's hand.

Despite the power I felt in the sociologically inspired activism, something was missing. And that something was Northwestern, whose pull was still strong. I decided to take a leap of faith and follow the voice within me and transferred. I moved into Willard Hall on the Evanston campus at the start of my third year. Although I loved its intellectual culture, Northwestern's political climate couldn't have been more different than what I experienced in Ann Arbor. That year, student dorms were defaced with epithets like "Die Negroes," "Kill All Jews," and "Die Fags."

No longer afraid, I was now angry. My first quarter at Northwestern, I enrolled in a sociology course called Social Inequality taught, as fate would have it, by Marika Lindholm, who put me on a path that shaped the rest of my life. Marika taught me the mechanisms through which inequality develops and comes to be seen as legitimate. Listening to one of her gripping lectures about Iris Marion Young, I learned that **oppression** has five "faces": **exploitation, marginalization, powerlessness, cultural imperialism,** and **violence.**

Armed with these conceptual tools and inspired by an event I attended in Ann Arbor, I co-organized with Jon, my dearest friend at Northwestern, a "Queer Kiss-In" on campus. A signature expression of queer politics, kiss-ins blend principles of nonviolence with an aggressive visibility action to assert that sexual minorities should have the same rights to express affection in public as heterosexuals. Jon and I designed our protest to confront all five faces of oppression—with the disarming simplicity of a kiss. That protest event stood in defiance to the violence that was so often directed at queer public displays of action, thus giving those of us who were there a feeling of empowerment and entitlement at the center of a public place, rather than forcing us to its margins.

On the first Friday of April 1997, twenty students joined Jon and me at "The Rock," an iconic boulder in the center of campus that students use as a location for activism, performances, and philanthropic efforts. Carrying signs reading "Love Sees No Gender" and "Kiss Me, I'm Queer," we gathered for an hour-long event that politicized public displays of affection. Straight people take for granted the ability to hold hands or share a kiss. When LGBTQ+ people do the same thing, they risk verbal harassment and physical violence.

The rally began with a speech by Rick Garcia, then the director of the Illinois Federation for Human Rights (known today as Equality Illinois). "We have seen the battered bodies, the bruised bodies, and the dead bodies of sexual minorities," he told the crowd of students who had gathered with curiosity about the event. "We must come out and be strong against the prejudice that sexual minorities face." The student paper, *The Daily Northwestern*, featured the protest in a front-page story entitled "A Kiss Isn't Just a Kiss." Jon and I gasped with glee when we learned that the *Windy City Times*, Chicago's queer weekly paper, printed a photograph of us kissing on its front page (we still have a copy, of course).

As I recall these moments of self-discovery in the many rooms I've inhabited in my life, I imagine myself dancing again with Brent in Ann Arbor and protesting with Jon at Northwestern. Rick's speech echoes in my ears, and I see Marika standing in front of the lecture hall inspiring us with lessons about inequality. Sociology connected me with all these remarkable people.

And now, just like that, I'm a young boy again, sitting in my room with feelings for Adam, trying to figure out what it all means. The memory takes me to a passage in Frank Browning's book *A Queer Geography*, where he reflects on coming to terms with his sexuality while living with his parents in Kentucky. Picturing the place where he brought his first lover, Browning offers a poignant account: "The room feels queer because it opts for the erotic over the utilitarian. Queer because it seizes sex from behind the bedroom door and throws it onto the center of the living room rug. Queer because it asserts an aesthetic of eroticism and pleasure as essential to the fulfillment of the room's possibility."

Frank's in his room, I'm in mine. Over the years, I figured out how to make the rooms of my life uniquely queer for me by embracing the "weird people" I was advised to avoid, by walking past my nerves and into the Nectarine on National Coming Out Day, by not allowing fear to stop me from holding hands with my first boyfriend, by learning about the multifaceted forms of social inequality, by organizing a kiss-in to protest those faces of oppression, and by using activism across all these places to draw public attention to the injustices that LGBTQ+ people face. Sedgwick was right: people *are* different. For me, this collection of my life's ephemera, stitched together by sociology, was essential to the fulfillment of queerness in each and every room.

KEY CONCEPTS

Five faces of oppression — Iris Marion Young expands our understanding of oppression by pointing out that it is maintained and exerted in five ways: (1) **exploitation**—using people's labor power without fair compensation; (2) **marginalization**—excluding and relegating certain groups to a lower standing, and subjecting them to profound material deprivation; (3) **powerlessness**—an inability to develop one's capacities, disrespectful treatment by others, and a lack of participation in decision-making; (4) **cultural imperialism**—the dominant group dictates norms and values, thereby rendering the oppressed invisible or deviant; and (5) **violence**—the threat of being hurt or attacked, which keeps the oppressed afraid and compliant. Together, these five forms are woven into our social structure, embedded in norms, habits, and symbols of oppression to dehumanize and subjugate nondominant groups.

Homophobia — Fear, hatred, and prejudice against individuals who are or are perceived to be gay, lesbian, or bisexual, and against other non-heterosexual people.

Intersectional lens — Examining society with the knowledge that our lives are impacted by multiple interacting identities. These complex identities can shape the specific ways we each experience oppression. For example, Ghaziani shares that his experience of queerness was intimately informed by being an immigrant who was bullied for the color of his skin.

DISCUSSION QUESTIONS

1. Ghaziani says that sexuality is "at once a life force and a world-making project." What does he mean by that? Are there other elements of human experience that work that way?
2. In his first year of college, Ghaziani says, he decided to use his fear

as motivation for social change. Is there a fear you have that could be motivation for social change? If so, what kinds of study, organization, or activism might help you do that? How might the family or community you are part of decrease or enhance your fear?

3. Ghaziani notes early in the story that anti-immigrant sentiment informed his experiences of sexuality. How is this an example of an intersectional lens? Have you had any similar experiences?

4. How did Ghaziani's search for community shape his self-discovery, sense of fitting in, and ultimately his work for social change?

LEARN MORE

The Brandon Teena Story. Zeitgeist Films Documentary, 1998.

Browning, Frank. *A Queer Geography: Journeys Toward a Sexual Self*. Rev. ed. New York: Farrar, Straus & Giroux, 1998.

Sedgwick, Eve Kosofsky. *Epistemology of the Closet* Updated with a new preface. Oakland: University of California Press, 2008.

Young, Iris Marion. *Justice and the Politics of Difference*. Princeton, NJ: Princeton University Press, 2011.

Amin Ghaziani is professor of sociology, Canada Research Chair in Urban Sexualities, and coeditor of *Contexts*, the public-facing magazine of the American Sociological Association. A faculty member at the University of British Columbia in Vancouver, Dr. Ghaziani is author of sixty articles, chapters, and essays, including publications in *American Sociological Review*, the *Annual Review of Sociology*, *City & Community*, *Social Problems*, *Theory & Society*, and *Urban Studies*. He also has authored or edited six books: *Long Live Queer Nightlife* (Princeton University Press, 2023), *Imagining Queer Methods* (NYU Press, 2019), *Sex Cultures* (Polity, 2017), *There Goes the Gayborhood?* (Princeton, 2014), *The Dividends of Dissent* (University of Chicago Press, 2008), and *A Decade of HAART* (Oxford University Press, 2008). Dr. Ghaziani has won several awards for this body of work, including a Best Article Award in Collective Behavior/ Social Movements; a Distinguished Article Award (honorable mention) in Sexualities; the Clifford Geertz Award (honorable mention) for Best Article in Culture; a Lambda Literary Award (finalist) for Best Book in LGBT Studies; and a Robert E. Park Award (honorable mention) for Best Book in Community and Urban Sociology. He has received international fellowships from the London School of Economics, the Princeton

Society of Fellows, and the Netherlands Institute for Advanced Study. Alongside his scholarly pursuits, Dr. Ghaziani also is an active public intellectual who has contributed to conversations in *The New Yorker*, *American Prospect*, and *Time* magazines, as well as the *Guardian*, *USA Today*, the *Los Angeles Times*, and the *New York Times*.

PART 4

Confronting Class and Status

Poverty is not just a sad accident, but it's also a result of the fact that some people make a lot of money off low-income families and directly contribute to their poverty.

Matthew Desmond

18

All in the Family

Myra Marx Ferree

My father had a factory job, and my mother had kids. That's the way we saw things in 1959. Eventually we were seven kids; I was the oldest. When I was ten and Kid #5 was six months old, Pop hurt his back on the job and was hospitalized for many months. Though the union provided good health coverage, our income dropped while Pop recuperated. We relied on the Salvation Army for our Thanksgiving turkey and maybe more. Mom landed an evening job as a census-taker for the 1960 count. I was drafted as babysitter-in-chief.

Mom came home late each evening with stories about the neighborhoods she visited. Some nights, she told me about the old mansions on the outskirts of town, homes hidden from the road by stone walls and long driveways. As a census-taker, Mom was invited inside houses with front lawns, garages, and no sidewalks, where the adults apparently drove everywhere and the children had their own playgrounds in their backyards. The nicest homes had fireplaces, fancy entryways, and chandeliers. The number of rooms was always much greater than the number of people Mom counted living there. I imagined some of the kids I went to school with might live in such houses, but they'd never invited me over. These were what I thought of then as "the rich people," who were not the same as the merely "well-off" in newer houses or the "not well-off" in our neighborhood.

Other nights, Mom would describe the poorer neighborhoods she visited. Even though our house was shabby, I never thought of us as poor. Naïve as I was at ten, I had internalized enough of the racial stereotypes of the dominant culture that I assumed only Black people were poor. Mom vividly described closely packed three-decker houses with rickety stairs and six-to-nine small apartments tucked in each building in "the Hollow," the part of town where the Black people lived. We lived less than a mile away, in a house that was in a constant but improving state of disrepair. My pop had been doing his best to rewire and re-plumb it, but this was to be a decades-long endeavor. Still, it seemed nice when I compared it to the ramshackle apartments Mom described in the Hollow. Our neighborhood was mostly a mix of Irish and Italian families—the former went to our church, the latter to the church across town—but excluded people of color.

The curiosity inspired by my mother's stories stayed with me when I went to college. Studying social class and life chances through the lens of urban sociology gave me insight into the solidarity as well as the struggles experienced in communities that were "not well-off." And it challenged those stereotypes I'd held about "urban" and "poor" being synonymous with Black, showing me that the kinds of **social mobility** and opportunity that Pop's white working-class buddies offered him—an otherwise unavailable mortgage, for example—were much harder for Black men to access. I could now understand that the movement of white families to those new houses on the outskirts of town was a matter of white privilege and resulted in Black families being left behind.

In college, from Richard Sennett and Jonathan Cobb's book *Hidden Injuries of Class*, I came to understand the resentment that men felt about the authority of their bosses and the injustice of their low incomes. This helped me make sense of the conflicts I'd witnessed between my parents. Mom had to decide which bills to pay each month and fought with Pop sometimes over his generosity to his buddies. I understood how the deference he had to show to his bosses explained his intolerance for insubordination at home, and that this was why he sometimes made us kids "feel the belt." I could see now why his self-taught home-building and car repair skills gave him such a sense of pride. It was work he could control, unlike his job. And it garnered him a kind of respect from his family and buddies that his job could not offer.

But Sennett and Cobb focused on the injuries men suffered because of the class system. Feminism burst upon the scene for me in a 1971 lecture by Kate Millett. The ideas she raised spoke to my questions about gender and power. Mom worked hard—just like my pop—at a combination of paid jobs and unpaid labor at home. I was almost through college when I learned that Pop's work, however problematic it was physically and emotionally, carried recognition that my mom's did not. Women were somehow supposed to be impervious to the injuries to self-respect that Sennett and Cobb described for men.

This wasn't the first time I'd noticed gender inequality, but it was the beginning of me gaining a language for it and understanding it as systematic. I'd known that, as a girl, I was excused from some, though not all, of the physical fights that took place among the kids in our neighborhood. As the oldest and biggest kid in the family, I had to defend myself and my little brothers if they got picked on. I also needed to contribute financially if I could. In those days, only boys could have newspaper delivery routes—jobs handed down from older brother to younger brother. I was a babysitter from the time I was eleven. I tried to hang around when Pop was changing the oil or using the radial saw, but he made it clear those were skills he only wanted to teach his sons. I was also excluded from Little League and the Soap Box Derby, the two most prestigious activities for kids in our neighborhood.

Just as I was graduating college, the word "sexism" emerged. I read everything I could on the subject, which wasn't hard to do: all the books about women one could find in the Harvard social science library filled one short shelf. I tried to bring these new insights home, along with the first issue of *Ms.* magazine. When I gave it to Mom to read, Pop grabbed it and threatened that if I ever brought "that kind of stuff" into his house again to "destroy his marriage," I would not be allowed in the door.

I didn't directly challenge Pop, but I did think more about the kind of power and political dynamics that had been marginalized in male-centered accounts about working-class families. While books on urban studies and class politics offered analyses that were sympathetic to my pop and his struggles, they suggested that women like my mom weren't interested in self-liberation or self-realization. Most social scientists at the time assumed that only middle-class educated women needed self-affirmation from paid work, and that male breadwinners of working-class families only needed better wages so their wives could stay home where they supposedly always wanted to be. The powerful contradiction embedded in these assumptions alone would have caused me to question the conclusions, but sharing my mom's excitement in her census job and sympathizing with her demand to stay employed after my pop was back at work convinced me that these diagnoses were wrong, as did my father's reaction to *Ms.* magazine.

I began to see in my pop a kind of white working-class masculinity that the male urban studies scholars hadn't recognized as a gender issue, but only one of class. It was true that Pop relied on recognition from his buddies and his self-taught skills for a sense of pride he could never get at work, but his insecurity, evident in his demands for exaggerated obedience at home, also complicated his efforts to love his wife and kids. These **injuries of class** were suffered by us all.

Because I couldn't find my mom in the ethnographies of the working class that I read in my courses in the '70s, I worked to write her back into the narrative. My doctoral dissertation was based on interviews with working-class mothers who told me about the strategies they used to get their husbands to help with household chores (such as having them do dishes rather than hang out laundry because their friends won't be able to see them). I learned that, as in my own home, these families engaged in less egalitarian talk about who did what but reported more egalitarian arrangements than I'd read about in many published studies of professional-class families. They didn't know much about this "new feminist stuff," but they were interested in ways of life that would recognize their aspirations as well as their contributions.

My mom's excitement when she came home from census-taking not only fed my preteen curiosity but also offered me a compelling example of how needing the money and enjoying the work were not found in two different *types* of women of different *class* positions but depended on the *conditions* of women's jobs. Sociology has grown to encompass insider stories of Black families in neighborhoods like the Hollow (such as Carol Stack's *All Our Kin*) while also building a rich literature on white working-class women's lives (Judith Stacey and Margaret Nelson have been especially insightful). Race, class, and gender limit these options in paid work, but also shape the kinds of unpaid work that have to be done and by whom. Meeting the continuing need for specific analysis of the **intersectionality** of race, class, and gender in practice still depends on students and scholars with truly diverse experiences being inspired not only by what sociologists have already written, but by what they themselves recognize as missing or wrong in what they read.

KEY CONCEPTS

Injuries of class — The personal and emotional impact of being a blue-collar worker in our stratified society, as described by Jonathan Cobb and Richard Sennett in their groundbreaking book *The Hidden Injuries of Class*. For example, Ferree notes that her father's strict insistence on obedience at home was connected to his lack of work autonomy and the deference demanded by his bosses. Their work set the groundwork for sociological research on the ways in which human dignity and respect are compromised by inequality.

Intersectionality — The reality that our lives are shaped by multiple interacting identities, forms of inequality, and systems of oppression. Ferree is heartened by scholarship that examines race, class, and gender from a variety of diverse perspectives and intersecting identities.

Social mobility — The opportunity for individuals and families to move up or down the economic hierarchy. Currently, in the United States, the rate of upward social mobility ranks behind that of several European countries.

DISCUSSION QUESTIONS

1. The idea that class systems cause injuries is sociologically important but also personally relevant. Have you or a loved one experienced psychological injury based on your class status?
2. A sociological lens helps Myra Marx Ferree reflect empathetically on the ways that gender roles influenced her parents in the 1950s and '60s. How much has changed? How does attention to gender roles help you understand choices made by the elders in your family?
3. Ferree describes how class and gender can intersect to shape a person's experience of family and work. What is the relationship between your class status, gender, and experience of family or work life?

LEARN MORE

Collins, Patricia Hill. *Intersectionality as Critical Social Theory*. Durham, NC: Duke University Press, 2019.

Millet, Kate. *Sexual Politics*. New York: Doubleday: 1970.

Nelson, Margaret, and Joan Smith. *Working Hard and Making Do: Surviving in Small Town America*. Oakland: University of California Press, 1999.

Sennett, Richard, and Jonathan Cobb. *The Hidden Injuries of Class*. Reissue of 1972 book. New York: Verso Books, 2023.

Stacey, Judith. *Brave New Families: Stories of Upheaval in Late-Twentieth-Century America*. New York: Basic Books, 1990.

Stack, Carol B. *All Our Kin: Strategies for Survival in a Black Community*. New York: Basic Books, 1983.

Myra Marx Ferree is the Alice H. Cook Professor Emerita of Sociology at the University of Wisconsin–Madison, where she was also a member of the Gender and Women's Studies Department. Her 1971 dissertation focused on working-class women's feminism and was conducted with the aid of a Woodrow Wilson Fellowship in Women's Studies. The intersection of class and gender remains a theme in her book *Varieties of Feminism: German Gender Politics in Global Perspective* (Stanford University Press, 2012), translated into German as *Feminismen* (Campus 2018). It also informs her recent work on intersectional structures for mobilization on both the right and the left (such as "The Crisis of Masculinity for Gendered Democracies," *Sociological Forum*, 2020, and "Under Different Umbrellas," *European Journal of Politics and Gender*, 2021) and historically grounded understandings of gendered stratification (such as "Theories Don't Grow on Trees," in *Gender Reckoning*, edited by Messerschmidt et al., 2018). Overall, her articles and books address feminist organizations and politics in the United States, Germany, and other countries; gender inequality in families; and intersectionality in sociological theory and practice. She reaches out to students with her coauthor, Lisa Wade, in *Gender: Ideas, Interactions and Institutions* (3rd ed., 2023). She is proud to have received prizes for her mentoring from Sociologists for Women in Society and from the University of Wisconsin–Madison. She is currently a resident of Newton, MA, and is affiliated with the Center for European Studies at Harvard University.

19

My Mother's Bequest

Douglas S. Massey

When I was growing up, I sensed that my grandmother did not approve of my best friend, but I didn't understand why. Only later did I become aware of the existence of invisible barriers imposed by social class and realized it was because his father worked in a factory, whereas mine (her son) was a white-collar professional.

I am the product of a mixed marriage, at least in terms of social class. My father was the son of two native-born, college-educated parents. In 1919, when my grandparents met as school teachers, only a tiny fraction of women earned college degrees. My grandmother and grandfather met in Colville, Washington, and got married in Spokane, where my father was born in August 1923. Shortly thereafter, the family moved west of the Cascade Mountains to Olympia, the state capital, where my grandfather got a job working for the Washington State Highway Department.

In contrast, my mother was the daughter of poor immigrants from Finland with grade-school educations. They had migrated independently to the United States for work in the early 1900s and met at the Anaconda Copper Mine in Butte, Montana, where my grandfather was a miner and my grandmother worked in the commissary. My mother was the valedictorian of her tiny high school class of seven students. After saving up money working in a salmon-canning factory, she took a steamer during World War II down the Alaska panhandle to Seattle, where she worked her way through the University of Washington, majoring in economics. It was there that she met my father, a business major specializing in accounting.

When my father began seeing my mother, his own mother was not at all happy. She perceived a second-generation immigrant from a poor, working-class family in Alaska to be beneath the dignity of the Massey family. In a desperate attempt to prevent my father from "going steady" with my mother, she confiscated his fraternity pin and locked it in a safe deposit box so he couldn't "pin" my mother. I am living proof that this gambit was unsuccessful. Over her objections, my parents went on to marry in Seattle in 1947, then moved to Olympia, where they both got jobs working for the state government.

In addition to being formed by our families, all of us are also products of the communities in which we were raised. Olympia in the 1950s was a small city, virtually all white, but with only one high school. I therefore came of age in a social world that was segregated and homogeneous in terms of race but diverse with respect to social class. Owing to the postwar economic boom, though, wages were constantly rising, and I remained blithely unaware of the challenges of poverty and racism throughout my childhood. I thought everyone was middle class and white.

As my calm 1950s childhood gave way to adolescence during the conflict and turmoil of the 1960s, my social and political awareness grew. I slowly became cognizant of the fact that my grandmother, the college-educated daughter of a rich merchant, looked down on my mother's immigrant origins. She also was strongly prejudiced against Jews, Catholics, and Blacks, and probably didn't think much of Finns, either. She was a snobby, self-righteous Presbyterian who held almost everyone else in contempt, including my mother. She believed that those less fortunate than herself were necessarily of low moral character and deserved their lot in life, exemplifying psychology's **fundamental attribution error**, which leads people to attribute people's outcomes to their dispositions rather than to their circumstances.

As I got older, I increasingly came to resent my grandmother's constant criticism of my mother and her patronizing attitude toward other human beings. She looked down on my high school girlfriend, whose mother had gone on welfare after her father deserted the family of four children. She made cutting remarks about my uncle's wife, who was Catholic. She made disparaging remarks about Olympia's one Black resident, a blind man who lived in a hotel and tuned all the pianos in town, and she disapproved of my mother letting him into our house to tune ours. Much later, I learned that throughout World War II, Olympia had been a "sundown town": a city ordinance stated that all Black people had be out of the city limits by the end of the day.

Sometimes people ask me how a middle-class white boy from a white town in a white state ended up studying Blacks, Hispanics, and Mexican immigrants for a career. Part of the answer is the zeitgeist: I was swept up in the civil rights, antiwar, and progressive political movements of the time. In my senior year of high school, my civics teacher had us read *The Autobiography of Malcolm X*. From television news, I thought I'd learned all about racism and segregation in the South. I'd seen racist Southern sheriffs unleash attack dogs on peaceful demonstrators and turn fire hoses on children protesting school segregation. Somehow, I believed things were better in the North. My grandmother aside, I thought most Northerners were "enlightened" and not racially biased or discriminatory. I did not yet see **racism as an institutionalized system** built into the structure of US society. But Malcolm X was raised in the North, and through his eyes I came to see that racism was pervasive throughout the country.

Many of my high school classmates came to that conclusion before I did. At our graduation ceremony, our class speaker referred to Olympia as "a white racist ghetto." Pandemonium ensued, with half the audience booing and screaming at her to "Go back to Russia" and the other half cheering and shouting for her to "Tell it like it is." It was a stark lesson to absorb about my hometown at age seventeen.

A more fundamental reason for my interest in racial and class inequality is the fact that I am my mother's son. Knowing where she came from, how hard she worked to get ahead, and how much she achieved was a source of pride for me. Witnessing the disrespect she experienced from her snooty, self-satisfied mother-in-law made me angry and resentful. As a result, I have always sided with the underdogs of the world: those who weren't born into privilege, who struggle against the odds to get ahead, but who are nevertheless looked down upon by those who have never had to worry about money.

Today, when I hear about Mexicans crossing the border in search of a better life, Black children growing up in poor, segregated neighborhoods, or first-generation college students struggling to manage social and academic life on elite campuses, I think of my mother. It was she who bequeathed to me the drive for education, instilling in me the desire to use it to understand how **systems of stratification** hold people back. She gave me the need to put this knowledge to work in service of making the world a fairer, more egalitarian place. For this reason, I dedicated one of my books to her with these words:

"To my mother, born Ruth Sylvia Matson to immigrant parents, who taught me the importance of education, and the importance of using it for good."

We are all a product of our circumstances, but sociology gives us the tools to understand how discriminatory social processes and biased institutional configurations can generate inequities in circumstances that produce widely divergent life chances. In so doing, sociology also provides us with the insights and awareness needed to transform institutions and practices through political action to create a more just and equitable world.

KEY CONCEPTS

Fundamental attribution error — The common tendency to discount or minimize situational and environmental contributors to someone's behavior while overemphasizing the role of personality or character traits. For instance, one might blame the poor for their poverty rather than recognizing the many structural barriers to upward mobility, as exemplified by Massey's grandmother's disdain for his mother.

Institutional racism — Discriminatory racial practices embedded in political, economic, and educational institutions. The disproportionate incarceration of men of color is an example of institutional racism that starts with unequal educational opportunities, compounded by a punitive legal and criminal justice system that disproportionately incarcerates Black men for low-level drug offenses.

Systems of stratification — Processes that sort people into enduring hierarchies. Systems of stratification are primarily based on race, class, ethnicity, gender, sexual orientation, education, religion, and disability.

DISCUSSION QUESTIONS

1. Massey links his grandmother's class bias to the fundamental attribution error, which he believes caused her to frequently assume that if a person was poor, it was their own fault. Where do you see the fundamental attribution error operating in contemporary discussions around social issues?

2. Have you ever been the target of someone else's class bias? What did it feel like?

3. In a society like the United States, where neighborhoods are often segregated by class, it's not uncommon for people to grow up knowing only people of their own class. How might this contribute to the fundamental attribution error and class bias? Does Massey's story give you any ideas about how to overcome the fundamental attribution error and class bias?

4. The United States is often characterized as a middle-class society, yet the gap between the wealthy and everyone else is widening. If most of us think of ourselves as middle class, does that make it easier or harder to address class inequality?

LEARN MORE

Grusky. David B., ed. *Social Stratification: Class, Race, and Gender in Sociological Perspective*. Abingdon: Routledge, 2014.

Ross, Lee. "The Intuitive Psychologist and his Shortcomings: Distortions in the Attribution Process." *Advances in Experimental Social Psychology*, no. 10 (1977): 173–220.

X, Malcolm, with Alex Haley. *The Autobiography of Malcolm X*. New York: Grove Press, 1965.

Douglas S. Massey is the Henry G. Bryant Professor of Sociology and Public Affairs at Princeton University, where he received a PhD in 1978. Formerly, he was the Dorothy Swaine Thomas Professor and Chair of Sociology at the University of Pennsylvania, where he also directed its Population Studies Center. He is coauthor with Nancy A. Denton of *American Apartheid: Segregation and the Making of the Underclass* (Harvard University Press, 1993), which won the Distinguished Publication Award of the American Sociological Association. Massey has also published extensively on Mexican immigration, including the book *Beyond Smoke and Mirrors: Mexican Immigration in an Era of Economic Integration* (Russell Sage Foundation, 2002), which won the 2004 Otis Dudley Duncan Award for the best book in social demography. His most recent book, coauthored with Camille Charles and two former students, Kimberley C. Torres and Rory Kramer, is *Young, Gifted and Diverse: Origins of the New Black Elite* (Princeton University Press, 2022). Massey has also served on the faculty of the University of Chicago, where he directed its Latin

American Studies Center and Population Research Center. He is an elected member of the National Academy of Sciences, the American Academy of Arts and Sciences, the American Philosophical Society, and the Academia Europaea. He is past president of the Population Association of America, the American Sociological Association, and the American Academy of Political and Social Science.

My Daughter Is Not a Bourgeois Girl

Gloria González-López

"*Papi*, daddy!"

I was a child, five or six years old, calling out animatedly and affectionately to my father during a conversation we were having. We lived in a modest house in a colorful, vibrant working-class colonia in Monterrey, Mexico. I remember well the stern warning he gave me and how it made me feel.

In a firm tone, he exclaimed:

Mi hija no es una niña burguesa, solamente una niña burguesa usa diminutivos para hablar con su padre. Dime papá o padre. Nosotros somos una familia de clase trabajadora.

My daughter is not a bourgeois girl, only a bourgeois girl would use a diminutive to talk to her father. You either call me dad or father. We are a *working-class* family.

I looked up at him, speechless and confused. He was tall and strong. I would not know what bourgeois or **working-class** family meant until I read Marx and Engels's *The Communist Manifesto* in the late 1980s. Then I finally understood: "bourgeois" came from bourgeoisie, the class of modern capitalists, owners of the means of production and employers of wage labor. My father was the sole provider with a wage salary, making us a humble working-class family—urban, non-Indigenous—which included my mother and five children; I was the fourth of them.

My father's powerful words started to make sense while attending a public elementary school, not far from my house: I was not *una hija de papi*, the daughter of an upper-class man, the wealthy girl with access to many privileges.

After that first lesson in **class consciousness**, I started to develop tremendous respect for my father. It was through him that I came to understand that labor and respect should go hand in hand. I began to use *usted*, the formal "you" in Spanish, in all my conversations with him, and did so until the day he died in 2007. I still talk to him in my imagination as *usted*.

My father was an idealist. My mother used to beg him to get a better job at a large company, where he could earn a better salary and benefits for the family. *Imperialista* and *capitalista* are two of the words I remember my father using in a heated argument with my mother, as he explained the many reasons why he had to stay at the small shop as a union organizer. Rich debates and analyses of Marx's theorizing on imperialism and capitalism abound across disciplines and languages. My father used *imperialista* and *capitalista* to identify the processes by which my hometown of Monterrey became not only a national icon of industrialization and a vibrant economy but also an example of the concentration of wealth in the hands of very few at the expense of the exploitation of the many. My father's commitment to the many kept him working at modest shops until he retired.

My father finished third grade and was deeply proud of knowing how to read and write. He devoured the local newspapers. I remember him reading the encyclopedias that my mother bought on installments for us, the children. He was better educated than many who had completed much more schooling. He enjoyed reading about different cultures and would talk with my oldest sisters' friends about their trips to Europe. "When did your father go to Spain?" they would ask us. I would crack up, clarifying that he had not traveled much in his life, but that he loved to read. I remember my father also gently intervening and correcting the tour guide every time we visited museums or other cultural spaces, either in Monterrey or in Mexico City. I would blush, embarrassed, which frequently would be followed by a kind tour guide saying, "Yes, I think your father is right."

He was a magnificent storyteller. Some of our neighbors called him "the storyteller man"—*el señor de los cuentos*. I remember him in his rocking chair in the late afternoon on our porch, surrounded by the children of our street, sitting on the floor and listening to him attentively. He was my first teacher on the skill of being an active and engaged listener to people's stories; I would then do my best later to write down the stories I heard with the same richness and respect. These were the seeds of my fascination with people's life stories, the qualitative methodology that has helped me conduct sociological research and nurture my academic career.

When I told him, "Today is my graduation day, Papa," I felt some sort of shyness and awkwardness. I had miraculously finished college with the support of my family, scholarships, college loans, and a full-time job. I was proud of myself, and I wanted my father to be proud of me too. But I didn't want to come across as arrogant or offensive, especially since he had only completed third grade. He replied assertively and sharply, with words that stung as a warning or even a reprimand: "I am happy for you, but that does not make you better than anyone else. Stay humble. Never forget where you came from." I will never forget that I come from a man with a third-grade education who could correct tour guides.

Concepts like *bourgeois*, *working class*, *imperialism*, and *capitalism* came together in my doctoral training in the 1990s. Back then, I was studying Marxist theory for the first time, and I was also learning feminist theory. The complex interconnections between capitalism and gender inequality started to make sense; Marxism and feminism became the two wings of a bird that was teaching me to fly. I eventually realized that I had learned my first lessons on feminism years earlier, from my own mother. Marxist theory and **Marxist feminism** offered more than knowledge; they warmed my heart. My father would have been shocked to know that I learned about all of this at a university in the United States, a capitalist, patriarchal, and racist collage made of painful paradoxes and contradictions, and the home of the wealthiest men on earth.

"I am taking my comprehensive exams soon; would you pray for me, please?" I pleaded with him. "Yes, of course!" He replied animatedly, but also made a request: "And if you pass your exams, would you promise to take me to the Basilica of the Virgin of Guadalupe in Mexico City?" I accepted enthusiastically.

I treasure the memories of that trip to Mexico City in the summer of 1997. Visiting the house of Frida Kahlo for the first time with him at my side was special, given the connection Frida had with Marxism and my father's own ideological history. Because of his Catholic faith, I think he identified more with liberation theology than with orthodox

Marxism. A Catholic theological approach, liberation theology has strong roots in the Latin America of the 1960s. It concerns the liberation of oppressed and marginalized populations, and at times has relied on Marxist concepts, creating tension and conflict with Vatican politics and other Catholic circles.

"I am graduating from the doctoral program in May, would you come to my graduation in Los Angeles?" I asked my dad in early 2000. He expressed his discomfort with US international politics and kindly excused himself. I deeply wanted him to be present that day. Completing a doctoral degree meant so much more than I could explain at that moment, and it saddened me that he was missing in my graduation pictures. But I kept a camera in my heart and took some imaginary photos. He is proud and smiling in those memories.

Days after my father turned eighty years old, and right after my first semester as an assistant professor, I video-recorded a conversation with him. "How would you like to be remembered the day you are no longer with us?" I asked.

"Think of me on December 12, the Day of the Virgin of Guadalupe," he replied.

I stopped identifying as Catholic, but I have honored his wish. That is the only day of the year when I visit a Catholic Church, and it is like being by his side.

Years before, while conducting fieldwork in Mexico, I visited my father, and a neighbor asked me if I was still single. "That's such a stupid question," my father exclaimed. "That is why she went to college, so she does not have to depend on a man!" I was moved by his angry reaction. It felt like a powerful feminist intervention, one coming from an adult man born in 1922 and raised in a patriarchal society, and that meant the world to me. Not only was he proud of my achievements, but he was defending my choices, though they had taken me far from his world! I simply told him: *Gracias, papá.*

In May 2007, I was getting ready to drive to campus and had my father on the speakerphone of my car. I was touching base to find out how he was doing. He sounded lively and happy, and we had the most beautiful conversation ever. I told him how much I loved him and how grateful I was for his presence in my life. He was similarly engaged and affectionate with me, and gave me his blessing. "Did he just say goodbye to me . . . forever?" I asked myself with teary eyes after we hung up. It felt like a premonition.

Days later, I got a phone call from my oldest sister. It was already dark, and I was still on campus, wrapping up a busy semester. She had sad news: our father had had a heart attack and had not survived. The next day, I drove to Monterrey to attend his funeral.

My father was popular in the colonia where he lived—charismatic, friendly, with explosive honest laughter. I was deeply moved while looking at the faces of so many people I'd never seen before sobbing at his funeral.

Cleaning his modest and well-organized closet brought a revelation a day later. As my oldest sister and I looked at the few belongings he left behind, she told me to pick whatever I wished to keep. My father was a minimalist, and I doubt he ever had a bank account. I went straight to his clean, well-folded red handkerchief, a nice lotion, his pair of dressing shoes, and the green fleece I've been wearing while writing different drafts of this essay. As I looked at my father's pile of books, I saw a thick notebook. With a deep sigh, I looked through the endless stories and poems he had written over the years. My father was a writer. I had not known.

Around that time, I was teaching an undergraduate course called Sociology of Masculinities. For their final paper, students had the option to write an essay I called "A letter to my father," which involved a feminist analysis. I explained to my students that, as feminists, I believed it was important for us to "resolve the unresolved" issues with our fathers. I realized at some point that I was inviting students to do what I'd never done myself: write a letter to my own father. Reading the letters my students wrote to their fathers gave me tears, memories, and important lessons about men's lives in patriarchal societies. Writing this essay is an opportunity to write the letter as the oldest student in a course I no longer teach.

I am getting ready for my daily walk. I get my walking shoes from the rack by my door and think of him: my walking shoes are next to my father's shoes, the ones I kept after he died. He never drove or owned a car, relying on public transportation his entire life. He walked and walked wherever he needed to go, until he could no more.

"The philosophers have only interpreted the world in various ways; the point is to change it," wrote Marx in his *Theses on Feuerbach* (1845). I have no doubt my father would have agreed with him. May my always-in-evolution feminist heart—nurtured by my mother and with its sprouted seeds of class consciousness that you planted in my childhood—remain focused on collective healing and transformation, always inspired by your sense of dignity, modesty, and integrity, just like you, Dad—*así como usted, papá.*

Thank you for the light of your knowledge, comrade Karl Marx.

Este ensayo es mi modesta ofrenda
en conmemoración de los 100 años de su nacimiento,
con todo mi amor y gratitud infinita por siempre,
para usted, papá.

KEY CONCEPTS

Class consciousness — Recognizing a shared economic condition. The term originated in Karl Marx's prediction that a working-class consciousness would lead to revolution against the bourgeoisie. Clearly, González-López's father was proud to pass on his class consciousness to his daughter.

Marxist feminism — Feminism grounded in Marxist theory, namely that a capitalist class system that promotes the exploitation of labor is oppressive to women. Marxist feminists analyze the gendered structures and ideologies linked to capitalism.

Working class — Described as the proletariat in Marxist analysis, the working class don't own or control the means of production, and their labor is exploited by capitalist industry.

DISCUSSION QUESTIONS

1. How have differences in education or class shown up in significant relationships in your life?
2. In Massey's essay, his grandmother has disdain for his mother, but in this essay, González-López's father inspires her respect for the working class. Were there adults in your life when you were a child who inspired you to think about the dignity of work or the importance of respect?
3. Why do you think González-López's father associated the use of diminutive language with the middle class and the use of formal language with the working class?

4. Part of the story occurred in the 1960s in a town in Mexico. Do you think it would be equally relevant in the town where you live today?

LEARN MORE

Gimenez, Martha E. *Marx, Women, and Capitalist Social Reproduction: Marxist Feminist Essays*. Boston: Brill, 2018.

González-López, Gloria. "The First Feminist Who Loved Me." *Ms. Magazine*, May 8, 2020. https://msmagazine.com/2020/05/08/the-first-feminist-who-loved-me-memories-of-my-mother-during-Covid-19/.

Marx, Karl, and Friedrich Engels. *The Communist Manifesto*. Originally published in 1848. Penguin Great Ideas. London: Penguin Classics London, 2015.

Smith, Christian M. *The Emergence of Liberation Theology: Radical Religion and Social Movement Theory*. Chicago: University of Chicago Press, 1991.

Gloria González-López holds the C. B. Smith Sr. Centennial Chair #1 in U.S.-Mexico Relations and is a professor of sociology at the University of Texas at Austin. She is a first-generation college student and a member of an extended family with a long history of transnational Mexico-US migration. She is the author of *Family Secrets: Stories of Incest and Sexual Violence in Mexico* (NYU Press, 2015) and *Erotic Journeys: Mexican Immigrants and Their Sex Lives* (University of California Press, 2005); she has published her academic work extensively in Spanish. She is a couples and family therapist by training and has worked with Latina immigrant women with histories of sexual violence. She is a consultant for professionals working in sexual violence eradication, prevention, and treatment programs at grassroots organizations and academic institutions in Mexico. Because of the kindness and generosity of students, colleagues, mentors, and supervisors, she received the 2021 Simon-Gagnon Lifetime Achievement Award and the 2022 Feminist Scholar-Activist Award, both from the Sexualities Section and the Sex & Gender Section of the American Sociological Association, respectively.

21

When a Harvard Degree Is Not Enough

Vivian Louie

I will never forget an eye-opening and disturbing conversation I had over lunch with a fellow Harvard employee. I was on the faculty, and she was a residential staff member whose job was to oversee the academic and social well-being of undergraduate students. "Harvard undergrads come in three groups," she told me when I asked about her job. "The bottom third are just as talented as the rest, but they struggle for lots of different reasons, mainly **socioeconomic**. They need help figuring out the Harvard-ness. Sometimes, they have family issues."

Internally cringing, I nodded, munching on my ham-and-cheese sandwich. As a Harvard College alum, fifteen years out, I was especially curious about her take on the students.

"Then there's the top third," she continued. "These are the students who are always at your office. They never let you forget their names. They are destined to be the Rhodes Scholars, Phi Beta Kappa. And they know it."

I nodded, realizing that "bottom third" was code for poor and mostly racial and ethnic minorities, and "top third" meant wealthy and mainly white. A Latino student of mine whose dad was a cab driver trying to survive in a high-poverty Bronx zip code flashed through my mind. Then I thought of a white student whose dad was a corporate lawyer and had grown up in the super-upscale suburb of Greenwich, Connecticut. "And the third group?" I asked, wondering what she might say next.

"Yes, the middle third," she replied. "These are the students who do well enough on their own. They could probably join the top third, but they don't ask for help. So, they don't get it."

Maybe it was the small shrug my colleague gave as she spoke so matter-of-factly, precisely folding the paper that had neatly wrapped her sandwich and then pushing it away, but it bothered me. We moved on to another topic, but my mind couldn't let go of the ease with which she classified the students. I was struck by how she did not mention race and ethnicity at all. Yet I knew that race, ethnicity, religion along with socioeconomic status informed the challenges facing the bottom third. I saw how Harvard could be an intense transition for Black, Latino, Indigenous, Asian American, non-Christian, low-income students. And I wondered about the middle third. I kept thinking, *My friends and I didn't even know we should have asked for help. We didn't know.* Was it because many of us were first-generation college students, children of immigrants, or barely in the middle class? After that lunch, when I spoke to those college friends, now spread across the country, I asked, "Did you know we were the middle third when we were at Harvard?"

I went to Harvard in the late 1980s. My closest friends and I developed our own rituals, like trudging through the snow and fierce winds up to Hilles Library in January to confine ourselves as we studied for finals. By junior year, we were thriving. Two of us took Shakespeare, and our volume of plays seemed to weigh a ton. Our grades were more than good. We loved our extracurricular activities. One friend was vice president of the Asian American Students club. Another was a DJ at the college radio station and in the band. Still another toured the world in a famed a cappella singing group. I edited a literary publication. The hard work was going to pay off. A Harvard degree!

We were not naïve. Our families were working or lower middle class, immigrants of color, or Jews only a generation removed from working-class immigration journeys. We knew our parents—factory and restaurant workers, public school teachers, a department store clerk—were very different from many of our wealthy classmates' parents and had more in common with the parents the residential staff member described as the bottom third. If our parents owned their modest homes, they were lucky; if they didn't, they lived in urban public housing or rent-controlled apartments. Still, in our first two years of college, we felt equal to our classmates from wealthy families, who were also our friends.

We were excited to graduate but were wrestling with sudden anxiety. I slowly realized I was learning things for the first time that others seemed to have known for a while. I knew about the cum laude tiers—and would end up graduating magna cum laude in history and literature. But it was not until junior year that I learned about Phi Beta Kappa.

By fall of senior year, I realized our family backgrounds mattered in ways that would affect our futures. Catching up from the summer, a classmate casually said, "Oh yeah, I took a Princeton Review LSAT course. You know, to prepare me for the LSAT." I dumbly nodded, though it was the first I was hearing of graduate school test prep. We were used to classmates going on fancy trips during school breaks. Now we were hearing about summer jobs or semester internships they'd landed at national magazines, architecture firms, and other seemingly unattainable places through their family networks. My friends and I reviewed the eligibility criteria for prestigious scholarships—Rhodes, Marshall—and applied, even as we realized we should have been preparing for them long before.

Our experiences spoke to the power of social class and the role of higher education institutions, including ones like Harvard, in reproducing the social hierarchy. These institutions position wealthy students to reproduce the social class of their families. For poor, working-class, and lower-middle-class students, the hope is that an undergraduate degree will be sufficient to vault them into similar professional success. But for my friends and me, a Harvard bachelor's degree was not enough—at least, not then.

The fine crack separating us from our wealthy classmates widened into a crevice those first few years after graduation. The contrasts were jarring. One day, I visited some old roommates in the two-bedroom Manhattan apartment they crammed into with their high school friends, still using futons and milk crates. There were bills to pay, loan payments coming due. One of them was working at a bank, learning about mortgages, and furiously saving so she could qualify for one in a few years. Another day, I ran into a college acquaintance and was invited to stop by her place, where she lived alone in a beautifully furnished, spacious two-bedroom apartment; all the costs were covered by her dad, an Ivy League law professor (and Harvard alum). Another friend slowly let go of his college dream of becoming the next Frank Lloyd Wright or Le Corbusier as he found himself stuck designing corporate bathrooms and parking garages. "I take those jobs for the money," he told me wistfully. "I can't starve for art." I moved back in with my family to save on costs and figure out my next moves. I visited the Harvard Club in Manhattan, a dimly lit, forbidding fortress of rich old white people, mainly men—I certainly did not feel that we were equal—and combed through NYC alumni lists to see if there was a connection I could capitalize on.

My close friends and I still had faith that our Harvard education was our way out, but if Harvard was the door, we were still missing the key: the ability to access and bridge the social capital needed to help us see and optimize all that Harvard offered. And if we were struggling, what were our classmates from even poorer backgrounds experiencing? We all needed information and guidance that we simply didn't have equal access to because of our class background. Our networks and **cultural capital** afforded us less opportunity and information than our wealthy peers. Unlike those students, whose class and status prepared and propelled them for professional careers, the journey was harder than we or anyone else had expected.

But eventually, most of us found our way, and that way was smoothed at least to some degree by the social networks we'd formed at Harvard. When I was a sociology doctoral student, I needed research experience. The older sister of a college roommate referred me for an opportunity as a research assistant in New York. That one opportunity was transformational. Beyond the amazing research training, I met people who would steer me to publishing, networking, and job opportunities for the next twenty-plus years. In fact, that's how I got my first faculty job at Harvard.

Now I am a professor at Hunter College, where most of our students are from working-class and lower-middle-class backgrounds. Many of them are the children of immigrants. I've written books about how **bridging social capital** is key to connecting immigrant, working-class students to the opportunities they didn't know they needed until other students landed them. It's possible to build bridges through mentors and collective strategies. For example, when students at a community college wanted to learn more about four-year colleges as their next step, with staff guidance, they formed a student club dedicated to doing just that. The club hired school vans to take them all over New York State to check out four-year colleges. Their efforts paid off when they applied and received school funding to attend.

At Hunter, I advise the students in my courses to sign up for my office hours, yet very few do. This semester, I will go one step further and require just one visit, even if it's simply to say hello and tell me a little about themselves. Uncomfortable as that may be, especially with an authority figure, it is a useful skill. I advise my students and relatives from working-class families to keep in touch with people who've helped them. Let them know what you're up to and where you'd like to go, I advise them. Not because they owe these people, but because if they cared enough to help once, they might be willing and able to do so again.

I also advise the academic staff and faculty at Harvard and elsewhere to reach out to their so-called middle-third students. They're easy to forget, as they're neither in crisis nor on the cusp of receiving a prestigious award, but please try, I say. Bring them to your door. And once they arrive, connect them to opportunity.

KEY CONCEPTS

Bridging social capital — Social capital is our network of relationships— the people we know and the resources they offer us. Bridging social capital refers to relationships that help us connect to new groups. This is in contrast to **bonding social capital**, which strengthens the ties within groups. Bridging social capital is important when our networks lack access to some valuable information; expanding them to include people with a diversity of knowledge and information is helpful for recognizing and finding new opportunities.

Cultural capital — Pierre Bourdieu coined the term to describe symbolic resources and social assets that communicate one's social status, such as style of speech, knowledge of the arts, education, and even leisure activities that can be used to one's advantage. For example, Louie describes that she lacked the cultural capital of her Harvard peers, who knew about Phi Beta Kappa and LSAT prep courses.

Socioeconomic status (SES) — One's place in the system of stratification based on a combination of social and economic factors. Currently, SES is the best predictor of educational achievement. Sociologists are interested in reforming the educational system so that students from any SES, and not just the wealthy, have unlimited educational opportunity.

DISCUSSION QUESTIONS

1. Louie describes the sorting of Harvard students into three groups. Do you recognize these groups? What was your reaction to read-

ing this? How should colleges and universities allocate support resources to students?

2. One conclusion we might draw from Louie's essay is that, while elite colleges and universities might help poor and working-class students move into the middle class, they still manage to maintain a bubble around the elite. Should it be the role of higher education institutions to help people climb the class ladder, and if so, how high should they help them climb?

3. Can you think of ways to help yourself or others build social capital that connects you to new networks? Where would bridging social capital be most useful in your own life?

LEARN MORE

Armstrong, Elizabeth A., and Laura T. Hamilton. *Paying for the Party: How College Maintains Inequality.* Cambridge, MA: Harvard University Press, 2015.

Jack, Anthony Abraham. *The Privileged Poor: How Elite Colleges Are Failing Disadvantaged Students.* Cambridge, MA: Harvard University Press, 2019.

Louie, Vivian. *Compelled to Excel: Immigration, Education, and Opportunity among Chinese Americans.* Palo Alto, CA: Stanford University Press, 2004.

———. *Keeping the Immigrant Bargain: The Costs and Rewards of Success in America.* New York: Russell Sage Foundation, 2012.

Vivian Louie is professor of urban policy and planning and director of the Asian American Studies Center and Program at Hunter College. Louie has been an associate and assistant professor, a postdoctoral fellow in education, and a lecturer in sociology at Harvard University, as well as a program officer at the William T. Grant Foundation. She has also worked as a newspaper journalist, journalism teacher, and youth magazine editor.

Louie studies what it means to be an American in public policies and discussions, civic participation, and civic education, as well as the role of race, ethnicity, immigration, social class, and gender. She also writes about the factors that shape success along the educational pipeline among immigrants and the children of immigrants, and in the workplace. She is the author or editor of three books—*Compelled to Excel: Immigration, Education and Opportunity Among Chinese Americans* (Stanford University Press, 2004); *Keeping the Immigrant Bargain: The Costs and Rewards of Success in America* (Russell Sage Foundation, 2012); and *Writing Immigration: Scholars and Journalists in Dialogue*

(University of California Press, 2011)—along with more than thirty academic reports, articles, book chapters, and scholarly commentaries. Her research has been featured in news outlets such as the *New York Times*, NPR's *All Things Considered*, and the *Leonard Lopate Show*. Louie comments frequently on why we need Asian American studies and racial and ethnic studies. She serves on the Board of Youth Communication and the Russell Sage Foundation's Advisory Committee for Race, Ethnicity, and Immigration. She is a lead scholar in *Hidden Voices: Asian American and Pacific Islanders in the United States*, a curriculum and resource guide from the NYC Department of Education. She previously served on the New York State Advisory Committee to the US Commission on Civil Rights. Louie earned her PhD and MA from Yale University's Department of Sociology, an MA from Stanford University's Department of Communication, and an AB from Harvard University in history and literature.

22

The Luxury of Knowing

Theresa Rocha Beardall

The Graduate Record Examination (GRE) is not required, but students are encouraged to take the examination and submit test results to be considered for fellowship programs. At least three letters of recommendation should be submitted, ideally from faculty members who know your work. Finally, students should submit a writing sample, usually a copy of a term paper (or some approximation thereof) that has been completed for a course.

I sat in a short row of clunky desktop computers in my local public library and read these words over and over again. I hoped to submit my grad school applications in the coming weeks but needed clarification about how to tackle any one of these three components. My mind raced. Thanks to the loud neon test-prep flyers plastered across bulletin boards between college classrooms and my bus stop, I knew that the GRE was a required exam to enroll in certain graduate school programs and that there were courses one could take to prepare. Tapping my foot on the old linoleum floor, I also worried about letters of recommendation. Whom should I ask and how? Sure, I participated in class, completed my readings, and dedicated time outside of class to polishing my written assignments, but was it enough? I also worked two jobs during college, commuted to campus by bus, and had a demanding home life that required a lot of my attention and any extra dollars I could spare.

Fueled by my desire to obtain graduate training to better serve my family and community, I took a deep breath and scribbled out a list of faculty who might be able to meaningfully articulate my talents, dedication, and potential in the classroom. Having typed all my coursework in the shared campus computer lab in San Francisco, I also scratched out a reminder to call the department's front office, hoping there would be some way to have a copy of my term papers sent to me in Los Angeles.

All of this felt overwhelming, and I wished I'd known more about applying to graduate school sooner. There was so much I would have done differently: timelines I could have followed, guidance I would have sought. Surely, I couldn't be the only person who didn't know what everyone else seemed to know about applying to graduate school. Why did it feel like my desire for more school was a luxury I couldn't afford, a path reserved for those with more financial stability or family experience navigating higher education? As my prepaid computer access minutes ticked down, it was as though the clock itself was urging me to just commit to a way, any way, forward.

As a first-generation high school graduate, born in San Diego to an American Indian mother and an undocumented Mexican father, I felt fortunate to be a new college graduate. Growing up, my siblings and I lived in poverty. Our neighborhoods and K–12 schools were all underserved, making my path to higher education difficult and unlikely. Despite these challenges, my siblings were committed to making sure that I, the youngest in the family, could move forward with my love of learning.

Once I'd saved up nearly enough to take the GRE prep course, I had to use some of that money to help my siblings with the rent after an emergency. Situations like this were always coming up, but without an awareness of the social forces and **interlocking inequalities** that were at work on my community, I couldn't help but blame myself for feeling confused, alone, and ultimately responsible for every "failure" or lost opportunity that came my way. I didn't understand what I now have come to fully understand: the paths toward upward educational mobility are often hidden from people like me.

Eventually, my introduction to the concept of **hidden curriculum** in my doctoral studies helped me begin to make sense of my feelings of frustration and exclusion, to finally understand how and why I continued to encounter new and seemingly endless obstacles to educational training and advancement. The hidden curriculum describes the knowledge, skills, and strategies that matter for success in higher education but are not explicitly taught. Access to this curriculum is unevenly distributed and intersects with other key social locations that subordinate and marginalize individuals, including race, gender, class, ability, age, and sexual orientation. Oftentimes, this curriculum is hidden from those who need it most, suggesting a strong relationship between social inequality and access to educational and professional advancement. Although this concept was discussed only in passing, I can vividly remember sitting in my graduate seminar, struggling to follow the conversation on another topic since my mind raced with the many ways this taken-for-granted concept affected every aspect of my life.

I also learned that one's ability or inability to navigate the world is largely structured by one's access to cultural and social capital. Cultural capital describes a set of behaviors, skills, and knowledge, such as style of speech, dress, and education, that can be used to demonstrate one's belonging and status in that society and to recognize the status of others. For example, a business suit and knowledge of golf might signify membership in the US business elite. A related concept, social capital, describes the resources we receive because of our network of social relationships. When trying to get into graduate school, for instance, it's a huge help to know people who have attended or worked in universities. Cultural and social capital are enormously useful in maintaining and advancing our societal positions.

As I came to understand these concepts and their profound impact on cumulative advantage and disadvantage, aspects of my own life story became much clearer, including my confusion and anxiety in striving for upward educational mobility. For example, knowing how to ask for help is considered a middle-class trait, whereas for working-class kids, it might be seen as a sign of weakness or vulnerability. In schools, asking for help can lead to more individualized attention and thus better access to learning the hidden curriculum. As Pierre Bourdieu tells us, we all arrive in school from different family environments and with different social understandings, and many students lack the "valued" cultural capital or "social wealth" that can make success a likely outcome. In this context, we might expect teachers to be more likely to invest in, and share resources with, students they find to be more compatible with their own class position. With all of these processes at play, my schooling denied me access to the hidden curriculum offered to my doctoral peers of middle- and upper-class status. Sometimes the hidden curriculum is so well hidden that students like me believe we do not know how to navigate school processes because there is something fundamentally wrong with us and our abilities, leading us to drop out of the formal education system altogether. It can be hard to persist when you are sure you don't belong.

The impact of the hidden curriculum infiltrates all levels of education. Grade schools in poorer districts tend to socialize students to obey authority and learn rote processing, while middle- and upper-class students are encouraged to collaborate and engage in critical thinking. These disparities continue through high school. Indeed, understanding how to succeed in an academic environment like college or graduate school is rarely taught in economically disadvantaged communities. This can be as simple as knowing how to speak to professors in a way that allows us to build relationships with them or knowing where to turn for help on campus. In a sense, many of the features we associate with the hidden curriculum in grade school are present in college and beyond, but with much higher stakes. Things like class status and parental resources can influence the colleges we attend, what we study, and our potential future earnings. These social and cultural processes, like the hidden curriculum, contribute to broader social trends of inequality.

The hidden curriculum profoundly affected my ability to understand and navigate the organizational structure of a university campus and build meaningful relationships with faculty through **socialization** within the language, culture, and etiquette of higher education. I was never properly introduced to the organizational structure of university campus life. My years as a student at both community college and later a four-year state school also sorely lacked programming that would have demystified ideas about disciplinary fit, opportunities for research training, and extracurricular activities. Too many of us were scrambling, working, commuting, and trying to live on our own with several roommates so we could afford to be in college in the first place. Conversations about financial aid and the importance of applying for scholarships constituted the bulk of our training; little time was devoted to exploring the higher education landscape, beyond an emphasis on learning to strategically finance our time on campus. As a result, too many of us lacked academic guidance when choosing our courses, majors, and minors. I followed preprinted checklists in topic areas that interested me and graduated mostly unaware of the names of major disciplines and their similarities and differences. Without this knowledge, I could not have known which faculty to seek out for coursework or which outside readings and extracurriculars might have helped me meet my academic and professional goals.

Not until many years later did I understand how the culture of advancement in higher education required me to develop meaningful interpersonal relationships with professors and more senior students who could help answer some of my seemingly impossible questions. Throughout my K–12 experience, we were pushed to be quiet and obedient, to solve problems on our own, and to independently choose the best path forward. Adults and authority figures were available in moments of crisis, less so for routine interactions and meaningful mentorship. I now recognize these interactions as both raced and classed. I never realized that my small questions—the topics and concerns I was afraid to ask faculty about—were, in fact, big questions that required the guidance and insights of those equipped to show me the way forward. In addition to mentorship expectations, K–12 socialization should have given me the language and technology necessary to email a professor to explain my interests and academic aspirations. Learning that building mentoring relationships is connected to success would have kept me from worrying that asking questions and seeking guidance was an intrusion on the time and energy of academic authorities.

It has taken me many more years to unlearn the lessons and skills necessary to navigate my K–12 experience than it did to acquire them. I hesitate even now to ask questions of my colleagues and do so only after I have exhausted my own research capabilities.

There continues to be an urgent need to reveal the hidden curriculum in higher education and to address its implications for students like me. As a professor, I mobilize this belief into action by positioning myself as a cultural translator and hidden curriculum tour guide. I encourage students to join my office hours each week and hold more than half of these hours in public spaces on campus, so students feel welcome to drop by. In a friendly and casual setting, we sort through any questions and concerns they might have. I also encourage students to remake campus spaces and conversations to fit their questions, dreams, and expectations about the world in which they hope to live and learn. And I work to advance their research skills, which are often masked in the hidden curriculum, by breaking down expectations into clearly defined segments—explaining the nuts and bolts by modeling how I complete my own work. Transparency and generosity guide my actions as I help students embrace uncertainty. I stress that while we each forge our own path, we are all shaped by the people, places, and values we encounter along the way. I tell them that lacking the cultural and social capital to access and decode the hidden curriculum is not a personal failing. The true failure is that institutions reward one group of students while disadvantaging the other. With the collective clarity of seeing things for what they are, we can all better navigate obstacles and find our way forward together.

KEY CONCEPTS

Hidden curriculum — Norms and values that are taught indirectly in school routines, such as punctuality and obedience, but also skills and strategies that matter for success in education but are not explicitly taught. For example, Rocha Beardall received lessons in obedience that prevented her from asking questions and seeking additional support. This hindered important mentoring relationships that other students knew to develop.

Interlocking inequalities — Systems of inequality based on categories such as race, class, and gender intersect and interlock to maintain privilege and promote discrimination. For example, sexism and racism interlock to put Black women at a greater disadvantage than white women or Black men. Interlocking inequalities are easier to see when we use an intersectional perspective.

Socialization — The lifelong learning process by which we learn the norms, values, and ideals of the groups, organizations, and societies to which we belong. Rocha Beardall is motivated to help students like herself whose socialization process didn't include transparency regarding the hidden curriculum.

DISCUSSION QUESTIONS

1. What kinds of cultural capital would a person need to acquire to fit into the social spaces you typically occupy? Where does a person typically acquire that cultural capital? How did you acquire it?
2. Are there places you aspire to fit in (think schools, careers, social circles, neighborhoods, classes)? What kinds of cultural capital would you need to learn to succeed there?
3. What lessons did you learn from the hidden curriculum in your own schooling? Think about hidden lessons about gender, race, and

class, but also about success, obedience, and fitting in. Have those lessons tended to serve you well or hold you back?

4. Have you ever had a teacher like Rocha Beardall, who has acted as a "hidden curriculum tour guide"? If so, what did they help you see? If not, where would one have been most helpful?

LEARN MORE

Adair, Jennifer Keys, and Kiyomi Sánchez-Suzuki Colegrove. *Segregation by Experience: Agency, Racism, and Learning in the Early Grades*. Chicago: University of Chicago Press, 2021.

Ardoin, Sonja, and Becky Martinez. *Straddling Class in the Academy: 26 Stories of Students, Administrators, and Faculty from Poor and Working-Class Backgrounds and Their Compelling Lessons for Higher Education Policy and Practice*. Sterling, VA: Stylus Publishing, 2019.

Bourdieu, Pierre. *Reproduction in Education, Society and Culture*. New York: Sage Publishing, 1977.

Calarco, Jessica McCrory. *A Field Guide to Grad School: Uncovering the Hidden Curriculum*. Princeton, NJ: Princeton University Press, 2020.

Kozol, Jonathan. *Savage Inequalities: Children in America's Schools*. New York: Harper Perennial, 1991.

Theresa Rocha Beardall is an assistant professor of sociology at the University of Washington. Dr. Rocha Beardall's scholarship examines how systems of law and agents of the state enact state violence. In one research thread, she analyzes the relationship between tribal sovereignty and family policing, and its implications for the social, political, and legal status of Native children and families. In the second thread, she studies urban policing at the intersection of race, class, and labor law, examining the limitations that police unions and their contracts pose to citizen control of the police. Dr. Rocha Beardall's ongoing research draws from her unique theoretical contributions in both areas to address criminal system contact for Native Peoples. In this multi-method work, she shows that the extractive and exploitative nature of settler colonialism has enduring impacts on the likelihood of Native exposure to state violence. Dr. Rocha Beardall's research can be found in several high-impact interdisciplinary journals, including *Criminology*, *Sociology of Race and Ethnicity*, the *Columbia Journal of Race and Law*, and *Native American and Indigenous Studies*.

PART 5

Crossing Borders and Ethnic Divides

People come here penniless but not cultureless. They bring us gifts. We can synthesize the best of our traditions with the best of theirs. We can teach and learn from each other to produce a better America.

Mary Pipher

Watch It, White Boy!

Tomás R. Jiménez

In eighth grade, I had my sociological curiosity about **racial and ethnic identity** knocked into me. I accidentally bumped into Rachel on the way to my third-period class. She didn't know me, but everyone knew her. Rachel was a tough girl who found trouble if it didn't find her. "Watch it, white boy!" she yelled at me when our shoulders brushed. I didn't respond. I knew that Rachel was capable of assembling a crew to exact physical and disproportionate punishment for anything I might have said.

That confrontation with Rachel was a dramatic version of a catalog of encounters I had about my racial and ethnic identity throughout my childhood. Mostly, people were vexed by the combination of my white skin, blue eyes, blond hair (which later turned brown; it now has some gray), and my very Mexican name—Tomás Roberto Jiménez—which I accented when I wrote and pronounced it. What was I, they wondered?

I certainly didn't seem white in my mind, given my family's history. My father is a Mexican immigrant who came to the United States at a young age. He and his family were farmworkers who traveled throughout California harvesting crops. He and his siblings missed school so they could work. Kids at school made fun of him because he was Mexican, because of his accent, and because he was poor. He was also undocumented. His family was deported when my father was in eighth grade (the border patrol came to his classroom to detain him). Later, the family returned to the United States with a visa. He ultimately got a green card and became a citizen. He even wrote about his experience in a series of autobiographies (see Jiménez, Francisco, in the Learn More section below).

When I was growing up, we were aware and sometimes directly felt the prejudices people held about Mexicans. White neighbors complained about too many "brown" people moving to California. Politicians ran campaigns based on stopping Mexican immigrants from coming to the States. People told me that my academic success was because I was Mexican and that I'd benefited from affirmative action. As a child, I couldn't precisely define what it meant to be white. But I knew my family's experience didn't seem all that white.

On my mother's side, I'm the great-grandson of four Italians who emigrated from northern Italy in the early twentieth century. They too were poor; they worked in agriculture and cleaned hotel rooms. They also experienced discrimination. My grandfather, the son of Italian immigrants, recalled being beaten up by kids who didn't like "dagos" in the neighborhood. My mother grew up in a distinctly Italian household. Raised by her grandparents, she spoke Genovese, an Italian dialect, participated in Italian institutions, and ate Italian food. I got to enjoy my Italian ancestry whenever our family got together. The anti-Italian discrimination my grandfather had experienced as a young person had largely disappeared by the time I was growing up. No one ever mistreated me or said anything offensive to me when they learned I have Italian ancestry.

My parents' origins swirled together smoothly in my childhood home. Both of my parents spoke fluent Spanish (my mother learned Spanish in college and honed it after marrying my dad), and some of our conversations were sprinkled with Genovese and Spanish. We ate Mexican and Italian food. Our holiday celebrations included elements from each ancestry. My parents routinely offered up stories from their childhoods to us.

And yet, I noticed something different in California about being a person of Mexican descent as compared to someone of Italian descent. My family visited Mexico easily; we had abundant opportunities to speak Spanish outside the home, regularly interacted with Mexican immigrants, and encountered representations of Mexican ethnicity everywhere. In addition, Mexican immigration was a focal point of local and national politics. Being Italian wasn't that way at all. My family ate Italian food occasionally; we sometimes engaged with Italian American institutions. Still, we never visited Italy, knew almost no Italian immigrants, and I rarely heard the language outside our home. To the extent that Italians came up in politics, it was celebratory.

My childhood and adolescent experiences—from the "watch-it-white-boy" moments to the trips to Mexico and big Italian dinners—collided in my mind during my senior year in college at Santa Clara University when I read Mary Waters's classic book *Ethnic Options*. It was as if Waters had taken a sociological lens, focused it on me, and then zoomed out to reveal the whole context that shaped my experiences.

Waters showed that later-generation descendants of European immigrants exhibited a form of ethnic identity—a sense of self anchored in a group with shared ancestry, history, and culture—like the one on my Italian side of the family. Ethnicity for the people in Waters's study was something they treated as a leisure pastime, displaying it when they wanted to feel different and stowing it away when they wanted to feel part of a larger whole undefined by ethnicity. This was precisely how we invoked our ethnic identity on the Italian side.

Waters's book and Richard Alba's *Ethnic Identity* were the capstones of **assimilation theory**, which also describes the trajectory of my Italian side of the family: each new generation born in the United States had more education and income than their parents. US-born generations moved outside ethnically concentrated urban areas and into suburbs, interacting with individuals from different ethnic origins. Those patterns diversified their **interpersonal networks**, leading to higher intermarriage rates and a population of individuals who trace their ethnic roots to multiple origins. Like my Italian family, these people became "white ethnics" through assimilation.

That account didn't resonate with what I knew of the Mexican experience. Being Mexican had different importance. It mattered to us in ways that being Italian did not. But why?

I started to figure it out my first year in graduate school at Harvard University. I took a class with the same Mary Waters who'd helped me understand my connection to my Italian ancestry. In one class meeting, Mary asked the class if descendants of immigrants from Asia and Latin America would ever have ethnic options. A consensus answer emerged in the class: no. My classmates reasoned that racial identity—a sense of self rooted in a connection to a group defined by its physical appearance—made it so that Asians and Latin Americans weren't white, and whites in the United States would always see them as different. They didn't have the option to identify as Mexican, Chinese, Puerto Rican, or Korean. Other people, the students said, would always impose those identities on them. That explanation seemed entirely plausible to me, but something was missing. I didn't say anything in the seminar, but I wasn't satisfied with the consensus we'd reached.

I spent the next couple of weeks going over Mary's question. I took seriously the idea that ethnic identities are socially constructed—individuals take from their environment symbols, experiences, and interactions with others to create an ethnic identity. Then I went back to my childhood experience. I realized that the large Mexican immigrant population in the Bay Area and the United States may have profoundly affected the symbols, experiences, and interactions in my childhood environment. Italian immigrants hadn't. A key difference is that Italian migration occurred during a defined period of time while Mexicans had been living in established communities annexed by the United States, thus less a story about immigration than one of colonization. And since then, Mexican immigration has been ongoing, continuously replenishing that original Mexican population.

For my dissertation, I interviewed dozens of descendants of Mexican immigrants—Mexican Americans—who came in the early twentieth century to understand how they constructed an ethnic identity. The people I interviewed didn't have ethnic options. Instead, their ethnic identity mattered because of the significant presence of Mexican immigrants who affect the symbols, experiences, and interactions they described to me. They saw some of that effect as positive. Just like I got to grow up around a vibrant Mexican culture, the people I interviewed felt like they had more profound connections with their ethnic identity, including opportunities to speak Spanish and engage in institutions, and greater access to the symbols and practices that came directly and more recently from the ethnic homeland. They also felt they had an opportunity to positively represent a population they cared about and were often under attack from xenophobes.

But they also had their own "watch-it-white-boy" experiences. The people around them had strong ideas about what it meant to act like someone with a Mexican ethnic identity: speak Spanish, be familiar with life in Mexico, and have tastes in food and music that resemble those more likely to be found among immigrants. When the people I interviewed failed to live up to those expectations, other individuals accused them of not being authentically Mexican. They also had run-ins with racial prejudice and discrimination at the hands of people who assumed that all people of Mexican descent were immigrants and even undocumented. Some reported losing jobs, being stopped by the Border Patrol, or ignored because their skin color made others assume they were immigrants and perhaps undocumented.

Looking back, I now see that my shoulder brush with Rachel in eighth grade wasn't about me. It was about all of us—how the symbols, experiences, and interactions in our daily lives shape our racial and ethnic identities. Pursuing the research questions my childhood experiences motivated gave me an understanding of how the human experience is shaped by racial and ethnic identity. In the process, I've gained an appreciation for the power of sociology to deepen our connections to each other by showing us how what we think is unique to our own experience is actually part of the human experience.

KEY CONCEPTS

Assimilation theory — An explanation of how ethnic minorities are brought into the American mainstream and achieve upward mobility, as in the case of Jiménez's Italian relatives, who became "white ethnics" by diversifying their networks, marrying outside their ethnicity, and embracing the norms of the dominant culture.

Interpersonal networks — Our web of social relationships, which can range from homogeneous to diverse. Within these networks, strong ties offer support, and weak ties offer information one might not normally have access to, such as job opportunities.

Racial and ethnic identity — The categories we apply to ourselves or that others apply to us, as well as the way we think of ourselves in relation to racial and cultural differences.

DISCUSSION QUESTIONS

1. Jiménez talks about ethnic options, including the option for ethnicity to be purely celebratory, something a person chooses to display when it will be valued and to put away when it would be seen negatively. Have you experienced this option in terms of your ethnicity?
2. Individual actions have collective consequences. When people can assimilate and choose to do so, it often opens up opportunities for upward mobility, but doing so also reinforces the power of the dominant culture. How do you think individuals should weigh their ethnic options?

3. Jiménez tells a story about Professor Waters asking her class about whether descendants of immigrants from Asia and Latin America would ever have ethnic options. Her students had said no. Having read this essay, how would you answer that same question?

4. What do you make of the fact that it was Jiménez's Mexican identity that was both more meaningful, in terms of symbols, experiences, and interactions, and more likely to lead to discrimination and stereotyping? Are there elements of your own identity that provide meaning while also leading to harmful consequences? How do you deal with this?

LEARN MORE

Alba, Richard D. *Ethnic Identity: The Transformation of White America*. New Haven, CT: Yale University Press, 1992.

Jiménez, Francisco. *The Circuit: Stories from the Life of a Migrant Child*. New York: Clarion Books, 1999.

Waters, Mary C. *Ethnic Options: Choosing Identities in America*. Oakland: University of California Press, 1990.

Tomás Jiménez is a professor of sociology and comparative studies in race and ethnicity, founding codirector of Stanford's Institute on Race, and director of the Qualitative Initiative in the Immigration Policy Lab. His research and writing focus on immigration, policy, assimilation, social mobility, and ethnic and racial identity. He has written three books: *States of Belonging: Immigration Policies, Attitudes, and Inclusion* (Russell Sage Foundation Press, 2021); *The Other Side of Assimilation: How Immigrants are Changing American Life* (University of California Press, 2017); and *Replenished Ethnicity: Mexican Americans, Immigration, and Identity* (University of California Press, 2010). His research has appeared in leading academic journals, including *Science, American Sociological Review, American Journal of Sociology*, and the *Proceedings of the National Academy of Sciences*. He has written editorials on immigration in major news outlets, including the *Washington Post*, the *Los Angeles Times*, CNN.com, the *Chronicle of Higher Education*, and the *San Diego Union-Tribune*.

Scars of Shame

Marta Tienda

In the summer of 1960, just before my tenth birthday, I realized how poor we were. Once the school year ended, my father, stepmother, grandmother, and siblings and I headed from Detroit to Monroe County, Michigan, to join hundreds of transient farmworkers who lived and worked in migrant labor camps. It was the first summer my siblings and I toiled alongside adults harvesting tomatoes. The days were long and hot; neither gloves nor hats were provided to protect us from the pesticides and searing sun. Only rainy days offered a respite from the drudgery. Communal outdoor pumps provided water for cooking and hygiene. We all dreaded the outhouse even more than the huge spiders lodged in the tomato plants. Camp accommodations consisted of single-room shacks with meager amenities. Our family had two large beds, a small refrigerator, a table, two chairs, and a two-burner hot plate, which was used for the daily ration of beans, rice, tortillas, and *guiso*, a Mexican stew for tacos. Plus, all the tomatoes we could eat.

Up at the crack of dawn, each of my siblings and I picked ten pecks before lunch and ten after. Our father probably picked more than all of us combined, but every peck added to the family coffers, and the prospect of new school clothes was motivating. I could hardly wait to head back to Lincoln Park—our working-class neighborhood outside Detroit. Our sparsely furnished shack that summer wasn't one of the big white farmhouses I saw from the fields, where I imagined kids with an endless stream of toys and indoor bathrooms, but it was a place to live. On Thanksgiving that year, I watched a powerful film on CBS, *Harvest of Shame*, that educated the public about the plight of impoverished migrant workers whose labor put food on their tables. Watching the documentary, I hoped never to return to farm labor. I was too young to understand that life on the margin would take the family back to the fields a couple of years later, this time to the cherry orchards outside Traverse City. To this day, seeing farmworkers stooped over vegetables elicits a flashback to my own painful experience.

My Mexican immigrant parents had moved from Texas to Detroit in 1950, first settling in a ghetto basement, then upgrading to public housing, and finally in the summer of 1956 realizing their dream of owning a home by securing a land contract, a purchase arrangement between seller and buyer that the poor use to bypass banks. Our joy didn't last long: just eight months later, my mother died from a botched routine surgery. At age twenty-seven, she left behind five children, ages sixteen months to eight years. The second child, I was four months shy of my seventh birthday when she died.

On her deathbed, my mother made my father promise that all five of us would graduate from high school, as neither she nor my father had finished primary school. My grandmother committed to raising us, so we were deposited without our father in Edcouch, Texas, a tiny rural community in the south of the state. My grandfather's disapproval of the arrangement was palpable, even to a six-year-old: we all understood that we were not welcome. On every long-distance phone call home, we cried, "Daddy, come get us! We want to go home."

Just weeks later, my father drove to south Texas and packed all five of us into his 1950 Chevrolet, leaving the young widower to balance work and childcare. We were among the 22 percent of families designated poor by the federal government, meaning that my dad's earnings from a full-time union job were insufficient to meet minimum living standards.

With limited understanding of the social welfare system and low proficiency in English, my father fended off social workers who counseled him to place his children in foster care. No one would likely take all of us, but several families might take one or two. Fortunately, he was stalwart in his refusal. "You not take my kids" was his standard broken-English response, despite the formidable odds he faced to keep us clothed and fed. After all, he had promised my mother five high school diplomas.

Despite his perpetual fear of being caught by Child Protective Services, my father sometimes left us alone while working the graveyard shift. After a close call (a neighbor reported him), he cobbled together the resources needed to secure a live-in sitter, who had a child of her own—which meant two more mouths to feed.

Although my father worked as much as childcare demands and steel mill schedules permitted, he was not too proud to refuse free food to supplement his meager earnings. A social worker certified us for surplus commodities—leftover agricultural foodstuffs that the US Department of Agriculture stockpiled to keep food prices and farm incomes stable. Once a month we received canned and boxed food. We welcomed the cheese, butter, and peanut butter, but detested the canned ground meat, institutional Spam, and dried milk, which tasted salty and never fully dissolved in water—even with a hand mixer.

The Catholic Church also came to our aid. Father Murphy's weekly sermons included appeals to help a newly widowed father of five whose children needed school clothes and supplies. Among the many who answered the call, one altruistic parishioner stands out: she took the three oldest of us to Sears, Roebuck to buy new school shoes. My excitement soured to disappointment when I came home with a pair of black-and-white saddle oxfords rather than the black patent leather shoes I'd desperately wanted. According to our benefactor, the oxfords were sturdier and had just the right amount of "growing room." Unlike the shame I would later experience over footwear, the saddle shoes fit and did not elicit ridicule from classmates.

In a provocative article, "The Positive Functions of Poverty," Herbert Gans explained that helping the poor allows the better off to feel good about themselves by practicing their Judeo-Christian ethic. He enumerated other ways the poor benefit the nonpoor that resonated with my early life: doing essential dirty work, like harvesting crops; creating jobs for social workers; consuming surplus commodities that benefit farmers; and purchasing secondhand clothes and other goods that are useless to the better off. In the past, I was the beneficiary; today, I am a benefactor. It gives me pleasure to donate goods to organizations that serve the poor. But discussion of the **positive functions of poverty** eschews questions about the tolerable limits of inequality in the richest nation in the world as well as the lasting socioemotional harm poverty inflicts on youth, often forging scars that last a lifetime.

I became more aware of deprivation as I grew older, especially on holidays, when my friends got new clothes. In our family, we pretended that used clothing purchased at the Salvation Army was new. **Material**

deprivation was emotionally taxing, and on many occasions, unnecessarily humiliating and stigmatizing. We often lacked basics, like shampoo, warm coats, and, yes, proper-fitting shoes. As a fourth grader, I was elated to receive a pair of ankle-height, fleece-lined boots that were all the rage that year. Expected to last two years, mine were too big and rather clunky. Because I had no other shoes, I was still wearing the oversized, tattered leather boots in late spring. As I skipped rope with my friends in a sleeveless summer top and cotton skirt, Mr. Schroeder asked in front of my classmates, "Why are you wearing those boots? Don't you know the snow is gone?" Children can be mean, but I never expected such flagrant ridicule from a teacher. The sting of that reckless insult in front of my peers remains seared in my psyche. The boots did not survive to see a second year, but the humiliation they brought lasted a lifetime.

Through adolescence, I remained self-conscious of my footwear. In eighth grade, our dog chewed the back of my new loafers, and I was forced to wear them taped for the rest of the year. In high school, my stepmother forced me to wear donated calf-high rubber boots that slipped over my shoes. By then, I was more rebellious. To avoid embarrassment—never mind cold, wet feet—I would bury them in the snow on the way to school and put them on before walking into the house. No one ever took them; who would want the ugly, stained white rubber boots? In high school, I resolved to prevent humiliation by saving my babysitting money to buy cheap shoes in many colors. I would stash them in my locker or under my bed so my stepmother wouldn't see them.

My many footwear insults left permanent socioemotional scars. Labor economists define **scarring** as the long-term effects of early experiences, such as the impact of a parent's unemployment on their child's job prospects as an adult. There is extensive empirical evidence of the long-term social and emotional consequences of growing up poor: child poverty scars both body and mind for a lifetime.

The ghosts of shoe scarcity haunted me for decades. To compensate for my scars, as an adult—even well into my sixties—I purchased more shoes than I ever needed: standing shoes, sitting shoes, walking shoes . . . way too many shoes. But this was possible because my father delivered on his promise to my mother that my siblings and myself would complete high school; we also picked up several college degrees. I ended up using the documentary *Harvest of Shame* and its sequel, produced fifty years later, in my Ivy League classroom to illustrate that the devastating plight of migrant children continues.

KEY CONCEPTS

Material deprivation — The inability to afford essential items, such as winter clothes, a heated home, and nutritious food. The 2021 US Census data indicate that 33.8 million people are living in food-insecure households in the United States.

Positive functions of poverty — In 1972, Herbert Gans wrote a provocative essay asserting that society needs the poor to function, as they provide a low-wage labor pool for jobs that support the middle and upper class. Tienda's childhood is an example of the poor benefiting the nonpoor by doing essential dirty work, like harvesting crops.

Scarring — A term labor economists use to describe the long-term traumatic emotional impact of material deprivation. Tienda writes eloquently about the ongoing impact of these scars from childhood.

DISCUSSION QUESTIONS

1. When did you first become aware of your class position? Was it an affirming or challenging moment?
2. The dominant narrative about poverty in the United States is that it is caused by individual flaws (laziness, lack of interest in education, etc.). Tienda's story illustrates the ways that structural factors like migration and low-wage work intersect with personal troubles like the death of a parent/partner. Why do you think that dominant narrative remains so powerful?
3. Tienda describes the lasting scars of childhood poverty and uses her shoe collection as one illustration. What childhood experiences echo in your adult life? Can thinking about those experiences as grounded in social arrangements (as hers was grounded in systems of economic inequality) help you put them in a new perspective? How did Tienda carry or move past some of the scarring she experienced?

LEARN MORE

Arulampalam, W., P. Gregg, and M. Gregory. "Unemployment Scarring." *The Economic Journal* 111, no. 475 (2001): 577–584.

Gans, Herbert J. "The Positive Functions of Poverty." *American Journal of Sociology* 78, no. 2 (1972): 275–289.

Gregg, P., and E. Tominey. "The Wage Scar from Youth Unemployment." *Labour Economics* 12, no. 4 (2005): 487–509.

Harvest of Shame. Television documentary. Presented by Edward R. Murrow on CBS, 1960.

Marta Tienda is Maurice P. During '22 Professor in Demographic Studies, professor of sociology and public affairs emerita, and a visiting senior scholar at the Center for Research on Child and Family Wellbeing at Princeton University. She is also an external fellow of the American Institutes for Research, president of the American Academy of Political and Social Science, and past president of the Population Association of America. She held appointments at the University of Wisconsin and the University of Chicago, where she served as chair of the Department of Sociology and editor of the *American Journal of Sociology*. Professor Tienda is coauthor of *The Hispanic Population of the United States* (Russell Sage Foundation, 1987), the first national comparison of the major nationality groups, and coeditor of two volumes about Hispanics and the future of America, published by the National Academies of Science (2006). She has authored over 200 scientific papers, research reports, and edited volumes. Her research has focused on various aspects of racial and ethnic stratification, immigrant integration, and, more recently, the well-being of youth. Currently she serves as an independent trustee of the Urban Institute (DC), the Holdsworth Center for Excellence in Public Education (Austin), and the Robin Hood Foundation (NYC). Professor Tienda holds a BA in Spanish from Michigan State University, an MA and a PhD in sociology from the University of Texas at Austin, and several honorary degrees, including from her alma mater.

25

K-Pop and Me

Grace Kao

I hope you will never give up. Remember there is a person
here in Korea, in the city of Seoul, who understands you. We
are all in different parts of the world, in different environments and circumstances, but at this moment I hope we can
all give each other a warm pat on the back and say, "It's OK."

*Jimin, BTS commencement speech for
the Class of 2020 (YouTube)*

As I write this, I'm listening to K-pop group NewJeans' song "Attention." I am a quantitative sociologist who has spent thirty years studying race, ethnicity, and immigration experiences, primarily of young
people in their educational outcomes. This semester, I'm teaching a
class titled Race and Place in British New Wave, K-Pop, and Beyond. I
think I'm Yale's resident expert on K-pop, a topic I knew almost nothing about before the COVID-19 pandemic. My newfound fascination
goes well beyond the music. I've come to believe that K-pop can play
a powerful role in society through its positive **representation** of Asian
Americans in the Western media, potentially even addressing negative
bias and hate crimes.

My first exposure to K-pop was via *Saturday Night Live* in April 2019. A
boy band called BTS (Bangtan Sonyeondan [방탄소년단], or Bulletproof
Boy Scouts) was the musical guest. I couldn't recall ever seeing an Asian
or Asian American musical guest on *SNL*. As it turns out, BTS were
the first Asian group on the show in its forty-plus-year history. As they
performed "Boy with Luv" and "Mic Drop," I was admittedly surprised

by how much I enjoyed their performance. But what stuck with me was the joy I felt watching Asian American musicians on US television.

When the COVID-19 lockdown began, being stuck at home led to more time on YouTube, which led me to watching BTS music videos. This took me deep down the rabbit hole that all BTS fans (known as ARMY) fall into, as not only do K-pop groups generate more content than anyone could ever consume, but their fans also churn out tons of other media. I was the chair of Yale's Sociology Department, and the pandemic disrupted my own research, as well as that of most members of my department. Everyone's stress levels were high, and most administrators' work increased. Many of us found new hobbies to alleviate the anxiety. For me, it was BTS.

As my interest in the group grew, my new collaborator and ethnomusicologist Wonseok Lee urged me to learn about a few other idol groups. At this point, the sociologist in me took over my K-pop consumption. I eventually made a spreadsheet that documented boy groups and the companies that generated them. I learned about the trainee system, which requires these young people to work so hard before they have a chance to debut. I learned about their contracts, studied many music videos, and took notes on their imagery and song structures. This led to learning about the history of the industry, which included generations of boy groups and, later, girl groups. I learned about fandoms, fanchants, and K-pop lingo. I learned that I had to have a "bias"—a favorite band member—and a "bias wrecker"—the member who makes you question your bias. I learned that all groups have a leader, a center, and a visual, as well as a *maknae*—the youngest member of the group.

It was fun to combine my skills as a sociologist with the passion every teenager has for their favorite pop musicians. My new interest also decreased my stress level. Not only was the subject matter interesting, but I grew motivated to write research papers on popular music. My new collaborator and I first wrote an essay about the importance of BTS in improving the image of Asian Americans during COVID-19. Maybe it was a premature call, but we thought that perhaps the increased visibility of K-pop in the United States would eventually dismantle the idea that Asians were to blame for the pandemic.

As an Asian American, I've never had pop musicians who looked like me to enjoy. MTV fed this child of the 1980s a steady stream of white musicians from the British New Wave. While I still love the music of my youth, I also somewhat resent its pervasive whiteness. It would have been unimaginable to my teenage self to have a favorite Asian or Asian American group to love. Only when I saw BTS and the many boy and girl groups from South Korea was I truly struck by what was missing from my own youth. I envy the first-year college students in my class at Yale, who have had the luxury of a steady diet of popular music from all over the world. Streaming services such as YouTube and Spotify also have allowed them to be less dependent on MTV and radio programmers for their music consumption. The students in my class were primarily people of color, and they felt proud of K-pop. I'm left to wonder how the absence of Asian American popular musicians affected me and my **ethnic identity** as a teenager.

I'm clearly not the only Asian American who felt this absence. K-pop is more important than ever, as is obvious from the recent success of BTS. With "Dynamite," BTS became the first K-pop act to have a number-one song on the US Billboard Hot 100, followed soon by five more as of the end of 2022. The band sold more albums than any other group worldwide in 2020, occupying seven of the Top 10 spots on the Billboard World Albums Chart by the end of 2020. Their video for "Dynamite" was viewed more than 100 million times in its first twenty-four hours, a new record. BTS's 2020 online concerts outearned all past online shows as well.

While we don't know how many K-pop fans in the West are Asian American and other people of color, the fans themselves believe most of them are. K-pop has elevated the visibility of Asians worldwide, as well as music and other media produced by Asians and Asian Americans. Thanks to K-pop, many more Asian Americans feel that they belong, especially in the West, where the lack of Asian Americans in the media is a painful reminder of our **marginalization** and invisibility. The space also offers many research possibilities. South Korea is creating a major shift in the production of popular music for a worldwide audience. There are interesting stories to be told about changing definitions of masculinity, musical production, and other topics.

I am excited that K-pop is helping a new generation of Asian Americans and other people of color become interested in Asia and Asian Americans. I still hope that the popularity of BTS and other groups can ease hatred and violence against Asian Americans. No matter what, the increased visibility of Asian faces can help minority students who might otherwise feel that they don't belong in US society. Meanwhile, I am already looking forward to watching the newest episode of the Korean TV show *Music Bank* on Viki tonight.

KEY CONCEPTS

Ethnic identity — Identifying with a group that shares a common ancestry and culture.

Marginalization — Social exclusion that denies groups of people equal access to social opportunity. Historically, Asian Americans have been marginalized by rigid stereotypes that limited their appearance in film and TV. Only recently has a fuller, nuanced, and diverse range of Asian Americans become more visible in the media. In 2023, Michelle Yeoh made history as the first Asian woman to win the Best Actress award at the Oscars.

Representation — The way in which the media portrays different groups, often relying on limiting stereotypes. Kao is heartened by the potential for K-pop to introduce examples of Asian male role models who don't conform to stereotypes and thus help lessen hate crimes and anti-Asian sentiment.

DISCUSSION QUESTIONS

1. Kao believes that K-pop can have the power to reduce violence against Asian Americans. How does she think it will do that? Do you agree?

2. In what ways do K-pop artists challenge commonly held stereotypes about Asians? Does K-pop reinforce any widespread stereotypes? If K-pop increases Asian and Korean visibility in the United States, does it start to affect the ethnic options available to Asian Americans, as described in the essay "Watch It, White Boy!" by Jiménez?

3. Music is a powerful cultural force. Often, popular music made in the United States has transmitted US cultural messages across the globe, contributing to what some call a kind of cultural imperialism (where the United States dominates other cultures through the spread of music, movies, etc.). Do you think the rise of K-pop is changing this pattern? Do you see evidence that Korean cultural messages are becoming widely accepted in the United States?

4. Kao reports a sense of loss when she reflects that she never had Asian or Asian American pop musicians to admire as a teenager. How important is it to see people who look like you represented in positive ways in popular music, movies, and television?

LEARN MORE

BANGTANTV. *BTS Commencement Speech | Dear Class of 2020* [video]. June 7, 2020. https://www.youtube.com/watch?v=AU6uF5sFtwA.

Kao, Grace, and Wonseok Lee. "Can BTS Protect Asian Americans from Xenophobia in the Age of COVID-19?" *Contexts*. April 1, 2020. https://contexts.org/blog/covid-19-impact-on-asia-and-beyond/.

Kao, Grace, and Peter Shinkoda. "Media Bears Responsibility for Reinforcing Asian American Stereotypes." *Variety*. April 12, 2021. https://variety.com/2021/film/news/media-asian-american-stereotypes-1234949658/.

Lee, Wonseok, and Grace Kao. "'Make It Right': Why #BlackLivesMatter(s) to K-Pop, BTS, and BTS ARMYs." *International Association for the Study of Popular Music (IASPM) Journal* 11, no. 1 (2021): 70–87.

———. "'You Know You're Missing Out on Something': Collective Nostalgia and Community in Tim's Twitter Listening Party During COVID-19." *Rock Music Studies*, 2020.

McIntyre, Hugh. "BTS Commands 70% of the Top 10 on the World Albums Chart." *Forbes*. April 17, 2021. https://www.forbes.com/sites/hughmcintyre/2021/04/17/bts-command-70-of-the-top-10-on-the-world-albums-chart/.

Grace Kao is IBM Professor of Sociology and Professor of Ethnicity, Race, and Migration (courtesy appointment) at Yale University. She received her PhD and MA in sociology from the University of Chicago and her BA in sociology and Oriental languages (Chinese literature) from the University of California, Berkeley. She is past vice president of the American Sociological Association. She has served on the boards of the Population Association of America and the Association for Asian American Studies. Her research focuses on: (1) racial, ethnic, and immigrant differences in educational outcomes and transition to adulthood; (2) interracial friendships and romantic relationships; (3) social relationships during the COVID-19 pandemic; (4) dating and marriage in South Korea; and (5) the sociology of music, especially K-pop and the Hallyu. Her most recent book (with Phoebe Ho and Hyunjoon Park) is titled *Diversity and the Transition to Adulthood in America*, published in 2022 by the University of California Press. She is also the author (with coauthors Kara Joyner and Kelly Stamper Balistreri) of *The Company We Keep: Interracial Friends and Romantic Relationships from Adolescence to Adulthood* (ASA Rose Series/Russell Sage Foundation, 2019). Her work has been cited more than 14,000 times.

A Bittersweet Graduation

Julie Park

"Do not make eye contact with Mom," I kept telling myself during my college graduation ceremony, waiting for my name to be called. I sat with mixed emotions as they called the names of over a thousand graduates who were waiting with me.

At the start of my last quarter of college, the completion of my bachelor's degree was a lock. I was on track to complete my honors thesis, selected to be an undergraduate teaching assistant for a sociology course on immigration, and preparing to attend graduate school in the fall. This all changed the second week of classes, when my father suddenly fell ill and was hospitalized. Neither of my parents spoke English, and my mom had to keep working to maintain health insurance coverage for my dad, so I had no choice but to move back home to be my dad's translator and advocate through a complicated labyrinth of medical services. I made arrangements with my professors to complete coursework from home, and since I'd put myself through college with financial aid, work, and scholarships, extending college into a fifth year was not an option. My professors and thesis advisor were extremely supportive, and I was able to complete all of my courses and requirements to graduate as scheduled.

Earlier in the year, the entire family had been excited for my graduation ceremony. I would be the first in my family to graduate from college. After my dad's hospitalization, I filed for graduation, but I no longer wanted to attend the ceremony. What was there to celebrate? My dad's health was touch and go, so we were not sure he could make the trip. Not to mention, graduate school was on hold indefinitely. Besides, the required graduation regalia was another expense that would put more strain on an already tight family budget. I resolved to just get my diploma in the mail.

One evening, in the car ride home from a hospital visit, mom asked me when commencement was and how we would need to prepare. I explained that I didn't plan to go and that this wasn't a big deal, since I would still get my degree. I tried my best to be nonchalant yet convincing while holding back tears. Thanks to the darkness, I didn't have to look my mom in the eyes. From the first phone call about my dad's emergency, I had taken it upon myself to be strong for the family, to somehow be the family leader. I thought that meant not showing how scared and sad I felt.

Mom had seemed physically and emotionally exhausted all evening, but her tone immediately changed from weary to one of strength and determination. She explained how important it was that we attend the graduation ceremony, which symbolized so much for her: the fulfilling of my parents' unmet dreams of an education that neither of them was able to pursue in South Korea. A way of reaffirming that their sacrifices and hardships were worth it. A sign that despite my father's illness, we were going to be okay. She asserted that we would all attend the ceremony. Her assertion as the parent made me feel so secure. More than the decision itself, I relished the feeling of security and the chance to feel like the child once again.

Now I understand that my mom's insistence on attending the graduation ceremony symbolized her fulfillment of the **intergenerational mobility** portion of the American Dream—the promise that the next generation would fare better than their parents, in terms of wealth and social class. It is important to note that in contrast to the American Dream, many American families do not achieve intergenerational mobility (hence, the concept of the **social reproduction of class**, where children remain in the same social class as their parents). Many immigrants are all too familiar with the social reproduction of class, since they come from countries where intergenerational mobility is also not guaranteed, and class rigidity is often impossible to overcome. Nonetheless, the promise of the American Dream and a greater chance for intergenerational mobility is compelling enough to induce immigration. Such was the case for many South Koreans, including my parents, who immigrated to the United States during the 1960s and 1970s.

My parents grew up during the Korean War and postwar era in South

Korea. The war had left the country in shambles, and neither of them could finish high school. They had to give up educational pursuits to help stem the tide of their parents' economic downward mobility. Living with their unrealized potential, they knew their occupational choices would be limited, especially in South Korea. Once in the United States, they tried various jobs, including cook, janitor, and auto repair, until Mom eventually settled on working on a computer motherboard assembly line and Dad became a general contractor and handyman. They experienced upward occupational and economic mobility themselves, which gave them more hope and determination for intergenerational mobility.

Without much economic resources or human capital, my parents encouraged my sister and me to accumulate the cultural capital (social assets or knowledge a person uses to signify social status or to facilitate social mobility) needed to succeed educationally. We moved around a lot in pursuit of better job opportunities, but my parents eventually landed and remained in the most affordable part of a good school district. They knew the school would provide not only an excellent education but also the cultural capital required to access higher education. They did not understand the American education system, apart from what they heard from friends, but they instilled its importance in us from an early age. They could not help with homework, SAT prep, or college and scholarship applications, but this didn't stop them from discussing with us how and from whom we could find the help we needed. In hindsight, sociology has helped me more fully understand how my parents aided me in attaining a college degree and therefore why it was so important for our family to participate in the ritual of a college graduation ceremony.

"Do not make eye contact with Mom," I kept telling myself as I looked for my family in a sea of celebrating families after the ceremony. For us, there was an odd mixture of emotions in the air. Joy and celebration were shadowed by the fact that Dad was still not doing well. He was able to attend, but he looked disoriented because of his constantly changing medications. We played the part of revelers while bottling up our stress and pain, knowing that one person's tears would lead everyone to start crying. The couple of months leading up to graduation had been fraught with so much pain, stress, fear, and uncertainty, but no one took the luxury of expressing how hard it was, at least not in public.

Everyone had their turn putting on a labored smile and posing for a picture with me in my regalia. Then I took off my cap and gown, and put them first on Dad, then on Mom, as a way of showing that they share in my achievement. It's a symbolic gesture that many children of immigrants make to thank their parents and to acknowledge that their accomplishment is shared.

The concept of intergenerational mobility is measured by individual education or occupation outcomes. But within many communities, and particularly working-class ones, the higher economic and social status attained by the younger generation is shared with their parents in various ways. Though parents may be *assigned* to a particular social class by their own educational and occupational attainment, they *experience* an elevated sense of social standing from the achievements of their children.

I thanked them for all their support. "But we didn't do anything," said my mom. It might sound like she was just being humble, but she had shared with me on several occasions that she felt as if she did not have anything to offer to help me advance. I distinctly remember her tearing up once as she shared how badly she felt that we could not afford expensive SAT prep courses. It always made me sad and frustrated that she and my dad did not stop to consider all their sacrifices, including working overtime and taking second jobs, and their encouragement as contributions to my success.

Neither of my parents wanted to keep the regalia on for too long. They were proud of me, but they didn't feel like they had contributed much to my degree. This is probably also why they didn't take a stronger stance against my plans to eventually go to graduate school. There were faint suggestions that I was educated "enough" and should find a good job (one with a consistent salary and important benefits, like health insurance), marry their friends' son, with whom I went to college (he's always been "the one who got away" in their eyes), and live nearby. They weren't opposed to me getting more education, but graduate school was even more foreign to them than college. To them, grad school just meant more time during which I would not be earning a salary, would be away from them, and would possibly grow more distant from them. This made me feel boxed in, suffocated. My parents' plans for my future revealed that intergenerational mobility is not always about going as far as you can. It is often constrained by the desire to keep the family close enough for everyone to enjoy the new elevated status.

The "celebration" was short-lived. My family started their long drive home, while I stayed behind to finish cleaning and moving out of my apartment near campus. After they left, I was so relieved not to force another smile. I'd succeeded in my goal of avoiding eye contact with my mom, or at least not too much of it, to prevent myself from crying on my "happy" day.

Alone in my apartment, I looked forward to releasing all the emotions I'd carried all day. But I couldn't, at first. I forced myself to think about all that had happened. A single tear eventually led to the "ugly," guttural cry that no one can ever anticipate or prepare for. I cried cathartically, and Mom told me much later that she got to do the same when she got in the car. So often, I wanted to cry in front of Mom and unburden my fears, anguish, and pain. I would sometimes get teary-eyed but reminded myself that I had to be strong for her, for the family. And I noticed the same restraint from her. She only recently shared that she felt the same pressure to be strong. We now cannot decide whether it would have been better to share our emotions back then or if the restraint helped us get through.

For me, mustering up the determination to finish college while moving back home to take charge of Dad's hospitalization made me more responsible than any of my friends—more responsible than I wanted to be. I did not get to finish college the way I had planned. I had to make peace with the fact that I would not be attending graduate school in the fall like I'd planned. I was not going to be free from the translating, advocating, and other responsibilities that I'd had since childhood. **Parentification**, or reverse parenting, is quite common in immigrant families, as children are quicker to pick up English proficiency and aid their parents in navigating life in the United States, starting with the education system. This was a difficult time that did not seem to have an end in sight. Achieving upward intergenerational mobility just didn't seem that important to me at that time.

In the past decade, I have come to realize that in many immigrant families, the parental role reversal is ongoing. Because I took on the parental role in the family, I may have consulted everyone in family decisions, but I also had the leverage to have the final say. My parents were not enthusiastic about me going to graduate school, but the decision was mine.

After months of helping with Dad and working two jobs, I applied to graduate schools again, but this time without telling my parents. My dad was hospitalized a couple more times during this period, and his doctors could not definitively say when or if his health would stabilize. After receiving several acceptance letters, I was in turmoil about whether I should quit working and go to graduate school and, if so, what the best timing would be. I struggled with the decision for months, as the "best" or "right" answer seemed to depend on "for whom?" With a heavy heart, I eventually enrolled in graduate school a year later, choosing one that was even farther away than where I'd attended college. I pursued graduate school for many reasons, one of which I understood only recently: I needed space to grow up and figure out my own way without being forced to be grown up for others—my parents.

I now study intergenerational mobility in immigrant families. I take a qualitative sociological approach, interviewing generations of immigrants to explore how intergenerational mobility works and what it means to them. Their stories are all too often familiar to me. But to my surprise, they bring me an odd mix of relief and lightness from knowing I am not alone in what I experienced. They help me better understand my parents and, to some extent, myself. I am reminded once again why I chose to be a sociologist. A sociological perspective helps me situate my personal experiences and those of others in broader societal processes and contexts. It's comforting and empowering to acknowledge that shared experiences mean we are not alone and not all that different. This perspective helped me gain a more holistic picture of my college graduation and immigrant family dynamics more generally. It has given me the ability to speak about the pain I felt without reliving it.

KEY CONCEPTS

Intergenerational mobility — A change in a family's class and status from one generation to the next. Compared to other advanced economies, the United States has relatively low rates of intergenerational mobility; in 2020, for example, the World Economic Forum's Global Social Mobility Index ranked the United States at number 27 out of 82 countries. For too many children, their chances of upward mobility have declined compared to those of their parents.

Parentification — A common phenomenon among children of immigrants in which the roles of the parent and child are reversed and in which the child provides financial and/or emotional support for their parent. For example, Park leaves school to work two jobs to help her family. It's only with a lot of guilt that, a few months later, she decides to apply to and attend graduate school.

Social reproduction of class — The passing down of class status through the generations. In the United States, despite the American Dream ideology, which asserts that if you work hard, you can get ahead, those who start off poor often end up in the same class or even poorer after working hard their whole lives.

DISCUSSION QUESTIONS

1. Park decided to skip her graduation for the sake of her family's finances and her father's medical care. But then we see her mother object and insist that the graduation is too important to the family to miss, something Park attributes to the symbolic importance of the ceremony in marking an important achievement. Have you ever had to make a decision in which symbolic and material needs were in conflict? What people or other influences shaped the decision?

2. Park discusses the disappointment she felt at not being able to complete her senior year of college the way she'd hoped. Sacrificing personal desires for family needs is a common experience, particularly for members of working-class and immigrant families. Have you sacrificed personal desires for your family? Are these sacrifices linked to your cultural or class identity? Do these sacrifices conflict with a culture that rewards individual success and upward mobility?

3. When you look at your own family story, do you see patterns of intergenerational mobility? What factors propelled it or limited it? How, if at all, do you see tensions between the individual and the family illustrated in your story?

LEARN MORE

Bourdieu, Pierre, and Jean Claude Passeron. *Reproduction in Education, Society and Culture*. Translated by Richard Nice. London: Sage Publications, 1977.
Jiménez, Tomás, Julie Park, and Juan Pedroza. "The New Third Generation:

Post 1965 Immigration and the Next Stage in the Long Story of Assimilation." *International Migration Review* (Fall 2017): 1–40.
Suarez-Orozco, Carola, and Marcelo M. Suarez-Orozco. *Children of Immigration*. Cambridge, MA: Harvard University Press, 2002.

Julie Park is associate professor of sociology and the Asian American Studies Program at the University of Maryland, College Park. She served as the director of Asian American Studies from 2017 to 2022. Prior to joining the Maryland faculty in 2008, she was a research assistant professor in the School of Policy, Planning, and Development and the associate director of the Population Dynamics Research Group at the University of Southern California (USC). She received her PhD and MA in sociology as well as a master's in urban planning from USC. She received her BA in sociology at the University of California, Davis. Professor Park's research focuses most broadly on the adaptation process of immigrants and their families in the United States, which includes the areas of immigration, demography, race, gender, and urban studies. Some of her work has been published in *Demography*, *International Migration Review*, *Ethnic and Racial Studies*, and the *American Journal of Public Health*.

Along with her parents and younger sister, Julie immigrated to the United States from South Korea just before she turned six years old. She attended nine different schools in several states before finishing the seventh grade, but she completed high school in California's Silicon Valley. Julie dedicates this essay to her parents, Kyong Ran and Song Sil, who passed away in 2022.

27

La Vida Chicana and the Art of Savage Discovery

Mary Romero

March 20, 1969, was not a usual Thursday afternoon spent waiting for the school bell to ring. Instead, our principal, Sister Benedict, announced over the intercom that Cathedral High School was on lockdown because riots had broken out and protesters were moving toward downtown, where the school was located. Dead silence filled our classroom. Chicano and Black students exchanged knowing glances. We were all aware of the increasing racial tension between our communities and the Denver Police Department. There had been recent demonstrations against the police shootings of an African American man and an eighteen-year-old Chicano. Chicano and Black activism on the issues of school and housing segregation added to the charged atmosphere. Many white students were shifting uncomfortably in their seats, avoiding eye contact with us. By the time Sister Benedict announced permission to leave the school, it was too late to catch any bus other than the one near a police station, which I'd hoped to avoid. On other days, my journey home normally included a stop at Woolworths to drink a coke with friends before catching the bus. This Thursday, however, I avoided our customarily interracial group of friends. Many of the white students headed out to meet worried parents waiting in nearby cars. While some students of color walked together to catch buses, I avoided joining them, figuring that walking alone was less likely to attract police attention.

While walking the eight city blocks to the bus stop, I heard the constant whine of police sirens. Older white riders at the stop avoided eye contact with me and other regular riders of color. As we waited, two young Chicano guys passed by quickly, swiveling their heads to check for police cars. Both appeared to have been beaten up. When my bus arrived, I was relieved to find an empty seat in the back that allowed me to avoid other passengers.

Not long after the bus began its route south, I found out that the "riot" began as a walkout by West High School students, who were joined by Chicano activists from the Crusade for Justice, an organization that encouraged cultural pride and provided resources such as bilingual schools and food banks for the Chicano community. West High was predominantly Mexican American and Black. At Lincoln, the public high school in my neighborhood, where I would have gone if I hadn't convinced my parents to let me go to parochial school, the students were divided—Mexican Americans lived on one side of the boulevard and whites on the other side. Inside the school, these groups were tracked into different types of curricula, which were supposed to group students according to ability, IQ, and achievement level. However, race was the dominant criteria used: Mexican Americans and Blacks were assigned to vocational training, whites to college prep. My older brother and sister attended Lincoln. All their friends were Mexican Americans, except one or two whites who lived on our side of the boulevard. Both my sibs were tracked, and I cannot remember either of them doing homework or even talking about going to college.

I knew Cathedral High School was not a utopia. Even though I was in the same curriculum as the white students, they were always mentored to attend a four-year college or university. When I expressed interest in college, the nuns advised me to apply to a community college. However, the dean of girls encouraged me to apply to Regis College, a private four-year school now called Regis University, and helped me obtain financial aid. Even if I'd gone to community college, I was much better off than the male Mexican American students in my cohort. The war in Vietnam was raging, and they were advised to enlist in the military. I still recall the day Doug Vargas was called out of class to receive the horrible news that his older brother, an alumnus of the school, had died in Vietnam. My brother enlisted in the navy to avoid being drafted into the army and becoming more likely to be placed on the front lines. While none of my cousins or neighborhood friends were killed in Vietnam, many returned with serious PTSD and drug addiction.

Sitting on the bus watching the Denver Police with billy clubs and weapons surround West school and the nearby park, I felt incredibly sad and angry. I couldn't forget the bleeding faces of some West High School students who had been beaten by the police. Before that day,

I'd felt joy, seeing only brown faces, Chicano murals, Chicano community centers, and shops in the surrounding neighborhood. As the bus pulled away from the stop, I began to see the neighborhood differently. Now I realized how old and run-down the West High School building had become. Instead of bright murals, I noticed the factories and pollution surrounding this barrio, the old buildings and cracked sidewalks, the highway dividing our communities.

A year later, I felt part of the Chicano struggle for better schools and housing, political representation, and equal rights. And these were my goals when I enrolled in my first college sociology course. I wanted to learn everything about the Chicano movement, Black Power movement, American Indian movement, and Vietnam War protests. Why did school segregation exist? Why weren't the streets paved in my neighborhood? Why were there no sidewalks? Why did I never have a teacher who looked like me? Why were the police so violent in our neighborhoods? As I read about Mexican Americans as a minority group, I was surprised to find us classified as an ethnic group instead of a racial group. After all, the Ku Klux Klan and police in Denver targeted visible African Americans and Mexican Americans. The students at West High School had not been demanding change as an ethnic group, but as a racial group—*Brown is beautiful!*

I was further confused by the sociological explanations given for social issues. I knew there were poor white people, so how did the concept of **cultural deprivation**, which was based on identifying cultural disadvantages, such as having inferior norms, values, skills, and knowledge, or the notion of a **culture of poverty**, which blamed the problem on a values system that perpetuated poverty from one generation to another, explain low wages, discriminatory hiring practices, poor access to healthcare, and disproportionate deaths in Vietnam? What did being tracked in elementary school, and my brother and sister's limited options in high school vocational training, have to do with our cultural practices at home? Certainly, Catholicism, listening to *corridos*, living in a household that included my grandmother and occasionally cousins, and eating tamales on Christmas were not why I experienced tracking in school. I couldn't accept the belief that **assimilation** (acquiring the cultural traits of white middle-class citizens in place of my working-class Chicano culture) was the great equalizer. This process of absorbing the dominant culture, or acting white, was not going to give me access to equipment in science class, college prep courses, or a well-funded library. These sociological concepts bore little resemblance to my experiences growing up in Denver in the '50s and '60s. I also knew that changing me was not going to change the community.

The first book I read in college that offered what I thought was a reasonable explanation for my experience and that demonstrated the connections between schooling, housing, and poverty was William Ryan's *Blaming the Victim*. Beginning with the first chapter, "The Art of Savage Discovery," I began to see how problems, defined as cultural deprivation and the culture of poverty, were actually theories used to blame Chicanos for the racial inequality they experienced. Poor housing conditions and lack of street and sidewalk maintenance were attributed to residents' disregard for personal property rather than to the negligence of landlords and the scarce resources allocated to communities of color. High dropout rates were frequently attributed to parents' failure to embrace educational aspirations for their children rather than to poorly trained teachers, segregated schools, and vocational tracking. Instead of connecting discrimination to exclusion and suppression, the lack of political representation was regarded as Chicanos' cultural tendency to follow others rather than to develop leadership skills. While reading later chapters, I began to better understand the structural changes that the West High School students demanded in their walkout: bilingual education, classes in Chicano history and literature, desegregation of schools, the hiring of teachers of color, and an end to the practice of advising students to join the military instead of pursuing college.

As I continued through undergraduate and then graduate education, schools, healthcare, media, and government programs slowly integrated in response to the Chicano movement's call for civil rights. I was particularly attuned to identifying the ways that responses emphasizing culture, cultural deprivation, and assimilation were a source of social control in our communities. Bilingual family members were frequently called upon to translate at work, but they were never paid extra and were more likely to be denied promotions so they would remain available to assist higher-paying management. As bilingual education expanded in Denver, my sister-in-law was recruited for low-level teaching positions, such as teacher aide and parent advocate. Although she was required to regularly enroll in training classes, she was never given the opportunity to acquire a teaching certificate. Consequently, bilingual Chicanas such as her were paid less, and they were supervised by monolingual English-speaking teachers.

I examined how assimilation programs in the Southwest controlled Chicano and Mexican immigrant workers, tracked schoolgirls into domestic science, and functioned as tools to erode solidarity. As the War on Poverty, affirmative action, and other initiatives developed around diversity and inclusivity, I began to develop research questions that examined the processes used to incorporate Mexican culture into white spaces where Chicanos remained subordinate. I found that removing Mexican culture from social spaces dominated by the Mexican community and appropriating them into white-dominated spaces served white diversity narratives and their interests, but ultimately functioned to subordinate Mexican people and culture. I continue to engage in research that aims to expose the mechanisms of social inequality and processes of marginalization.

As I revisit Denver, I'm dismayed to see the persistent inequality in schooling and housing. In response to desegregation mandates, white families moved to the suburbs, and more than half of the Denver School District remains segregated. A large portion of the community surrounding West High School was demolished to expand the University of Colorado at Denver and Metropolitan State College. Several other Chicano and Mexican immigrant neighborhoods are undergoing gentrification, forcing residents to move to the neighborhood I grew up in, located in southwest Denver. An enormous police station has taken the place of the K-Mart, and there is a constant police presence throughout the area. There are also positive changes that mark the advances gained from the Chicano movement and Civil Rights movement. Among a visible Chicano middle class are lawyers, doctors, administrators, school principals, teachers, and professors. It has been a long and difficult journey since the day I rode the bus past West High School, but there have been advancements in racial equality. Still, the work is far from over, and we must journey onward.

KEY CONCEPTS

Assimilation — The process by which racial and ethnic groups are absorbed into the dominant culture of society, a process that often leads them to change their beliefs, values, and behaviors to fit into the new culture. The policy goal of assimilation, according to

Romero, was to exercise social control over groups to ensure that they complied with the norms and values of the dominant culture.

Cultural deprivation — A theory of poverty that claims people remain poor because they lack skills and knowledge.

Culture of poverty — Similar to cultural deprivation theory, the culture of poverty perspective blames the poor for their condition, but in this case for their supposed deviant norms and values instead of for a perceived lack of knowledge and skills. Romero is skeptical of both perspectives for not acknowledging the role of structural factors, such as low wages and lack of opportunity and resources, in perpetuating poverty.

DISCUSSION QUESTIONS

1. Romero identifies a set of structural changes that students at West High School were demanding. Do you see evidence of similar changes in the schools you or your children have attended? What impact have they had? If they haven't been implemented, why do you think that is?
2. Segregation remains a persistent problem in US communities. How integrated are the neighborhoods and schools where you live? What are your own attitudes toward integration of communities by race and class?
3. Have you seen or experienced victim blaming in your community? How is victim blaming a form of social control?

LEARN MORE

Oakes, Jeannie. *Keeping Track: How Schools Structure Inequality*. 2nd ed. New Haven, CT: Yale University Press, 2005.

Rosales, Arturo F. *Chicano! The History of the Mexican American Civil Rights Movement*. Houston: Arte Publico Press, 1996.

Ryan, William. *Blaming the Victim*. New York: Knopf Doubleday, 1976.

Mary Romero is professor emerita, justice and social inquiry, in the School of Social Transformation at Arizona State University. She served as the 110th president of the American Sociological Association. She is the 2022 recipient of the ASA W. E. B. Du Bois Career of Distinguished Scholarship Award, 2017 recipient of the Cox-Johnson-Frazier Award,

2015 Latina/o Sociology Section Founders Award, 2012 Julian Samora Distinguished Career Award, the Section on Race and Ethnic Minorities 2009 Founder's Award, and the 2004 Study of Social Problems Lee Founders Award. She was selected as the 2021 SWS Distinguished Feminist Lecturer. She is the author of *Introducing Intersectionality* (Polity Press, 2018), *The Maid's Daughter: Inside and Outside the American Dream* (NYU Press, 2011), and *Maid in the U.S.A.* (NYU, 1992). She is the editor of *Research Handbook on Intersectionality* (Edward Elgar Publishing, 2023) and coeditor of *When Care Work Goes Global: Locating the Social Relations of Domestic Work* (Ashgate, 2014), *Blackwell Companion to Social Inequalities* (Blackwell, 2005), *Latino/a Popular Culture* (NYU, 2002), *Women's Untold Stories: Breaking Silence, Talking Back, Voicing Complexity* (Routledge, 1999), *Challenging Fronteras: Structuring Latina and Latina Lives in the U.S.* (Routledge, 1997), and *Women and Work: Exploring Race, Ethnicity and Class* (Sage, 1997). Her work has also been published in numerous social science journals and law review articles.

PART 6

Resisting Racism

Systemic racism is a machine that runs whether we pull the levers or not, and by just letting it be, we are responsible for what it produces. We have to actually dismantle the machine if we want to make change.

Ijeoma Oluo

28

High Yella

Angela Jones

In elementary school, a popular white girl was friends with several kids I also hung out with. So, imagine my excitement when I was invited to her sleepover, too. Now, at age ten, I guess, these white children (thankfully) did not feel they needed to tell their parents that I was Black preemptively. However, she probably should have. Because while I was not asked to leave that night, I *was* told after the fact that I was not welcome back. Even more remarkable, when she found me on Facebook decades later and I asked, she had no recollection of an event I would remember for the rest of my life.

I grew up on the south side of Jamaica, Queens, a Black working-class neighborhood in New York. At home, among my Black friends, I was "high yella" on account of my light skin, something my darker-skinned friends liked to remind me of—especially when we argued. "Step-off, Oreo," they'd say, or "You're playing yourself, mulatto."

Their weaponization of race was eclipsed by the racism I experienced as I navigated white spaces. As a young biracial girl, I felt nomadic, navigating what often seemed like two different worlds. Despite the advantages of my light skin, or what Alice Walker called colorism, and my white mother's attempts to shield me from racism, I was no stranger to bigotry from a young age.

As some working-class families do, I used my grandmother's address to attend a school with a talented and gifted program across town—where, except for one other Black girl and a couple of other token South and East Asian kids, all my peers were white. The other Black girl in class was from Jamaica Estates, an affluent Black enclave in Queens—her mother was a doctor and her father an engineer. In this school context, I was no longer high yella, but the Black girl from the "bad side" of Queens—a racist and classist euphemism that I didn't understand as such until much later. White kids in my class excluded me, made fun of my clothes and hair, and regularly engaged in a wide range of what we'd now call **microaggressions**. I'll never forget the day they put glue on my seat—nothing about that felt micro. White kids outside my "special" class branded me a nerd and teased and bullied me—my Black genius an affront to their internalized white superiority.

When I was young, I didn't have a vocabulary or knowledge of conceptual frameworks to help me understand why I was unwelcomed at that popular girl's house or why white kids in elementary and junior high school teased and bullied me. So, I'll never forget the first time I read Du Bois's *The Souls of Black Folk*, particularly its first chapter, "Of Our Spiritual Strivings." Du Bois's prose and theoretical insights into the white supremacist world were life-affirming. He opened the essay by discussing an exchange he had as a boy with a young white girl at school. The class was exchanging visiting cards, and the girl refused to engage with him. The girl was new to the school and only saw him through what Du Bois called a *veil*. Under white supremacy, according to Du Bois, race operates like a veil—it covers our character and soul. As a result, all people see is the observable and socially constructed meanings attached to the racial category one inhabits.

Analyzing the veil in *Souls*, Du Bois writes:

> Then it dawned upon me with a certain suddenness that I was different from the others; or like, mayhap, in heart and life and longing, but shut out from their world by a vast veil. I had thereafter no desire to tear down that veil, to creep through; I held all beyond it in common contempt and lived above it in a region of blue sky and great wandering shadows. That sky was bluest when I could beat my mates at examination-time, or beat them at a foot-race, or even beat their stringy heads. Alas, with the years all this fine contempt began to fade; for the words I longed for, and all their dazzling opportunities, were theirs, not mine.

In the emotional exchange Du Bois experienced at school, all the young girl could see was his Blackness and the anti-Black socially, politically, and historically constructed discourses fettered to his melanated skin.

Falling deeper into the words on the page, I was brought back to that sleepover, the schoolyard, and the torment I faced from white bullies.

The young girl who rebuffed Du Bois's card felt so familiar. I imagined she looked like the many young white girls who looked at me just as that girl in Great Barrington, Massachusetts, looked at Du Bois. That girl Du Bois describes reminded me of Allison.

When I was young, I went to a sleepaway camp in upstate New York that catered to affluent white kids from Long Island, New York. My mother, a white public elementary school teacher and single mother, worked at the camp so I could attend for free. All the girls had designer jeans and shoes, and my working-class Black aesthetic was the source of bullying and marginalization. Black feminists, too, have gifted us an important legacy in developing **intersectional frames** for analysis. I learned from my foremothers that a combination of racism and classism shaped the exclusion I experienced in school and at this camp.

Allison had long straight brown hair. I can see her now—a white Champion sweater, Cavaricci Z brand pants, and white Keds shoes. She looked like a lot of the girls in the popular white magazines of the time, like *16, Teen Beat*, and *Bop*. I myself only read magazines for Black youth, like *Right On*. At camp, my race and class often made me feel like an outsider. Allison reminded me of my outsider status like it was her job. For a while at camp, I tried to get her to see underneath my veil—it was exhausting and painful.

In hindsight, I understand my mother's motivations for sending me to the camp. Once again, Du Bois helped me reach this understanding. Chile, I was a little Black girl from Jamaica who, after the few years I attended, knew how to sail a boat and was a Red Cross–certified advanced swimmer. I even played Annie in the big summer musical—a big fuck-you to all my racist haters. My mother wanted me to have "all their dazzling opportunities." And when kids bullied me or rolled their eyes at a Black Annie, it was like Du Bois said: This was their world, and I was a visitor. And yes, "that sky was bluest when I could beat my mates at examination-time, or beat them at a foot-race, or even beat their stringy heads."

My Black Girl Magic did not change how some kids saw or treated me. But, like Du Bois, when I look back, "I [have] no desire to tear down that veil, to creep through; I [hold] all beyond it in common contempt, and [live] above it in a region of blue sky and great wandering shadows." It took me decades to look back and see that Allison and her ilk's investments in white and class supremacy were to blame. Not to absolve her or any of my childhood bullies, but they are one example of how the systems of white supremacy and capitalism shape individual-level thinking and behavior.

Du Bois's work laid the groundwork for what critical race theorists argue today. The system of white supremacy is deeply embedded across social institutions like elite schools and camps, and race shapes social interactions and how we see others and ourselves. Growing up, it was interesting how white people, including my own family, would remind me that I was "half-white." At countless extended-family functions on my mother's side, I wondered, if I'm half-white, how come I feel so out of place here? Why am I the only Black person here? Do they even recognize how I feel? Can they see me? I still don't think most of them realize that their attempts at "not seeing race" were not helpful to me. While racial privilege cloaked their vision of my experiences, I always felt different and out of place, even in the absence of overt racism. Especially as I got older, it was hard for me to exist in spaces with people who, while kind to me, had refused to attend my mother's wedding to my Black father, Clyde.

Reading Du Bois, it dawned upon me that without intervention, I would forever understand myself through the eyes of white folks—who, regardless of how high yella I am, saw me as non-white, as Other. For much of my life, I identified as mixed, and as Black and white. However, I never genuinely understood what it meant to be biracial. Then I learned from Du Bois that how others see, recognize, and categorize us is critical to our social experiences, especially those of inequality, marginalization, and discrimination. So, yes, I am mixed, but as Du Bois reminds us,

> After the Egyptian and Indian, the Greek and Roman, the Teuton and Mongolian, the Negro is a sort of seventh son, born with a veil, and gifted with second-sight in this American world, — a world which yields him no self-consciousness, but only lets him see himself through the revelation of the other world. It is a peculiar sensation, this double-consciousness, this sense of always looking at one's self through the eyes of others, of measuring one's soul by the tape of a world that looks on in amused contempt and pity. One feels his two-ness, — an American, a Negro; two souls, two thoughts, two unreconciled strivings; two warring ideals in one dark body, whose dogged strength alone keeps it from being torn asunder.

Despite ostensibly being "half-white" (as if we can measure race in this way anyway), there is no context in which I am read as white—Puerto Rican, maybe; Egyptian or Indian, perhaps—all guesses people have made throughout my life because guessing racially ambiguous people's race and ethnicity is a pastime for white people. I can identify as mixed, half-Black, or half-white all day long, but while I can capitalize on colorism, I cannot capitalize on whiteness. Comments such as "But you're half-white" are divorced from reality. How people identify us does not always jibe with how we see ourselves—a lesson I learned from Du Bois in his thoughtful discussion of **double consciousness**. Under US white supremacy, dark skin *is* penalized more than light skin, but white supremacy doesn't always care about the hue of our Blackness—just that we are Black.

KEY CONCEPTS

Double consciousness — According to W. E. B. Du Bois, Black members of society not only maintain their own sense of self, but also see themselves as they are seen by whites.

Intersectional frames — Analytical approaches that connect and overlap with one another. For example, to understand the experience of Black women, one needs to see where racism and sexism connect with one another to shape their experience. This means one might apply the intersecting frames of feminism and critical race theory to understand the lives of Black women.

Microaggressions — Seemingly small and frequently unintended slights routinely aimed at a minority or stereotyped groups. For example, asking someone with East Asian features, "Where are you from?" sends the message that you don't assume they were born in North America because of their appearance.

DISCUSSION QUESTIONS

1. Jones shows us the difference between racism and colorism in this story and describes ways they have benefited from colorism while still being targeted for discrimination by racism. How do you understand the relationship between these two systems of inequality?
2. *The Souls of Black Folk* was published in 1903. Are you surprised that a book written over 100 years ago resonated so strongly with Jones

and helped them understand their experiences of the late twentieth and early twenty-first century? When you read the passages Jones quoted, did they feel relevant to you today?

3. Can you remember a time when you experienced feeling different or "other"? How might tapping into this memory help build your empathy for others?

4. Jones claims that Du Bois's concept of double consciousness helped them understand that the way "people identify us does not always jibe with how we see ourselves." Does this ring true for you? If so, when is it particularly important to be aware of double consciousness?

LEARN MORE

Collins, Patricia Hill. *Intersectionality: As Critical Social Theory*. Durham, NC: Duke University Press, 2019.

Du Bois, W. E. B. *The Souls of Black Folk: Essays and Sketches*. Chicago: A. C. McClurg & Co, 1903.

McBride, James. *The Color of Water: A Black Man's Tribute to His White Mother*. New York: Riverhead Books, 2006.

Walker, Alice. *In Search of Our Mothers' Gardens: Womanist Prose*. San Diego, CA: Harcourt Brace Jovanovich, 1983.

Angela Jones is professor of sociology at Farmingdale State College, State University of New York. Jones's research interests include African American political thought and protest, sex work, race, gender, sexuality, feminist theory, and queer methodologies and theory. Jones is the author of *Camming: Money, Power, and Pleasure in the Sex Industry* (NYU Press, 2020) and *African American Civil Rights: Early Activism and the Niagara Movement* (Praeger, 2011). They are a coeditor of the three-volume *After Marriage Equality* book series (Routledge, 2018). Jones has also edited two other anthologies: *The Modern African American Political Thought Reader: From David Walker to Barack Obama* (Routledge, 2012) and *A Critical Inquiry into Queer Utopias* (Palgrave, 2013). Jones is the author of two forthcoming reference books: *African American Activism and Political Engagement: An Encyclopedia of Empowerment* and *Black Lives Matter: A Reference Handbook* (ABC-CLIO). They are also the author of scholarly articles, which have been published in peer-reviewed journals such as *Gender & Society*; *Signs: Journal of Women in Culture and Society*; *Sexualities*; *Disability Studies Quarterly*; *Porn Studies*; *International Jour-*

nal of Gender, Sexuality, and Law; *Culture, Health, & Sexuality*; *Sociology Compass*; *Fat Studies: An Interdisciplinary Journal of Body Weight and Society*; *Sexuality and Culture*; *Sociological Focus*; *Journal of Historical Sociology*; and *Interalia: A Journal of Queer Studies*. Jones also writes for public audiences and has published articles in venues such as *Contexts* (digital), *The Conversation*, the *Nevada Independent*, *Peepshow Magazine*, *PopMatters*, and *Salon*.

29

Growing Up White in a Black Neighborhood

Tanya Golash-Boza

My brother Ian and I were the only two white children at Rudolph Elementary School in Washington, DC. Most white kids don't grow up conscious of their whiteness because they live in majority-white communities, where being white is the norm. That was not the case for me. Our family was one of the few white families in our majority-Black neighborhood. I did not experience exclusion because of my skin color, although I was aware I was white, and my neighborhood friends were Black. I felt accepted and embraced as a member of my community. I can't recall a single instance from my childhood where my race was a barrier to forming friendships with neighborhood children. No one ever told me they would not play with me because I am white.

I spent two years at Rudolph, but after my father had a disagreement with the principal over a school fundraiser, Ian and I transferred to Lafayette Elementary School—a public school that was a bus ride away. Although less than 4 percent of the children in DC public schools were white in 1980, white students were in the majority at Lafayette. The day I transferred, my father picked me up from school in our rusty Volkswagen. I sat in the back and was delighted that I could see the asphalt through a small hole in the floor of the car. Even as a small child, I rarely got a ride anywhere. My father was a city bus driver, and he expected me to take the bus wherever I needed to go. The next day, my brother Ian and I took the E4 city bus over to Lafayette. Ian resented having to escort me, so he walked on the other side of the street from me as we made our way to the bus stop. I took that bus through twelfth grade.

Being white meant I didn't face discrimination based on my race when I transferred to Lafayette. The thing about *not* being discriminated against is that this is not something one generally notices. Most white people grow up completely unaware of white privilege because, in a racist society, it is a privilege to *not* face discrimination. I did not notice *not* facing discrimination at school any more than I notice it now, when cashiers do not ask me for identification or when police officers do not pull me over.

I did notice racial inequalities, however. The differences between Rudolph and Lafayette were stark. Lafayette is laid out in an open format—the school was carpeted, inviting, and colorful, in contrast to Rudolph's linoleum floors and institutional feel. When I arrived at Lafayette, my second-grade language arts teacher had us read essays from a reader. I recognized the book from Rudolph—it was the same reader students in the fifth grade were using at Rudolph. And, whereas Ian and I were the only white kids at Rudolph, there were only a handful of non-white kids at Lafayette. Two other children took the E4 bus with us—Elise and Delisa, both of them Black.

In junior high and high school, my ties with my neighborhood friends deepened. In the ninth grade, my two best neighborhood friends, Monique and Nmadilaka, enrolled in my junior high school. From that point on, I hung out exclusively with my neighborhood friends. As teenagers, we mostly chilled at each other's houses or in the neighborhood or went to parties. But my parents were activists, so my family also went to protests regularly, and my best friend, Monique, often came along. When I was in middle school, Monique and I went to the South African embassy to protest against apartheid in South Africa, without realizing we were living our own version of apartheid right in the nation's capital.

Sociologists Douglas Massey and Nancy Denton described segregation in US cities as "American apartheid." They chose this label because racial segregation in cities did not happen naturally. Instead, specific laws and policies promoted segregation, and people worked to maintain it. By focusing on laws and policies as well as people, Massey and Denton wrote about the intersection between individual racism (when one person discriminates against another on the basis of race or ethnicity) and institutional racism (policies, laws, and institutions that reproduce racial inequalities).

When I was growing up in DC, the city was segregated. As Richard Rothstein explains in *The Color of Law*, this was due to a series of practices, policies, and laws that made segregation possible. After DC was established as the nation's capital in 1791, free African Americans settled in an area that came to be called Brightwood.

After the Civil War, Brightwood and neighboring Petworth, where I lived, remained sparsely populated, but a decade later, real estate developers purchased large tracts of land and began to build all-white subdivisions in these areas. By 1940, tens of thousands of white people lived in these all-white subdivisions. Developers put racially restrictive covenants in the deeds to these homes that indicated they could not be sold to people who were not white. Developers did this because they believed segregation would increase the prices of these homes and thereby their profits.

In 1948, the Supreme Court ruled that racially restrictive covenants were illegal, and Black people began to move back. For many Realtors, this presented an opportunity to make a profit. Once a Black family moved into a home, Realtors began to use scare tactics to frighten white families into selling their homes before a neighborhood "turned," claiming that property values would plummet. They assailed white residents with junk mail, phone calls, and door-to-door solicitations for them to sell their homes. Once Realtors got white homeowners to sell their properties to them and move out of the neighborhood, they resold the homes to Black people at inflated prices. This tactic, known as **blockbusting**, happened across the city. Between 1950 and 1970, half the white residents of DC left the city. Petworth became majority Black by 1960.

At the same time that neighborhoods were changing, so were the schools. In 1954, the Supreme Court ruled that children should be able to attend their neighborhood school, no matter their race. Schools that had been exclusively white, like Rudolph Elementary School, became exclusively Black within a year or two. Some schools in DC, such as Benning, Emery, and Wheatley elementary schools, transformed from zero to nearly 100 percent Black in just one year. In the decade following school desegregation, nearly one-third of DC's 500,000 white residents left. This process happened across the country and came to be known as **white flight**.

As the city's white population decreased, so did property values, and thus the tax base. This, in turn, led to a decline in the quality of the schools. Data from the National Center for Education Statistics show that in 1991, the year I graduated high school, the dropout rate in DC was four times that of the adjacent majority-white suburban areas of

Montgomery County and Fairfax County, and fifteen times that of the wealthy suburb of Falls Church, Virginia.

Petworth and Brightwood also became **redlined**—which refers to banks' reluctance to issue loans in majority-Black areas. The term *redlining* comes from the fact that, in the 1930s and 1940s, the federal government created maps of cities and outlined in red those areas it considered to be high risk for investment—those with "undesirable populations," such as Jewish, Asian, Mexican, and Black families. Once Petworth became majority Black, potential homebuyers and small businesses had trouble securing loans from banks, and homeowners had difficulty refinancing their homes to pay for repairs and upkeep.

I was too young to understand institutional racism and the intricacies of housing and lending policies that led to neighborhood segregation or the nuances of school funding that led to significant disparities between Lafayette and Rudolph, but I was old enough to see that there were inequalities and that these inequalities were along racial lines. My parents were anti-racist and anti-capitalist activists, so, when I asked them about these inequalities, they would try to explain in ways they thought I'd understand. Nevertheless, as a child, I always had trouble understanding why, as Rodney King would later famously say, we couldn't all just get along.

One afternoon I brought a white friend home from Lafayette Elementary with me on the city bus. I was thrilled to have a friend over, as I mostly went to my school friends' houses. We didn't have a television, much less a video game console at my house, so my friends usually suggested we play at their houses, where they at least had a television. My friend was excited to take the city bus for the first time.

When we got to my house, my parents weren't home yet. That wasn't a big deal to me, and I sometimes looked forward to being locked out, as my neighbors often invited me over for a bowl of chili or ice cream if they saw me sitting on the porch. However, when my friend's parents found out we were sitting outside waiting for my parents in our Black neighborhood, they were incensed, and that friend never got to come over again. At that moment, the racist policies that had segregated my neighborhood collided with my friend's parents' prejudices. After that incident, I only went to my school friends' houses and didn't invite them to my place. I lived two separate lives—one with my school friends in their large homes in Chevy Chase, and one with my neighborhood friends in their row houses or apartments in Petworth. Living two lives did not bother me, but likely helped me become an expert at compartmentalizing my life and my feelings.

Growing up aware of these unfair disparities in Black and white neighborhoods in DC inspired me to become not only a sociologist but also a critical race scholar. The purpose of a critical theory of race and racism is to advance our understanding of racial and racist dynamics in ways that bring us closer to ending racism. In my view, there is no good reason to study race other than working toward ending racial oppression. My hope is that my life's work moves us toward that goal.

KEY CONCEPTS

Blockbusting — A racist real estate practice that involves scaring white homeowners in predominantly white neighborhoods into selling their homes, then selling those homes to Black homebuyers. This feeds racist fears about falling home values and spurs more sales. In this way, real estate brokers created high levels of sales and reproduced racial segregation by turning white neighborhoods into Black neighborhoods.

Redlining — A racist practice in banking that involves refusing to offer mortgage loans to buyers who wish to purchase houses in areas the bank has deemed too risky. Banks often associate risk with homes in lower-income, predominantly Black neighborhoods, which results in the reduced ability of Black homebuyers to secure loans to purchase houses.

White flight — When white homeowners fear that property values are dropping as a result of recent sales to people of color, they sell their homes and move to areas they perceive as more stable. This rapid selling of homes by whites produces the very effect homeowners are afraid of: decreased property values and a declining tax base.

DISCUSSION QUESTIONS

1. Golash-Boza explains the policies behind the neighborhood segregation she witnessed as a child. Thinking about your own childhood, are there inequalities or social realities that you didn't understand then—or perhaps that you took as natural—but now see had structural or policy-directed causes?

2. How would you have felt in Golash-Boza's place if your friend had been prohibited from visiting your house because of something that you felt quite comfortable doing, like sitting on the steps of your house in a neighborhood where most people were not the same race as your friend?

3. Whites often contribute to the reproduction of racism by making individually rational decisions, like buying homes in neighborhoods that are largely white, which often have higher property values and stronger tax bases than those that are primarily Black. Golash-Boza's parents did the opposite. Do you think that if more white families made such choices, this would help dismantle structural racism?

LEARN MORE

Golash-Boza, Tanya. "How to Kill a Neighborhood and Make a Profit." TEDx. January 29, 2021. https://youtu.be/eakUZX-pRCQ.

Massey, Douglas S., and Nancy A. Denton. *American Apartheid: Segregation and the Making of the Underclass.* Cambridge, MA: Harvard University Press, 1993.

Rothstein, Richard. *The Color of Law: A Forgotten History of How Our Government Segregated America.* New York: Liveright, 2017.

Taylor, Keeanga-Yamahtta. *Race for Profit: How Banks and the Real Estate Industry Undermined Black Homeownership.* Durham: University of North Carolina Press, 2021.

Tanya Golash-Boza is the founder of the Racism, Capitalism, and the Law (RCL) Lab and a professor of sociology at the University of California, Merced. She has spent her scholarly career working to understand why racial and economic disparities exist, how racism intersects with capitalism, and how our legal system upholds these inequities. She has published six books and seventy peer-reviewed articles and book chapters. She has received several awards, including the Distinguished Contribution to Research Book Award from the Latino/a Studies Section of the American Sociological Association for her book *Deported: Immigrant Policing, Disposable Labor and Global Capitalism* (New York University Press, 2015). Her textbook, *Race and Racisms: A Critical Approach*, published by Oxford University Press in 2022, is now in its third edition. The research for her latest book, *Before Gentrification*, published by the University of California Press, was funded by the National

Science Foundation. Professor Golash-Boza is also the creator of the blog "Get a Life, PhD," which focuses on faculty success and well-being, and has over four million pageviews. For this and other mentoring work, she received the UC Merced Senate Award for Excellence in Faculty Mentorship in 2019.

April 29, 1992

Adia Harvey Wingfield

April 29, 1992, began as an ordinary day. It wasn't until my last class period at school that I heard the rumors, and even then I thought there must have been some kind of mistake. Surely someone had misheard or misinterpreted. But no, the initial word going around was correct: the four officers who had been charged with beating Rodney King had all been acquitted on all charges.

I was a high school sophomore. I lived in Raleigh, North Carolina, on the other side of the country from Los Angeles, where the trial took place. Raleigh was and is a very different city than LA. It's not internationally known, has no major entertainment industry, and has a fraction of LA's population. But it's still part of America, which means it is subject to the same broad history of racism, segregation, and systemic inequality. So later that evening and the next few days, when I watched the riots unfold and the City of Angels burn on TV, the news prompted familiar emotions in me—the need to understand why and to make sense of what it meant to be Black in America.

It wasn't the first time I'd had questions about race. Growing up as a transplanted Northerner and a Black middle-class girl in 1980s North Carolina, I wondered why I felt like I'd never really fit in. I was different from most people I knew in a number of ways, and this sense of being an outsider pushed me to ask what I would later discover were sociological questions: why my school, the city, and even social groups like my Girl Scout troop seemed so divided along racial lines. Sociology, as I came to learn, was the study of human behavior at the group level. It involved understanding the institutions that could affect behavior—the criminal justice system, family structures, neighborhoods—and their impact on various groups. While I didn't know it at the time, it was a framework for thinking about things that were becoming increasingly apparent in my life.

Being Black, I stood out from the mostly white kids in my classes; being solidly middle class, I was different from most Black students I knew, who lived in a different part of town; and having moved from Long Island, New York, I was unlike virtually everyone I knew in North Carolina, in that I was not originally from the state and didn't go to church.

All this put me in a position to notice differences early on. Some of these were small things, like the fact that Southerners don't wear "sneakers" or drink "soda"; they wear "tennis shoes" and drink "Coke." Others were more significant, such as the way many in the city identified as Christian and voted, socialized, and interacted based on this affiliation—especially when it came to attitudes about gender and sexual identity.

But by far the biggest factors that I consistently noticed were the intersections of race and income, and what these meant for me, growing up Black and middle class. Coming from a family with a certain amount of middle-class cultural capital meant I had educational opportunities unavailable to a lot of other Black kids. But being Black meant that, while I could be a friend to my white classmates, even welcome at their homes and birthday parties, I could never entirely escape their occasional casual expressions of overt racism. Sometimes this meant kids using racial slurs in my presence to describe other Black people—followed immediately by their assertions that I shouldn't be bothered by that language because I was "different." Other times it meant classmates justifying slavery or segregation as benign forces that benefited Black people by providing a civilizing influence. Even at a young age, experiences like this always made me angry, both because of the distance they put between classmates and me, and because even though I knew I and other Black people were just as good as they were, they somehow remained willfully oblivious to that fact and insisted on trying to demean me.

Being an outsider gave me the perspective needed to observe these patterns, but I lacked a way to understand them. How to make sense of the way that race and class affected my education, friend groups, social interactions, and opportunities? How to explain to my drama teacher why casting me—the only Black student in the theater group—as a servant in the school play was absolutely wrong and that it was not a part I was going to accept or perform? How could I bridge the gaps that sometimes emerged with other Black students when they found out I lived in a predominantly white middle-class suburb across town—and why were our neighborhoods so segregated, anyway? These things happened to me, but I also had a vague sense that they weren't happening *because* of me. There were bigger forces at play here. How could I make sense of them?

April 29, 1992, gave these questions terrifying clarity. The Rodney King verdict wasn't just about my own personal experiences but something much larger. How could twelve people watch that video and conclude that those four officers had done nothing wrong? How could peers, teachers, kids who'd invited me into their homes and who I considered friends, really not see how abhorrent the verdict was? What explained the visceral connection I felt to a man I'd never met, who lived in a different part of the country from me, whose life experiences were mostly dissimilar to mine? Why did I feel that his experience could be mine and that if he wasn't safe, I wasn't really either? How could I make sense of my fear, horror, and confusion?

I got answers the following school year when I signed up for Mrs. Ellington's sociology class. It quite literally changed my life. I enrolled in the class during the spring quarter of my junior year because it sounded vaguely interesting. I didn't really know what sociology was, other than that it wasn't psychology but had something to do with studying people. Going in, I had absolutely no idea what a treasure trove of information I would gain in that class. I don't remember anymore what specific books or articles we read, but whatever they were, they were enough to hook me. By the end of the quarter, I knew this was what I'd been looking for: the answers to questions I had asked my whole life.

Sociology gave me the language I needed to make sense of race relations. Learning about concepts like **systemic racism** explained to me why, no matter how much time we spent together, there was always a barrier between my usually well-meaning white classmates and me. Theories of systemic racism argue that racial inequalities are not an incidental byproduct of an otherwise neutral social structure but an intended outcome of how our schools, workplaces, and political systems are designed to function. At the same time, systemic racism reinforces the idea that whites come out on top not because of structural advantages but that they are fundamentally more moral, intelligent, and hardworking than people of color, and ultimately superior to them. When my classmates (or their parents, or sometimes my teachers) felt they could rationalize American slavery or tell me how to feel about their use of racial slurs in my presence, this explained why.

Understanding this concept helped crystallize bigger things, too. It clarified why, despite the passing of the Civil Rights and Fair Housing Acts several decades earlier, neighborhoods in the city remained racially segregated. What I didn't see, but what systemic racism explained, was that mortgage lenders continued to deny Black families access to loans, Black households lacked intergenerational wealth due to the legacy of slavery and segregation, and white homeowners engaged in white flight when neighborhoods became too nominally integrated for their liking.

Systemic racism gave me the tools to analyze segregationist senator Jesse Helms's infamous attack ad that aired repeatedly during his 1990 reelection campaign. The "White Hands" ad, as it came to be known, showed a white man's hands crumpling up a rejection letter while a voiceover suggested Black workers and "racial quotas" were unfairly taking jobs from more deserving white Americans. The message and language fit right into the systemic racism framework. After all, in the wake of centuries of **institutionalized labor market advantages** for whites, attempts to create more racial equity could easily be recast as harmful racial quotas for supposedly unqualified Black workers.

Fundamentally, systemic racism helped me understand how a so-called justice system could excuse and exonerate four white police officers caught on video mercilessly beating King, an unarmed Black man. It also shed light on why my white classmates seemed unaware of or indifferent to this verdict, while my Black peers observed in horror and with an all-too-familiar sense of history repeating itself. Systemic racism meant that this long history of violent policing was completely foreign to many of my white peers. My Black classmates could afford no such obliviousness. And, as much horror and disgust as I felt about seeing the endless loop of King being beaten nearly to death, it helped to have the words to explain what I was seeing and why.

Nearly three decades later, I write this piece in the aftermath of yet another high-profile case of police violence. The fear, sense of dread, and agonizing worry that, once again, systemic racism would mean no accountability for another Black life needlessly lost wasn't mine alone. It was palpable across the country. But unlike April 29, 1992, the Derek

Chauvin trial had a different outcome. The former officer was convicted on all charges related to his killing of George Floyd.

Does this mean systemic racism has been eliminated? Hardly. The deaths of Breonna Taylor, Tamir Rice, Eric Garner, Aiyana Stanley-Jones, Terence Crutcher, Rekia Boyd, John Crawford III, and too many other Black men, women, and children make that painfully clear. The persistent **residential segregation** that still characterizes most American cities shows that the ongoing effects of systemic racism still remain. And the accounts of Black students who still face hostility, exclusion, and marginalization in predominantly white schools show that the issues I confronted growing up haven't gone anywhere. Derek Chauvin's guilty verdicts indicate that some things have changed since April 29, 1992, when I was a high school student trying to make sense of a massive racial injustice. But the questions sociology teaches us to ask about why such injustice persists—questions about race, social institutions, and systems of power and inequality—remain as relevant and prescient as ever. I hope the answers lead us toward solutions.

KEY CONCEPTS

Institutionalized labor market advantage — People who are identified as white and male have historically experienced an advantage over workers of color and women in the labor market because whiteness and maleness are both unfairly associated with ideal worker qualities. For example, men are systematically viewed as ideal workers because of the assumption that they do not have childcare responsibilities that take them away from their work.

Residential segregation — The pattern in which neighborhoods tend to be predominantly occupied by members of a single racial or ethnic group. Formal segregation is against the law, but the pattern continues (de facto) because of systemic racism in real estate and banking, and because neighborhoods also tend to be class segregated. Given that whites in the United States have an institutionalized labor market advantage, as a category, they are more likely to earn higher incomes and be able to afford housing in wealthier neighborhoods.

Systemic racism — Policies, practices, beliefs, and attitudes that are collectively held and practiced to provide unfair advantage to white people while unfairly disadvantaging people of color. Residential segregation contributes to systemic racism because racially segregated neighborhoods tend to have unequal tax bases that give rise to educational inequality, which advantages white communities and disadvantages Black and Brown ones.

DISCUSSION QUESTIONS

1. In what ways or in what places have you felt like an outsider? Was that outsiderness connected to your race or class, or to something else?
2. Can you recall a time when a story in the news felt deeply relevant to your own life and experience? What was the subject? How did you respond?
3. What evidence of systemic racism do you witness in your own community? What, if anything, are people doing to address it? Do you think these attempts go far enough, and, if not, what else should be done?

LEARN MORE

Bourdieu, Pierre. *Reproduction in Education, Society and Culture*. New York: Sage Publishing, 1977.
Camp, Jordan T., and Christina Heatherton, eds. *Policing the Planet: Why the Policing Crisis Led to Black Lives Matter*. London: Verso, 2016.
DuVernay, Ava. *13th*. Documentary. Netflix, 2016.
Pattillo-McCoy, Mary. *Black Picket Fences: Privilege and Peril Among the Black Middle Class*. 2nd ed. Chicago: University of Chicago Press, 2013.

Adia Harvey Wingfield is the Mary Tileston Hemenway Professor of Arts & Sciences and vice dean for faculty development and diversity at Washington University in St. Louis. Her research examines how and why racial and gender inequality persists in professional occupations. Professor Wingfield has lectured internationally on her research in this area, and her work has been published in numerous peer-reviewed journals, including the *Annual Review of Sociology*, *Gender & Society*, and the *American Sociological Review*. She has served as president of the American Sociological Association, Sociologists for Women in Society, and the Southern Sociological Society. In addition to her academic scholarship, Professor Wingfield writes regularly for mainstream outlets, including *Slate*, *The Atlantic*, *Vox*, and *Harvard Business Review*. She is the recipient of multiple awards, including the 2013 Richard A.

Lester Award from Princeton University for her book *No More Invisible Man: Race and Gender in Men's Work*; the 2018 Public Understanding of Sociology award from the American Sociological Association; and the 2019 C. Wright Mills Award from the Society for the Study of Social Problems (SSSP) for her book *Flatlining: Race, Work, and Health Care in the New Economy* (University of California Press, 2019).

31

White Supremacy and Grandma

Nicola Beisel

I'd invited Kathleen Blee to speak at Northwestern's sociology collo-
quia series because most social movement scholars studied movements we admired, like the Civil Rights movement and feminism.
Kathy studied Skinheads. The people we now call White Nationalists
had become more prominent after Timothy McVeigh blew up the Al-
fred Murrah Federal Building the year before. Kathy opened her talk
by saying her first book had been on Women of the Ku Klux Klan,
adding, "but those people are all dead or dying now"—to which one
of my colleagues quipped, "good riddance." I was dumbstruck—my
grandmother, Aldine Mickle, had recently had a heart attack, and she
was dying. She and her husband, the man I knew as Pappy, had been
in the Klan. I was ashamed that such people were my blood relatives,
but I was also shocked that I had colleagues who saw them as so vil-
lainous that they were beyond understanding and empathy. It made
me realize that my discipline had a blind spot when it came to people
like my grandparents—deeply religious rural white people who lived
in a house trailer in a dying town in central Pennsylvania.

Kathy Blee's talk released quite a can of worms for me. First, there
was simply the issue of how I thought about my ancestors. The second
was (and remains) understanding what, if anything, the racism of the
1920s can tell us about people espousing similar beliefs a century later.
And the third, and hardest for me, is how I think about my own career.
I was a professor at an elite university—but how was the "merit" that
netted me my dream job related to the racism of ancestors that came
before? Decades later, I still struggle with questions about the **reproduction of privilege**.

Let me start by telling you about these ancestors of mine. Aldine

Mickle, my grandmother, had actually been in Klan Haven, a philanthropic arm of the KKK devoted to helping orphaned children of Klansmen. Her mother, who died in 1928, had been a member of Women of the KKK, at least according to her newspaper obituary. Aldine's husband, the grandfather I knew as Pappy, had been in the Klan.

I hasten to add that I was not close to my mother's parents. Not because of my finely hewn sense of racial justice, but because Grandma Mickle did not like me. She did like my three male cousins, which became blindingly obvious the day she pulled out a bag of candy, saying, "I have a treat," but looked at me and added, "it's not for you." I was eight at the time, and the injustice that rankled was candy-centric and personal. My family lived in Pennsylvania until I was twelve, but after that I very rarely saw, or interacted with, those grandparents. But Blee's talk made me think hard about these people and the role they played in my life.

I have very few memories of things my grandmother said. Mostly I remember her working—canning endless jars of fruit from their orchard and working as a cook at Ed's Steakhouse to make extra money. She had little use of her left arm—her shoulder had been wrecked when she was dropped as a baby—so in retrospect I marvel at how much work she did. In contrast to my more reticent grandmother, Pappy had lots to say, but his attempts at ideological indoctrination were mostly religious. Given that his every opinion, including racially heinous ones, was justified with a biblical quotation, his attempts at religious indoctrination created my profound skepticism about religion. But I did not understand how his comments about Catholics—which were frequent and scathing—were related to his clearly racist comments about Black people. To do that—and to understand why this matters now—I needed to learn more about the history of the Klan.

I've been asked if I was angry when I learned about the Klansmen in my family tree. Mostly I was perplexed. When I learned about my grandparents' Klan membership, I understood the Klan to have been an organization of men in the South hell-bent on terrorizing Black people. By then I was well aware that my grandfather was a racist. But the Klan? I looked around the tiny rural town of Fishertown, Pennsylvania, where my grandparents had owned the General Store, and wondered "how"? Everyone in Fishertown was white. Many years later the works of two scholars—Kathy Blee and Nancy MacLean—helped me understand what the northern Klan was in the 1920s—rural, enormously popular, viciously anti-Catholic, antisemitic, anti- immigrant, and the self-proclaimed defenders of morality.

But this left me with two puzzles. First was the link between anti-Black racism and anti- immigrant xenophobia. Second was understanding what appeal this would have to people like my grandparents. The historian Louise Newman revealed the key to understanding the complexities of racial categories when she argued that nineteenth-century racial ideology united race, religion, class, and geographic origin, so that "'Anglo-Saxon,' 'American,' 'white,' 'civilized,' 'Caucasian,' 'Christian,' and 'Protestant' frequently served as interchangeable terms, with each of these categories encompassing the others" (Newman 1999, p. 11). We sometimes speak of "white privilege" as if race in America is the process of sorting people based on the color of their skin. But if we want to understand the Klan in the 1900s, or the Christian Nationalism that is part of contemporary politics, we need to understand that who counts as "white" has been, and is being, contested.

But why would the Klan appeal to people like my grandparents? When Kathy Blee spoke at Northwestern, I had just finished a book about Anthony Comstock and his supporters. I was interested in Comstock because the Comstock Laws made birth control illegal in a number of states (the last state-level Comstock Law was overturned by the Supreme Court in 1965). The federal Comstock Act, first passed in 1872 and still in effect, made it illegal to use the postal service to distribute "obscenity," including information about, or devices that caused, abortion or contraception. Comstock was successful because he enlisted men of enormous wealth and social status in his campaign to stamp out obscenity. My grandparents were far from wealthy, and I did not see what they could have in common with the nineteenth-century economic titans who supported Comstock. Now I do.

Comstock sought support from the elite men of Boston and New York by appealing to their fear of the immigrant hordes—and specifically, how those hordes might tarnish the moral purity and endanger the social standing of upper-class children. So why would the fabulously rich industrial titans of the late nineteenth century support Comstock? I eventually realized that the nineteenth-century rich people I studied were like any parents who "want to do what's best for their children"—meaning, they wanted their children to achieve a social and economic position similar to, or perhaps better than, that of their parents. I called this process "family reproduction." I had never thought about my grandfather's racism when I wrote about the anti-immigrant beliefs of the Gilded Age upper class. But the beliefs about immigrants were similar and so, I think, was the underlying desire to ensure the economic welfare and social position of one's own children.

My grandfather, I believe, wanted to recreate a world where people like him, and his children, would be successful—success being defined by local social norms. The white supremacy practiced by my grandfather would have denied jobs and schooling and social status to people most of us now consider white—Catholics, Jews, eastern and southern European immigrants—as well as to people we now call "persons of color." (Let us pause to consider the rich irony that my grandfather would not have thought of Brett Kavanaugh and Amy Coney Barrett as "really white," even though people like my grandfather are now fervent Trump supporters.) But the white nationalism of the 1920s is so very similar to the anti-Muslim, anti-immigrant white nationalism that is flourishing a century later that I have to wonder if it is motivated by a similar fear—that the world that rural working-class parents hoped their children would succeed in has changed so much that the strategies parents embraced, and taught in hopes of ensuring their children's success, the values they had attempted to imbue and the norms they had upheld, are obsolete.

I am the granddaughter of those 1920s nationalists. Irony of ironies, when I think about the influence my mother's parents had on me, it was mainly in my determination to be "not like them." But when I think about my education, the pathway to the job I held at Northwestern, well, here is where reality bites. Because while I abhor the ideology that is white supremacy, I am very much the product of a (limited) meritocracy that was built on a basis of racist exclusion.

I am not my grandparents—I did not grow up as a working-class girl in rural central Pennsylvania. For this I thank Penn State University, which got my father from being a farm kid to having a secure place in the middle class. Because of Penn State I had parents who had the income to live in suburbs chosen for their "good schools." One of those good schools was my path to Bowdoin College, and then to the University of Michigan, with one of the best sociology departments in the country. When my father climbed the ladder from the farm to the middle class that Penn State offered him, less than 2 percent of the students at Penn State were Black—in part because lack of dormitories meant that students had to live off campus, and many businesses in

State College would not serve African Americans. So as much as I'd like to think that I held my position as a faculty member at an elite university because I am smart and worked hard, the doors that opened education to my father were largely closed to black people. The history of "meritocracy"—from which I have so greatly benefited—includes a history of racial exclusion that some of my ancestors promulgated.

And today, meritocracy is based on class exclusion. The defunding of state universities has made the ladder to the middle class increasingly inaccessible. Those "good public schools" that got me into Bowdoin are in increasingly expensive and class-sorted neighborhoods. Of course there are still ways to work the system, but that takes knowledge of how the educational system works—a specific kind of cultural capital, acquired and passed on in our social networks.

So what did I learn from Kathy Blee—and from my grandmother? First, Kathy forced me to think about my shared humanity with people whose beliefs I find despicable. As a sociologist, my job is to put aside that anger and try to understand these beliefs in a social context. We are all people trying to make sense of a world that is constantly changing around us. I have ideals about what the world should be—that is what brought me to sociology—but if I think about that shared humanity for a while, I might better understand why people who are my political adversaries think differently. And maybe with that humanity comes some humility as well. If **social mobility** is a game of chutes and ladders, the privileges that I was born to were very much a roll of the dice. Understanding how those chutes and ladders came to be, though, that is my job as a sociologist.

KEY CONCEPTS

Reproduction of privilege — Privilege is an unearned advantage. Privileges are reproduced through individual choices and institutional practices. For example, in the United States, schools vary in quality, and often schools in wealthier neighborhoods provide better educational opportunities than those in poorer neighborhoods. This means that children who grow up in wealthier neighborhoods are more likely to be admitted to prestigious colleges and to have higher incomes as adults. Our education system reproduces privilege by providing better opportunities to people who already have privilege.

Social mobility — Movement from one position to another in the class system. Social mobility can be upward or downward. It can be measured within a person's lifetime (intragenerational) or from one generation to another (intergenerational). It can also be the result of a person's own actions (individual) or it can be the product of a shift in the economy, a natural disaster, or some other large-scale event (structural).

DISCUSSION QUESTIONS

1. How does Beisel link her father's upward mobility to race? How have your parents and grandparents' opportunities been hindered or helped by race? Do you think this is a part of your story?
2. Applying a sociological lens, why would Beisel's grandparents join the KKK? How might exploring this help us understand today's political climate?
3. Why does Beisel encourage us to find our shared humanity with people whose beliefs run counter to ours, as challenging as this might be? Why is this important when thinking sociologically?

LEARN MORE

Beisel, Nicola. *Imperiled Innocents: Anthony Comstock and Family Reproduction in Victorian America*. Princeton, NJ: Princeton University Press, 1997.

Blee, Kathleen. *Inside Organized Racism: Women and Men in the Hate Movement*. Berkeley: University of California Press, 2002.

———. *Women of the Klan: Racism and Gender in the 1920s*. Berkeley: University of California Press, 1991.

Hayes, Elton. "Revisiting History: Penn State Returns to Bowl It Desegregated in 1948." *The Register-Herald*, December 27, 2019.

Hochschild, Arlie Russell. *Strangers in Their Own Land: Anger and Mourning on the American Right*. New York: New Press, 2016.

MacLean, Nancy. "White Women and Klan Violence in the 1920s: Agency, Complicity and the Politics of Women's History." *Journal of American History* (September 1991): 285–303.

Newman, Louise Michele. *White Women's Rights*. New York: Oxford University Press, 1999.

Nicola Beisel retired from Northwestern University in 2016, where she was an associate professor of sociology and a Charles Deering McCormick Professor of Teaching Excellence. Her work focuses on the politics surrounding reproduction, most recently on how America's racial politics and abortion conflicts are intertwined. She has been a John Simon Guggenheim fellow and a fellow at the National Humanities Center; her work received prizes from five different sections of the American Sociological Association.

.

32

Dancing in White Spaces

Heather M. Washington

I grew up in a small, majority-white town in Appalachia. I lived on a majority-white street, attended majority-white churches, and spent my summers attending vacation Bible school with my white contemporaries. I was the only Black girl on the swim team, in my Girl Scout troop, and in my youth group. More often than not, when I was not with my family, I was the only Black person in the room. I was aware that my family looked different from the other families around us and that my skin color was darker than that of my classmates. But despite the racism they had experienced in my hometown, my parents taught me that my family was the same as the white family down the street, and that my skin color would not determine my friendships or my future.

For a while, my parents were successful at shielding me from the realities that confronted Black families in my hometown. I spent my preschool years blissfully unaware of the ways in which race structured my parents' daily interactions and routines while in the white space I called my home. My perspective changed when I enrolled in school and began to experience **white spaces** alone, beyond my parents' protective shield.

In kindergarten, I was informed by a classmate that I could not play with him because, as he put it, "Black kids aren't allowed on the merry-go-round." I attempted to get on the play equipment anyway. My refusal to take him seriously caused him to widen his legs and stretch out his arms to block my way. I moved to another place on the merry-go-round to gain entry and then another, but each time he would run over and plant himself firmly, arms and legs outstretched, to make sure I could not enter. I watched as he allowed my white classmates onto the play equipment. I became frustrated and angry that I was denied access, not because of something I had done to provoke him, but simply because I existed in my Black skin. I plowed my way onto the play equipment despite his sprawled-out limbs, toppling both of us. The commotion prompted my teacher's attention. She took me inside to the secretary's office, where I sat doing my best to hold in my emotions while I waited for the secretary to call my parents. My classmate continued recess on the playground outside.

Unaware of the concepts of race, racism, and white spaces, I did not have the vocabulary to express why I was so angry at my classmate. My outrage about being denied access to the playground equipment was obvious to those who witnessed the conflict. Less apparent were the humiliation and injustice I felt about the reason I was denied access. Perhaps even worse, my teacher shamed and punished me for standing up for myself. When my parents were called to collect me from school that day, my teacher refocused the discussion by bragging about my fighting prowess. She assured my parents that I was not the victim here, but that I "got the best of him." She did not acknowledge or problematize the role that race played in the conflict. My teacher also failed to recognize my most noteworthy transgression on that day: being a Black person in a white space, a setting where Elijah Anderson (2015) describes Black people as typically absent, not expected, or marginalized when present.

My anger was replaced with feelings of rejection, shame, and sadness. These feelings covered me like a weighted blanket. Why would my skin color determine my access to the merry-go-round? Were there other playground rules about which I was unaware? Back at home, I told my parents about my classmate's statement. The stillness in that moment was unfamiliar to me. It was as if the air had been removed from my home and replaced with my parents' sadness as they confronted the realization that school would not be a safe space for me. Reluctantly, and in a way a kindergartner could mostly understand, my parents explained my classmate's behavior by tying it to the larger issue of racism in my hometown and their experiences with it. My father, who attended a racially segregated elementary school, talked to me about the racism he faced when schools were desegregated. My mother confirmed that she too had experienced racism as the only Black cheerleader at her high school. I found comfort in knowing that my parents understood my pain. Nevertheless, I still felt unprepared and anxious, wondering about the next time I would be excluded because of my skin. I was certain there would be a next time. And, though they did not say it to me directly, I could tell from the uneasiness in their voices that my parents shared my concern.

As Black residents of a predominantly white area, learning how to "dance" became an essential part of my family's socialization. Anderson (2015) explains the "dance" in this way: "Strikingly, a black person's deficit of credibility may be minimized or tentatively overcome by a performance, a negotiation, or what some blacks derisively refer to as a 'dance,' through which individual blacks are required to show that the ghetto stereotypes do not apply to them; in effect, they perform to be accepted. This performance can be as deliberate as dressing well and speaking in an educated way or as simple as producing an ID or driver's license in situations in which this would never be demanded of whites."

My instinct to **"dance"** while in white spaces was reflexive and strengthened by years of training. Like most children, I watched my parents closely. I watched my mother's daily attempts to carefully straighten and then curl her hair so that no strand was out of place before she entered her predominately white workplace. I remember her painstakingly trying to control my naturally curly hair, coaxing it into two perfect ponytails or pressing it straight for important events and photos. I never questioned why all these preparations had to be made, but I received the messages embedded in the actions: Black hair had to be tamed. It had to adhere as closely to white beauty standards as possible if we were to have any chance of acceptance in the white spaces that dominated my hometown. I internalized the messages I received about my hair, and I later took up the challenge of controlling it myself, trying an endless list of smoothing products and spending hours flat-ironing my hair until it was perfectly straight.

I now recognize these preparations as part of the "dance" and an example of the insidious way in which racism seeps into our daily lives. The dance was automatic and internalized, and while I was uncomfortable with the performance, I excelled at it. As a child, I learned that gaining admission to the white spaces my classmates occupied required me to make compromises. For example, getting an invitation to a sleepover or get-together with my classmates required a certain level of familiarity with sitcoms featuring majority-white casts when I actually had little interest in them and preferred to watch television shows that featured casts that looked more like my own family. Another part of my "dance" centered on my speech and demeanor in white spaces, especially around my teachers, all of whom were white. My **socialization** taught me to speak carefully and properly to teachers and to always defer to school administrators' authority.

My "dance" also incorporated the same survival strategies my family deployed in these same white spaces during the civil rights era. In my small Appalachian town, failing to "dance" and stay in one's physical and proverbial place could come with significant costs for Black families, including physical harm. My parents' experiences informed my knowledge about safe locations in and around my hometown. They reported being chased out of areas deemed white-only spaces, including sections of the river where Black people were not welcome to swim. As an adolescent, my awareness about the potential for danger while visiting or traveling through white spaces caused me to alter my routes to ensure that I made it through those areas before dark and without outside contact with community members and officials. Pervasive displays of Confederate flags, rumors about Ku Klux Klan gatherings nearby, and the occasional distribution of Klan recruitment pamphlets stoked fears, daring Black people and other non-white people in my hometown to stray from their "place." I was envious of my white counterparts who had fewer worries than I as they traveled through certain areas when the sunlight began to fade.

I traded my hometown for a new predominately white space—college. This new space afforded me an opportunity to learn about myself and the language that I did not have to express myself on the playground and in other earlier encounters with racism. Reading Elijah Anderson's article "The White Space" (2015) helped me process and understand my socialization, my efforts to fit into white spaces, and the persistent uneasiness that often accompanies me to those spaces.

A significant part of my socialization and my family's socialization centered on being taught how to dance—to make white people comfortable with our Blackness. Learning to dance was a matter of survival for Black people navigating the white space of Appalachia in which we all were raised. And while a performance could help ensure one's safety, it was accompanied by costs. A cost I incurred was a profound change in the way I thought about myself and about my relationships with my white peers and teachers. The dance was a constant reminder of my precarious status in the unavoidable white spaces I visited on a regular basis. I carried that understanding with me even as I navigated white spaces beyond my hometown.

My experiences to date confirm to me that whether I am on the playground or seated at the conference table, my access to white spaces is provisional, conditional upon my continued performance, and subject to revocation at any time. As Anderson explains, "In the general scheme of the white space, it matters little whether such acute disrespect is intended or unintended. The injury most often has the same effect: deflation and a sense of marginalization, regardless of the black person's previous negotiations, putative achievements, or claims to status; the person is reminded of her provisional status, that she has much to prove in order to really belong in the white space." My experience as a Black faculty member at a historically white institution is illustrative of Anderson's assertion. In my role, I advocated for the recruitment of faculty from diverse racial and ethnic backgrounds as well as the adoption of anti-racist pedagogy and policy. There were instances when I would interrupt my dance to challenge a colleague who did not see the value of these efforts. The uneasy and disappointing looks I received from my white colleagues each time I refused to dance served as a warning to me that my access to the white space is not immune to revocation regardless of my tenure. In those moments, the same feelings I felt on the playground came rushing in, reminding me that no matter how accomplished I am, how many degrees I earn, and how noteworthy my contributions to my workplace, my admission to the white space is not guaranteed or permanent.

It has taken years to undo the habits I learned from my childhood socialization and to love my authentic Black self. Years of socialization caused me to view my natural hair as unprofessional. Now, there are days when I decide to forgo my hair-straightening routine. Each time I sport my natural curls, I feel strong, confident, and beautiful; I feel like myself. I was once silent, refusing to make waves and conscious of the prescribed script I was taught to follow while in white spaces. Today, I use my voice to advance issues of diversity, equity, and inclusion. And as a professor and a mother, I dedicate my attention to making sure my students and children are well prepared for discussions about and experiences with racism.

KEY CONCEPTS

Dance — The mental and interactive steps a Black person needs to take to be accepted in predominantly white spaces and to avoid, as much as possible, being targeted with discrimination, which can range from microaggressions to deadly violence. The dance can involve altering one's appearance or speech, closely monitoring one's emotions, and deciding where one will or will not go.

Socialization — The process through which we learn our culture. Institutions like family, education, religion, and media are called agents of socialization because they help teach us how to be members of our societies. Our peer groups are also powerful agents of socialization. It is through interactions and observations in all of these spaces that we learn which behaviors, attitudes, and beliefs are valued in our cultures and subcultures.

White spaces — Spaces that are controlled by and occupied predominantly by white people. These might be organizations like workplaces and schools or geographical spaces like towns or neighborhoods. Despite residential segregation, many Black people spend much of their days navigating white spaces.

DISCUSSION QUESTIONS

1. "The dance" is a powerful metaphor for the work that Black people must do to be accepted in white spaces. Why do you think Anderson describes efforts to assimilate as a dance?
2. How many of the spaces that you move through in your everyday life are white spaces? Why are these still white spaces?
3. Think about a specific kind of white space: a school, for example. What can white teachers, administrators, and students do—individually or at the level of school policy—to make "the dance" unnecessary?

LEARN MORE

Anderson, Elijah. *Black in White Space: The Enduring Impact of Color in Everyday Life*. Chicago: University of Chicago Press, 2022.
———. "The White Space." *Sociology of Race and Ethnicity* 1, no. 1 (2015): 10–21.
Smith, Ella Bell, and Stella M. Nkomo. *Our Separate Ways with a New Preface and Epilogue: Black Women and the Struggle for Professional Identity*. Cambridge, MA: Harvard Business Review Press, 2021.

Heather M. Washington is deputy director at the American Sociological Association (ASA). She has served as director of diversity, equity, and inclusion at ASA. Prior to joining ASA, she was an associate professor with tenure. Dr. Washington received her PhD in sociology from The Ohio State University. Her areas of expertise include race, inequality, family, criminology, and incarceration. Dr. Washington's primary area of research focuses on the consequences of mass incarceration for family life, child outcomes, and individuals' life course.

Why Aren't You Pregnant Yet?

Linsey Edwards

"Why haven't you gotten pregnant yet? I'm so surprised."

"I would have thought you would have popped out at least two kids by now . . . Look at all those kids in your husband's family!"

"Breathe, Linsey," I recall telling myself as I stepped out of the yellow cab that dropped me off at the fertility center for the first time. "One step at a time." The entire ride involved me replaying people's comments over in my head. Comments from family, friends, and even acquaintances surprised by the fact that we had not grown our family after five years of marriage, perhaps assuming that fertility could not be the issue.

These comments were likely not meant to be malicious, but they stung nonetheless. As a Black woman, I could not help but feel they reeked of what Patricia Hill Collins calls **controlling images** of Black women: cultural images and stereotypes that shape the perception of Black women. For example, images of the "Jezebel" or the "Welfare Queen" proliferate via television and social media and are used to blame Black women for the poverty they experience. As Dorothy Roberts demonstrates in her work, such images portray Black women as hypersexual with hyper-reproductive capacity. These racist stereotypes were used to justify slavery, and provide the basis for the ongoing exploitation, objectification, and othering of Black women.

Today, these images continue to shape perceptions that Black women are inherently promiscuous and can easily get pregnant if their urges are not contained. These controlling images were constant in the content I consumed and the spaces I inhabited and engaged in as a girl growing up in the 1990s—so much so that I, too, assumed getting pregnant would be easy for me. Until it wasn't. The controlling images shaped not only others' perceptions and treatment of me, but also how I perceived myself.

"Breathe, Linsey."

The sting of people questioning why we didn't have kids reverberated in my head as I sat in one of the deep maroon chairs in the waiting room of the fertility office. It was the kind of chair you immediately sank into and didn't want to get up from. Warm wood paneling with an orange tinge adorned the walls, and a late June glow shone through the window.

Like many Black women having trouble conceiving, I was mostly silent about our struggle, lest I subject myself to further scrutiny. Nonetheless, the comments continued even from the small group I did confide in. "I know you'll get through this . . . You're so strong," I heard more than once. I certainly did not feel strong. Although I maintained a convincing façade, internally I was screaming, angry, and sad. From an early age I had been socialized to internalize and project another controlling image, that of the Strong Black Woman (SBW)—the idea that I could do it all, be self-reliant, and get through it with emotional resilience. As Dawn Dow writes in her article "Negotiating 'the Welfare Queen' and 'the Strong Black Woman,'" while the SBW image is meant to subvert more negative images, reduce stigma, and celebrate Black women's strength, it can be both empowering *and* constraining. In the fertility office waiting room, I felt like I was failing because internally I was struggling.

"Breathe, Linsey."

I glanced around the waiting room for signs of others similarly struggling. While the furnishings and design seemed explicitly intended to engender warmth and a sense of welcome, the energy was not. Those seeking care and their occasional partners—all white or white presenting—were scattered around in a protective bubble of silence, avoiding eye contact and social interaction. The tension was palpable. Some people were buried in a book or magazine. Others scrolled intently on their phones. Though I'm sure these individuals were also struggling, the outward message was loud and clear: *Don't talk to me.*

I looked around for something to distract me. On the table beside me was a neatly arranged stack of pamphlets. I flipped through one of the various treatment options for individuals experiencing infertility, only to find that all the people pictured in the pamphlet were white. Later, the orientation video new patients watched also featured mostly white heterosexual couples, and it was hard to identify a Black or Brown baby in the sea of pictures behind my doctor's desk (meant to signal all the successful births at the center). It was overwhelming and isolating not to see my experience reflected in the very medical space where I was seeking care, to be instead surrounded by hetero-sexual white consumers. Even the "success stories" centered white-ness, reinforcing the pervasive idea that Black women don't have this problem, that this was a space for white, heterosexual, middle-class, cisgendered women.

"Lin-sey! Linsey . . . Edwards?" A middle-aged white woman emerged from the back of the waiting room, summoning me to get my blood drawn. This would be the first of over one hundred moments/inci-dences/invasions in the process of in vitro fertilization (IVF) where I would be poked and prodded, leaving behind a seemingly endless trail of needles. Nonetheless, this first time would be one that stayed with me.

The nurse silently gestured for me to sit in a chair. Coldly, she asked for me to roll up my sleeve to reveal the veins on my left arm and make a fist as she tightly tied an orange band around my bicep. "Okay, I'm go-ing to draw some blood now," she said matter-of-factly. Before I could ask any questions, the nurse drove the needle into my arm and pulled it back out. "Hold still," she said. I had not moved. She stabbed me again, this time successfully, and drew three vials of blood. As each vial slowly filled with the red, viscous material from my veins, the nurse sat silently staring at the wall behind my head. In the stall next to mine, I could hear a jovial conversation about cats. "Okay, finished," she said, interrupting my eavesdropping. She glanced at my arm to see if I was bleeding, swiped it with a cotton ball, and sent me on my way.

"Um, can I get a Band-Aid?" I asked.

She quickly slapped one on and instructed me to return to the wait-ing area, where I was left with the uncomfortable feeling that the in-teraction was not quite right.

*Was she especially cold and abrupt, or was that just her demeanor? Was it weird she had to poke me multiple times and did not apologize? Was this an instance of racism, microaggression, or **implicit bias** (an unconsciously triggered belief, perhaps via a controlling image, toward Black patients)? Or was that just normal? Did she mean to not offer me a Band-Aid? Should* *she have offered for me to sit for a minute in case I felt dizzy from all the blood taken? Was I reading too much into it?*

Breathe.

The content, sequencing, tone, and meaning of this potentially racist interaction occupied space in my thoughts long after I left the fertility office that day. I was distracted during a Zoom conference call. I couldn't seem to get my writing going. And when I picked up a book, I reread the same sentence several times before I grasped it.

The thoughts milling in my head following the interaction—and its effect on my performance—are common, everyday encounters for many underrepresented minorities in white spaces. Research has demonstrated that Black participants experience reduced cognitive performance after being exposed to implicit bias or ambiguous signs of racism. This is due in part to the deliberation that follows an event, when we continue to think about the potential intent of the perpetrator. For my own experience, the context also mattered. That I did not see or interact with any other Black patients during my entire IVF journey meant I had no community in which to create a greater sense of belonging in the space, and no community to deliberate with about microaggressions or racist interactions. I felt singled out and alone.

Besides this interaction with the nurse, however, my overall experience with the fertility clinic was positive. The other nurses and my doctor were all fantastic—patient, understanding, interested, and effective at their jobs. I was able to become pregnant and give birth to a beautiful baby girl. Nonetheless, the experience of infertility is hard, filled with uncertainty, and can feel lonely for anyone. Reproductive technologies and innovations, like IVF, are incredibly effective and even empowering, but are also time-consuming, expensive, invasive, and painful. These experiences are exacerbated for Black women by negative interpersonal interactions with care providers, like assumptions about their pain threshold, sexual promiscuity, or ability to pay, as well as lack of representation in infertility spaces and treatment materials.

As a sociologist, I was deeply aware of the ways that racial bias and controlling images directly affect these provider-patient interactions and representations by shaping ideas about who fertility assistance is for. Having been unable to draw motivation and hope from the treatment environment, I knew alternative spaces that provide racially specific support for infertility were crucial. Spaces—like the one I eventually found—where Black and Latinx women as social agents were creating and engaging in what Dow describes as a "process of self-definition and valuation as a survival strategy within a society that might not share those beliefs." The physical and symbolic space we cocreated is part of what Marcus Anthony Hunter and his coauthors call **Black placemaking**.

However, as a sociologist, I also know that structural issues matter. Data show that access and outcomes related to IVF are racially unequal, leading to what some scholars call "stratified reproduction." Black and Hispanic women are less likely to have access to fertility care, whether due to affordability, differences in insurance coverage, or stigma; less likely to have a successful IVF cycle; and more likely to experience infant death, even after having a successful cycle. The onus to improve this situation cannot fall solely on the backs of individual Black and Latinx women. Structural and institutional transformation is also necessary if my daughter is going to live in a world where she can approach motherhood without the physical and psychological dangers that Black women face today.

KEY CONCEPTS

Black placemaking — Black people in the United States face discrimination, exclusion, and erasure in predominantly white spaces. One powerful response is to create spaces, whether symbolic or physical, for belonging and resisting white supremacy. These might be digital, like #blacktwitter, or they might be physical locations, like a coffee shop. They might be formally organized, like a sports league, or informally organized, like a certain table in a university cafeteria where Black students routinely gather to eat and socialize.

Controlling images — Powerful stereotypical images and narratives about a group—in this case, Black women—that shape the perception and treatment of members of that group by members of other groups, particularly dominant ones. Edwards notes the competing images of "Welfare Queen" and "Strong Black Woman" as two examples.

Implicit bias — Prejudices we hold without being aware of them. They often operate at the level of the subconscious. It is possible to consciously hold beliefs about the equality and dignity of all people and still be affected by implicit biases that we learned through the process of socialization. These ideas take a long time to unlearn!

DISCUSSION QUESTIONS

1. How did the controlling images of Black womanhood shape Edwards's ideas about pregnancy? What controlling images impact your sense of self?
2. What are some of the consequences when implicit bias and racism aren't clear-cut acts of racial bigotry? Have acts of implicit bias affected you in ways similar to or different from the ones Edwards describes?
3. The white space of the fertility clinic increased Edwards's discomfort during a vulnerable time. Have you been in situations where you felt like you didn't belong because of your identity? What would have helped?
4. Edwards's personal story might seem unfamiliar to those who haven't undergone fertility treatment, but can you think of other examples when medical treatment or healthcare isn't given equally to Black people? Do controlling images contribute to that differential care?

LEARN MORE

Ceballo, R., E. T. Graham, and J. Hart. "Silent and Infertile: An Intersectional Analysis of the Experiences of Socioeconomically Diverse African American Women with Infertility." *Psychology of Women Quarterly* 39 (2015): 497–511.

Collins, Patricia Hill. *Black Feminist Thought: Knowledge, Consciousness, and the Politics of Empowerment.* 2nd ed. New York: Routledge, 2000.

Dow, Dawn. "Negotiating 'the Welfare Queen' and 'the Strong Black Woman': African American Middle-Class Mothers' Work and Family Perspectives." *Sociological Perspectives* 58, no. 1 (2015): 36–55.

Hunter, Marcus Anthony, Mary Pattillo, Zandria F. Robinson, and Keeanga-Yamahtta Taylor. "Black Placemaking: Celebration, Play, and Poetry." *Theory, Culture, and Society* (2016): 1–26.

Murphy, M. C., J. A. Richeson, J. N. Shelton, M. L. Rheinschmidt, and H. B. Bergsieker. "Cognitive Costs of Contemporary Prejudice." *Group Processes & Intergroup Relations* 16, no. 5 (September 2013): 560–571.

Remster, Brianna, Chris Smith, and Rory Kramer. "Race, Gender, and Police Violence in the Shadow of Controlling Images." *Social Problems* (2022): 1–24. https://doi.org/10.1093/socpro/spac018.

Roberts, D. E. "Race, Gender, and Genetic Technologies: A New Reproductive Dystopia?" *Signs: Journal of Women in Culture and Society* 34 (2009): 783–804.
Wingfield, Adia H. "The Modern Mammy and the Angry Black Man: African American Professionals' Experiences with Gendered Racism in the Workplace." *Race, Gender and Class* 14, no. ½ (2007): 196–212. New Orleans: University of New Orleans.

Linsey Edwards is an assistant professor of sociology at New York University. Her research examines the complex set of factors that contribute to persisting racial inequality and poverty in the United States. Empirically, she focuses on schools, neighborhoods, and bureaucratic institutions as critical contexts that reproduce social disparities. In her article "Homogeneity and Inequality: School Discipline Inequality and the Role of Racial Composition," published in *Social Forces*, she seeks to untangle school-level mechanisms contributing to racial inequality in school punishment. Her in-progress book examines the ways that poverty, race, and neighborhood context shape how people use and experience their time in ways that reproduce inequality. Professor Edwards accidentally discovered sociology when she took a class as an undergraduate at the University of Maryland after the class she originally wanted was overenrolled. The class truly sparked her sociological imagination.

PART 7

Rewriting the Rules of Sex and Gender

Bodies are not only biological phenomena but also complex social creations onto which meanings have been variously composed and imposed according to time and space.

Katrina Karkazis

My First Girlfriend's Kitchen

Tey Meadow

I grew up in an upper-class Jewish suburb of New York City, born into a family of women who prioritized beauty and seemed good at producing it. At first it appeared I had the potential to join them; people praised my honey-blonde hair, blue eyes, and porcelain skin. But I was heavy-set, squinty, and clumsy from visual impairment, and I always seemed to be taking up too much space. My mother and her mother coached me on ways to starve myself into the body they thought I should have, scrutinizing my diet and exercise, how each article of clothing hung on my awkward frame. At thirteen, after an excruciating season of being wrangled into an endless succession of patterned party dresses for bar and bat mitzvahs, I retreated from femininity. I think of this as the beginning of my "gray sweatsuit period," a several-years-long project of hiding myself beneath the largest swaths of fabric that could conceivably pass as early nineties fashion. I was deeply miserable, at war with my body, in hiding. I walked around like a ghost.

I left home at eighteen for Bard College. I gravitated almost immediately to the weirdest smart kids I could find: boisterous theater geeks, pasty philosophers, stoned computer programmers, and, eventually, the core group of campus feminist activists. I cut my hair short, tore holes in my jeans, came out as queer, and began working for the collective, peer-run rape crisis response program on campus. I knew the activists had some form of self-knowledge that I craved. They seemed to own their bodies in ways none of the other women I knew did. They took up space. They spoke in class. They tried to make the world safer for women. They felt more awake to the world than the women in my family did.

My education in the language of gender began there, and it was all-consuming. I read books and watched films, listened to indie folk music, and spent a lot of time in coffeehouses. Little by little, I began discarding the gendered artifacts of my childhood. I bought flannel button-down shirts from the thrift store, layering them over concert T-shirts. I acquired the red Converse All Stars and Doc Martens my mother had deemed "too clunky" for my thick calves in high school. I threw out all my underwire bras and began binding my chest. With each successive stylistic innovation, I felt more entitled to my body and the space it occupied. I was finally able to transfer my gaze away from my own self-loathing and toward the universe of experience that awaited me in college.

I didn't discover sociology until my senior year, but I remember reading Candace West and Don Zimmerman's pivotal article "Doing Gender," which led me down a long path toward understanding the relational nature of our personal identities. We **do gender**, they told us, in interaction with our significant others. We fashion our appearance, speech, modes of dress, choice of vocation, erotic orientations, and more in ways that reference the social worlds we inhabit. And we are always, always looking to see how those microscopic choices are received by those we care about most.

When I first read that essay, it helped me frame the nearly constant negative feedback I received as a girl as part of the way my mother and grandmother tried (and failed) to make me into a woman. And it helped me understand in a new way how the gendered choices I was making, in interaction with the interlocutors I chose in college, were helping me remake myself into someone new, different, and more self-actualized.

By the time I entered my first long-term relationship at twenty, I was fully out as a lesbian, identified as "a butch," and had transformed my appearance dramatically. I was routinely read as male in public. This was a source of pleasure and validation for me, but it also caused tremendous discomfort for my family, and those relationships became intensely stressful. I was excluded from family events and felt dizzy with anxiety whenever I was in their presence.

We do gender, say West and Zimmerman, always "at the risk of assessment." Negative gender assessments lead to social exclusion, violence, and emotional pain. I experienced all of these. In the 1990s, there was no language I could use to explain myself to my family. I wasn't a "transsexual" (that is, I didn't identify as male), and I was something more than a "dyke." Store clerks would call me "Sir," and my mother would bristle with humiliation, then correct them angrily. She would instruct me to grow out my hair, to dress differently, to spare us both the stares at restaurants, the reprimands in public bathrooms. Because they were already so distressed, I could share with my family neither the difficulties of being visibly gender nonconforming in a cisgender world nor the absolute delight of coming into a self, into a self-articulation, that felt sweet and hot and empowering. All my family knew was that I was embarrassing and confounding.

These were classic negative assessments, often delivered without mincing words. Yet I did not retreat from my gender or from my family. And I did not cover (Erving Goffman's term for de-emphasizing stigmatized identities). Instead, I worked with and through the trauma of rupture with my family into what the queer theorist José Muñoz called **disidentification**. I neither identified with men nor against them, with the idea of the **gender binary** or against it. Rather, I borrowed from the practices of men and masculinity, repurposing them for my own uses.

When I met my first girlfriend in 1997, she didn't merely tolerate my gender presentation, my awkwardness, and my size; these were precisely the things she enjoyed in a lover. She called me her "boyfriend," and I felt the kind of freedom to move and to eat that I imagined the men in my family felt. It wasn't male, but it did feel masculine, and I liked it.

My girlfriend shared a tiny one-bedroom basement apartment in Brooklyn with a roommate, who slept behind a curtained-off area of their living room. The place was dark and sparse, but cheerfully adorned with Broadway memorabilia, a rainbow flag, and some Christmas lights. Nearly a quarter century later, I vividly remember sitting cross-legged in front of the low coffee table, eating boxed mac and cheese, and feeling more at home in my skin than I'd ever felt in my life. I was not "undoing" the gender I had been given or escaping the trauma of negative assessment. Rather, I was refashioning them into a self I could rest in.

Gender theory in sociology evolves at breakneck speed. Newer work on undoing gender, redoing gender, and doing transgender all formulate means of understanding the complex ways individuals negotiate and resist gender's mandates. Perhaps it is generational, or particular only to some, but I have come to understand my gender as an intricate engagement with the social order, with pain, and with trauma. My gender is constituted by both the pain of my failed attempts at femininity and the loss of a sense of belonging to the world of my family. It is also articulate, highly self-actualized, and shot through with pleasure and desire. I have many words to describe it and many ways to live and embody it. It animates my emotional and erotic orientation to my significant others. By negotiating the ways my masculinity provokes curiosity for some; discomfort, fear, or anger for others; and attraction for yet others, I have come into a self that feels fully mine.

KEY CONCEPTS

Disidentification — An idea associated with José Muñoz's theory that people who are historically marginalized can understand themselves by resisting the categories of the dominant group. For example, Meadow takes on many of the practices of masculinity but doesn't see herself as a man. She has disidentified with femininity without identifying as a man, thus rejecting the binary categories of the dominant gender ideology.

Doing gender — A term coined by Candace West and Don Zimmerman to refer to the way that gender is produced and reproduced through the performance of many everyday actions. We can do gender in ways that support and reinforce the dominant ideas of masculinity and femininity, or we can do gender in ways that challenge those ideas. We can do gender in ways that others view as consistent with our gender assignment, or we can do gender in ways that are viewed as nonconformist.

Gender binary — A system of gender based on the idea that there are only two gender options and that they are mutually exclusive and opposite. Like a light switch that can either be on or off but not in between, the ideology of the gender binary is grounded in the belief that a person can be either male or female, that males will all grow up as boys and become men, and that females will all grow up as girls and become women. In this way of thinking, there can be nothing in between.

DISCUSSION QUESTIONS

1. What are some of the ways that you "do" and "undo" gender in your daily life?

2. Meadow quotes from a famous essay by West and Zimmerman, noting that we do gender "at the risk of assessment." In what ways do you participate in assessing the gender performances of others? How do others assess yours? Are there ways we can reduce our tendency to assess people's gender performances?

3. For Meadow, gender is "an intricate engagement with the social order, with pain, and with trauma." Do you think this is true for many people, even if they don't think of it this way? Do you think it is true for other aspects of identity as well?

LEARN MORE

Bornstein, Kate, and S. Bear Bergman. *Gender Outlaws: The Next Generation.* New York: Seal Press, 2010.

Muñoz, José Esteban. *Disidentifications: Queers of Color and the Performance of Politics.* Minneapolis: University of Minnesota, 1999.

Risman, B. J. "Doing to Undoing: Gender as We Know It." *Gender & Society* 23, no. 1 (2009): 81–84. https://doi.org/10.1177/0891243208326874.

West, C., and D. H. Zimmerman. "Doing Gender." *Gender and Society* 1, no. 2 (1987): 125–151. http://www.jstor.org/stable/189945.

Tey Meadow is associate professor of sociology at Columbia University. Her research focuses on a broad range of issues, including the emergence of the transgender child as a social category, the international politics of family diversity, the creation and maintenance of legal gender classifications, and newer work on the erotic life of social categories. She is the author of *Trans Kids: Being Gendered in the Twenty-First Century* (University of California Press, 2018) and the coeditor of *Other, Please Specify: Queer Methods in Sociology* (University of California Press, 2018). She lives in Brooklyn with her daughter and a vast menagerie of multi-legged creatures.

And Just Like That, She Was Gone

Katharine M. Donato

I was ten years old when my mom died. It was the end of June. The last words I remember her saying were that she was going on a hospital vacation to rest. We were a family of eight: my father, my mother, and six children. I was the second oldest. Six days after she was hospitalized, my younger brother and I were at my grandparents' house. We were in the backyard when I heard the phone ring inside and then my grandmother scream. Before that moment, she'd never shed a tear in front of us. She called me in, handed me the phone, and I heard my father tell me, "Your mother died earlier today at the hospital." And just like that, my mother was gone.

The loss accelerated my path to adulthood. The years flew by in a blur. I had no time to figure out what had happened and why, or to manage the trauma of losing a mother at a young age. Despite my sadness, I pushed on, because that is what everyone around me appeared to do.

Fast-forward to years later, when—in my late twenties and early thirties—I finally began to make sense of what happened and why my adolescent years and responses to later-life challenges were the way they were.

I was in graduate school when I first thought about gender and the ideology of separate spheres, which asserts that home is a space best tended by women, and work outside the home best tended by men. Historically, separate spheres were reinforced in breadwinner/homemaker marriages and they were reflected in men's and women's work despite the inroads that married women had made in the US labor market since 1960. Generally, men had received greater benefits than women in the formal workplace. Within families, men earned more because they needed a family wage—a salary large enough to support his household, which included a non-employed wife and children.

After more married women began working outside the home, Arlie Hochschild taught us that women overwhelmingly bear the burden of a second shift, or the unpaid domestic work that includes housekeeping and childcare. Sandra Lipsitz Bem showed how hidden assumptions about gender perpetuate male power and the oppression of women, identifying three lenses through which men and women are viewed. Androcentrism defines the male experience as the standard and norm. Gender polarization is the tendency to superimpose the male-female difference on all our experiences, starting at birth. And biological essentialism rationalizes and legitimizes the other two perspectives by treating them as natural and inevitable based on male and female biology.

Developing my own **gender lens**, I thought a lot about **feminization**, first as a graduate student working on a project that examined women's inroads into occupations that were once largely composed of men, and then on my dissertation, asking why some countries sent immigrant men while others sent women to the United States. Much later, I explored this concept in a coauthored book with Donna Gabaccia on gender and international migration.

With a gender lens, I began to understand my mother's death as embedded in a larger context of separate domestic spheres. Her mothering role began when she married at age nineteen and ended at her death at thirty-four. Consistent with gendered expectations, she was pregnant eleven times, with five miscarriages and six children. She ended up being hospitalized with thrombosis, or blood clots in the veins of her legs. Mom told us gleefully that her hospital vacation would offer complete bed rest without young kids underfoot. Yet, several days later, she developed a pulmonary embolism when, after physicians allowed her to get out of bed too soon, a blood clot lodged in her lungs, and she suddenly died.

Although her death would be less likely today, multiple back-to-back pregnancies come with risk. With every pregnancy and birth, a woman's risk of dying increases. In addition, in the United States, the number of women experiencing both pregnancy and childbirth complications has continued to rise. Women in the United States are also three times more likely to die in childbirth than women in other high-income countries. And the maternal mortality rate for non-Hispanic

Black women is 2.9 times higher than for white or Hispanic women. My mother didn't die in childbirth, but her eleven pregnancies contributed to her thrombosis and, ultimately, to the pulmonary embolism that took her life. Some of you may also recall that Serena Williams almost died from a pulmonary embolism after giving birth.

I didn't realize until I was in graduate school how a sociological perspective on gender could offer insights into what had happened in my own life. Not only did gender help contextualize my mother's death, but it also made me see how the expectations of motherhood and care work operated in my family across generations.

Immediately after my mother's death, both my grandmothers stayed at our house and split the week to keep the house running and provide childcare because of my father's work schedule. One grandmother stayed at our house from Monday through Wednesday, and the other stayed from Thursday to Saturday. My oldest sister and I quickly learned that we too had to step up. We learned how to cook and clean, and how to care for our younger siblings. We also learned which housekeeping items and activities were safe for us to carry out and which were dangerous. Clearly gendered assumptions influenced the decision that the women in the family, young and old, were the appropriate family members to perform these roles.

Years later, after both grandmothers passed away, I realized how their gendered socialization and expectations laid the foundation for our (and their) family's experiences. My father's mother had created a strong shield of armor from an immigrant experience that involved domestic violence, poverty, and many young siblings. Having never shed a tear in front of her grandchildren until the day my mother died, she took care of her family and made money from piecemeal garment work, beading luxury evening gowns and handbags for the ultra-rich in New York City from her (or our) living room. My mother's mother shored up her strength—despite an earlier cancer diagnosis—and equally shared in the caretaking of us as children after her daughter's sudden death. She saw us through the time when we were without a mother in the house and passed away just a year after my father remarried.

Understanding gender from a sociological perspective was a turning point for me. I saw how my mother's death occurred in a family context that both influenced and reinforced gendered expectations about the roles of women and men. That my grandmothers, my sister, and

I were expected to keep house and care for the children while my dad worked isn't shocking, but it is telling. Although the ideology of separate spheres made women's unpaid work feel "natural" and "normal," as an adult I now appreciate how hard it must have been for my grandmothers at their age to care for so many grieving children.

Women universally step up when it comes to unpaid caregiving. Even employed women with male partners take on more of the unpaid activities related to elder and other forms of care work. When a parent gets sick, it's usually the woman who takes on these duties—even if it's the man's parent, and even if she earns more money and works more hours than her husband. This **gendered division of labor** is changing slowly, but the androcentrism, polarization, and biological essentialism that give rise to and reinforce separate spheres continue to disadvantage women in their pursuit of equity in employment and family caregiving. It is time to shed age-old gendered expectations that overwhelmingly burden women.

Processing my mother's death in the context of her role as a mother and wife was painful. Her short life was dictated and likely cut short by strict gender expectations that encouraged multiple pregnancies and put her at risk. Today, women in countries such as the United States are less constrained by such gender roles, but change is still needed to allow men and women to equally flourish in both domestic and employment spheres. Moreover, countries worldwide also must push beyond gendered ideologies and divisions of labor to create equity for women and men.

My deep understanding of gender helped me heal by putting my childhood experiences in a larger context. To ensure the future success of subsequent generations, we must support research that reveals how gender nuances and influences behaviors and beliefs today.

KEY CONCEPTS

Feminization — The process by which something becomes associated with women or femininity. For example, some jobs have become feminized as women have entered them. Flight attendants were all men during the very early days of commercial flight. They were referred to as stewards and projected strength and confidence to help people see flying as safe. As air travel became more common and airlines strived to appeal to businessmen, they began hiring women who were generally young, white, and conventionally attractive. These women were then called stewardesses, and the image became grounded in pleasure and hospitality. In response to feminist activism and lawsuits, the work has continued to change, and we now generally use the term "flight attendants," which is less sexualized.

Gender lens — Sandra Bem coined the term "lenses of gender" to refer to the multiple ways that gendered ideology shapes the way we see the world. Bem's theory says these lenses shape our vision in three ways: (1) we see the masculine as the standard (androcentrism); (2) we see genders as opposites (gender polarization); and (3) we see all of this as a function of natural difference (biological essentialism).

Gendered division of labor — Whether it is unpaid household work or jobs we do for pay, much work is divided between people in ways that align with gender categories. Looking at household labor, women do more childcare, cooking (indoors, at least), and cleaning than men, but men are more likely to take out the garbage, handle auto service, and do lawn care (in the suburbs). Interestingly, when it comes to paid work, chefs are more likely to be men than women, despite women's overwhelming responsibility for cooking at home.

DISCUSSION QUESTIONS

1. Thinking about your own family, how is the unpaid household labor divided by gender and/or age? Is there any household work you or your family outsource (pay others to do)? If so, how is that gendered?

2. Donato references the ideology of separate spheres. Ideologies are systems of thought that are geared toward supporting specific social arrangements. How strongly held is this ideology of separate spheres in the community where you live?

3. Young people in the United States today generally say that they aspire to relationships where household work and paid employment are equally shared. What social factors might make it hard to achieve this kind of equal sharing of responsibilities? What can be done to make it easier?

LEARN MORE

Bem, Sandra Lipsitz. *The Lenses of Gender: Transforming the Debate on Sexual Inequality*. New Haven, CT: Yale University Press, 1994.

Donato, Katharine M., and Donna Gabaccia. *Gender and International Migration: From the Slavery Era to the Global Age*. New York: Russell Sage Foundation, 2105.

Hochschild, Arlie, and Anne Machung. *The Second Shift: Working Families and the Revolution at Home*. New York: Penguin Publishing Group, 2012.

Hoyert, Donna L. "Maternal Mortality Rates in the United States." CDC Division of Vital Statistics, 2020. https://www.cdc.gov/nchs/data/hestat/maternal-mortality/2020/maternal-mortality-rates-2020.htm.

Power, Kate. "The Covid-19 Pandemic Has Increased the Care Burden of Women and Families." *Sustainability, Science, Practice & Policy* 16, no. 1 (2020): 67–73.

Taub, Amanda. "Pandemic Will 'Take Our Women 10 Years Back' in the Workplace." *New York Times*, September 26, 2020.

Katharine M. Donato is the Donald G. Herzberg Professor of International Migration and serves as the Chair of the Faculty Council in the School of Foreign Service at Georgetown University. She has also served as the director of Georgetown's Institute for the Study of International Migration. She examines many research questions related to migration and gender; US and global migration policies; health consequences of migration; consequences of the great recession and COVID-19 for migrant workers; refugee and migrant integration; environmental drivers of out-migration; and the use of organic data sources to understand the drivers of forced migration. She has coedited eight refereed journal volumes and published more than one hundred journal articles and book chapters. In 2015, the Russell Sage Foundation published her first book, *Gender and International Migration: From Slavery to Present*, coauthored with Donna Gabaccia. With Elizabeth Ferris, she coauthored a second book, *Refugees, Migration and Global Governance: Negotiating the Global Compacts* (Routledge, 2020). She is currently writing a book on the treatment and management of unaccompanied children entering the United States.

No Such Thing as a Paper Girl

Ruth Milkman

Growing up in Annapolis, Maryland, in the 1960s, I got around mostly on my trusty one-speed bike. In what was then a well-preserved colonial town with clogged, narrow streets on which cars could only crawl, cycling was safe and relatively speedy. It also was a potential source of income during my adolescence, when I was desperate for spending money. My Depression-generation parents were not forthcoming in that regard. "When I was in high school, I had one skirt," my mother replied when I told her I longed for the kinds of clothes other girls had.

That led me to the office of the *Evening Capital*, where I put in an application for a paper route. In those days, newspapers were delivered by teenaged paper boys, whose bikes, with their oversized baskets, were a familiar sight in the neighborhood. It struck me as the perfect after-school job.

When I announced that I'd applied, my mother predicted, with her typical pessimism, "They'll never hire you—you're a girl!" As ever, she was right on the mark. Still, I couldn't believe I'd been rejected for the job. I was an experienced, skillful bike rider; I was organized and reliable; and I knew the town's geography like the back of my hand. It seemed not just unfair, but irrational that I wasn't hired, even if I was a girl. I was outraged not only by the stupidity of the decision but also by the fact that there was nothing I could do about it. This was my first encounter with what I now think of as garden-variety **sexism**, and also with the naked power of employers—both of which would become major preoccupations for me in later years.

Eventually, I turned to babysitting instead. I enjoyed taking care of kids, and the work had other advantages, too. I especially liked getting out of my parents' house and seeing how other families lived. Thanks to my parents' frugality, we didn't acquire a television until I was a teenager. At some point, I inherited a phonograph from my older brother, but I had only a few records. I could listen to all kinds of music in the homes where I babysat, and there were sometimes interesting books lying around as well.

Back then, the going rate for babysitting was only 25 cents an hour—much less than a paper route. The insult of the *Evening Capital*'s rejection continued to rankle. I didn't have the tools needed to understand this at the time, even if the colloquial job title alone—"paper boy"—should have clued me in. I was confronting the deeply entrenched system of **job segregation by gender.** Women (and girls) were confined to a limited number of low-wage jobs, while men and boys monopolized the ones that paid the best.

In those days, newspaper classified ads were still divided between "Help Wanted: Male" and "Help Wanted: Female," and lots of jobs had explicit gender labels: mailman, fireman, milkman, to name a few. Other jobs without such labels also were—and remain—part of the same system of gender segregation. Even today, if you close your eyes and imagine a truck driver or a carpenter, you probably think of a man; if you conjure up an image of a secretary or a childcare worker, it's likely to be a woman.

I first began studying sociology in the 1970s, part of a new generation of gender scholars. At the time, I didn't fully appreciate what a privilege it was to be involved in a new academic field, although I certainly shared in the collective excitement. My first research project was a study of the impact of the Great Depression on women workers. In my head, that choice of topic was tied to my budding commitment to socialist-feminist theory. In retrospect, it's obvious my interest in the subject also reflected the endless stories I'd heard as a child about the deprivations of the Depression—especially from my mother. She was the youngest child in a once-affluent Brooklyn immigrant family that was plunged into poverty soon after the 1929 crash, the year she turned thirteen. Her parents' real-estate holdings became worthless, and they resorted to renting rooms to lodgers in their Brownsville, New York, home to make ends meet. Hence the one skirt! My mother could attend college only because Brooklyn College—part of the City University of New York system, where I now teach—didn't yet charge tuition.

As I began to study women's experiences during the Great Depression, I learned that popular sentiment overwhelmingly favored prioritizing male "breadwinners" for the few jobs available amid the economic devastation of the 1930s. Some industries had formal bans on hiring married women, who were supposed to be supported by their husbands. I was also taken with the Marxist claim that women were a **reserve army of labor**, pulled into the workforce in response to labor shortages and expelled in periods of labor surplus. Indeed, I expected my research would demonstrate that women workers bore the brunt of the 1930s surge in unemployment.

But as I dug deeper, I was surprised to discover that the Marxist orthodoxy was wrong. In fact, women's jobless rate was *lower* than men's in the 1930s! I eventually figured out that this was due to the extraordinary rigidity of job segregation by gender. In male-dominated sectors, like manufacturing and construction, employment collapsed dramatically after the 1929 crash. But in female-dominated clerical, sales, and service jobs, unemployment rose less and later.

I was stunned to discover that, even in the face of the deepest crisis of capitalism in the twentieth century, job segregation by sex persisted unaltered and trumped the popular consensus that men should get priority for the jobs that did exist. It turned out that employers almost universally considered male and female labor distinct and non-interchangeable—even though employing women was usually far less expensive. Most workers (including women) accepted this view, too. For employers and workers alike, the division of labor between women and men seemed utterly natural and unalterable. Although women are sometimes paid less than men for the same job—the problem that "equal pay for equal work" policies are meant to remedy—more typically, women don't have "equal work" to begin with. The gender gap in pay mostly reflects the fact that the jobs in which women are concentrated pay less than those dominated by men, even if the work involved is similar. Childcare workers, for example, are typically paid less than zookeepers (and paper boys).

That early research on women in the Great Depression got me hooked on sociology. It led me to wonder *why* job segregation by gender was so deeply entrenched in the labor market and how it came to be repeatedly reproduced even in the face of dramatic historical changes—a subject I would be obsessed with for years to come.

Job segregation has been reduced since the 1980s (especially for college-educated workers), but it remains the linchpin of gender inequality in the labor market. In the Great Recession of 2008, women's unemployment once again rose less and later than men's, replicating the pattern of the 1930s. And my childhood experience of being turned down for a "boy's job" is still an all-too-common occurrence more than a half century later. I carry the scars of that old wound to this day. As an adolescent, I couldn't do much about it, but in college, I became a feminist activist, leading a campaign for expanded childcare on my campus. And in graduate school, I helped lead an early effort to win protections for students against sexual harassment. Finally, I was in a position to fight the injustices I'd first encountered in my teens! Those injustices also deeply informed my academic research and writing, through which I've had the satisfaction of helping illuminate the systemic roots of gender inequality in the workplace.

KEY CONCEPTS

Job segregation by gender — Many jobs are performed primarily by people of a single gender. For example, in the United States, nurses and childcare workers are overwhelmingly women, while airline pilots and construction workers are overwhelmingly men. This reflects a gendered ideology about what women and men are like and what kinds of work they are most suited to do.

Reserve army of labor — Despite the gendered ideology referred to above, some sociologists have theorized that women have been used as a labor force that can be called up when men are not available. A classic example is the recruitment of middle-class women into factory work during World War II and then the pushing of those same women back into middle-class housewife roles after the war. Here, Milkman takes issue with that theory, noting that during the Great Depression, men lost employment at much greater rates than women did and did not displace women from their work because they primarily held jobs associated with femininity or womanhood.

Sexism — A system of inequality that privileges men over women.

DISCUSSION QUESTIONS

1. What is the first memory you have of injustice? Was it something you experienced or something you observed? How did you react to it?
2. In what ways are jobs or tasks, whether paid or unpaid, still segre-

gated by gender? How does the segregation or integration of jobs by gender affect your own life, household, or workplace?

3. Ruth Milkman writes of fighting back against the gendered injustices she faced as a young girl and beyond. How can you do the same in your own life?

LEARN MORE

Charles, Maria, and David B. Grusky. *Occupational Ghettos: The Worldwide Segregation of Women and Men*. Redwood City, CA: Stanford University Press, 2005.

Milkman, Ruth. *On Gender, Labor, and Inequality*. Champaign: University of Illinois Press, 2016.

Solnit, Rebecca. *Men Explain Things to Me*. Chicago: Haymarket Books, 2015.

Ruth Milkman is a labor sociologist and Distinguished Professor of Sociology and History at the Graduate Center of the City University of New York and serves as chair of the Labor Studies Department in CUNY's School of Labor and Urban Studies. She served as the 2016 president of the American Sociological Association, where her presidential address focused on Millennial-generation social movements. Her most recent books are *On Labor, Gender and Inequality* and *Immigrant Labor and the New Precariat*.

Hard Lessons at Yale

Pepper Schwartz

Graduate school at Yale was a shock. I was there to get a PhD in sociology, and I did. But the informal lessons I learned about sexism, class, and power were just as instructive.

I was very aware at the end of my master's year at Washington University that I'd lived an intellectually stimulating but rather cloistered midwestern experience. Having studied elites in my sociology class, I understood the advantages conferred by prestigious East Coast schools and imagined how they could help me make my way in the world. Yale, Harvard, and Princeton were only figments of my imagination; I'd never visited them or known anyone who did. My parents, first-generation Americans, had prospered, but in the way that many people from poor backgrounds do. My father had worked during the day and gone to school at night, getting the education he could rather than one he wanted. He earned his BA and law degree from Loyola University—a good school, to be sure, but not the elite education that would put a person on a path to becoming a captain of industry or joining the **power elite**. I craved the mysteriously powerful, rarefied experience of an elite eastern education. So, when I got into several excellent graduate schools, I chose Yale—-not because it had the best sociology department, but because I thought it would bring me into an unknown world in which I wanted to prove myself.

I knew at once that my understanding of class, status, and power (thank you, Max Weber) was exactly right when I told my father I'd been admitted to Yale. I stood on the steps to our second floor, and he was on the landing. In a tone that seemed to take us both by surprise, he said, "Well, now I'm going to have to take you seriously." I was stunned. I'd been bringing home academic accolades all my life, laying achievements at my dad's feet like a cat bringing her owner one mouse after another. Yet, unlike my brothers' accomplishments, which clearly meant something to my father, mine did not. Once Yale took me seriously, though, my father clearly felt he had to follow suit. I'd catapulted myself into such a prestigious category that I not only captured his respect but was now on the same level as my brothers. My father's newfound pride was my first lesson in how classism could trump sexism.

Armed with this new information, I went off to Yale. I arrived with two objectives: to earn a prestigious Yale PhD and to have some fun. I was ready to expand my world intellectually and socially. As a heterosexual woman, the male-to-female ratio at Yale was on my side, and I planned to take advantage of those statistics. While Yale started to officially admit women into some of its professional schools as early as 1892, the ideology of separate spheres for men and women remained powerful, such that Yale undergrads were all male when I began my graduate work there in 1969. Women's presence on campus was still rare and, in many ways, inconvenient. In fact, the sociology department didn't even have a women's bathroom!

Once I was at the school that had produced more presidents than any other, it became clear to me that I was seen as a visitor, an outsider. My vision of Yale started to shift. Sexism and classism dictated my experience. Perhaps I would gain a marketing advantage by going to Yale, but that didn't mean Yale thought I belonged. First of all, there was a general assumption that any woman on campus was in the Master's of Education program. This was a negative assumption in two regards, as both education programs and master's degrees were seen as marginal. Sociologists have observed that when a field is occupied primarily by women, it generally has less prestige than male-dominated fields. Women's work—even upper-class women's work—is undervalued, while the work of upper-class men is held in high esteem. In fact, the white men at Yale were given a glass escalator to success while the rest of us faced a glass ceiling. The hallowed law school had so few women you could identify each one by name. (By the way, one of them was Hillary Rodham Clinton.)

It was also clear that male undergraduates, graduate students, and many professors, though unwilling to view women as leaders, were more than happy to try to get into our pants. Kingman Brewster, the president of Yale at the time, seemed to be creating what Dr. Janet Lever and I would later refer to in our book *Women at Yale* as the "Geisha girl theory of co-education." That meant Yale women were worthy of being wives and colleagues of Yale men but not worthy of being their intellectual and professional peers. It was the men who would rule the world and win the global prizes. Would a Yale degree really change things for me, or would my sex continue to hold me back as doors started to open?

We women students had to hold a protest to get one bathroom out of more than four in our building designated for women so that we didn't have to go next door to pee. Professor Jackie Wiseman, a visiting woman professor, lived at the Graduate Union and found out that she was the only resident who wasn't getting maid service: after all, they told her, women should and could make their own beds. I'd received a four-year fellowship as an enticement to come to Yale, but it was not needs based. Sociologist Stan Udy, an otherwise kind professor, knew my family could afford to pay tuition and actually asked me if I would be willing to give up my fellowship "to help some male student who might need to support a family." I did not give it up.

Perhaps the most shocking of these insults was the fact that Elga Wasserman, the newly appointed dean of women, who had a PhD in chemistry, was asked to swallow her pride and go to administration meetings at Mory's, an all-male eating and drinking club on the Yale campus. Since Mory's didn't allow women as members or guests, the Yale administration asked Dr. Wasserman to use the back steps. When she protested quietly, they told her to get over herself. Frustrated and humiliated, she wrote an open letter to the campus protesting this treatment. Not long thereafter, she was removed from her position, a strong message of **social control** from Yale. The very structures of the institution were sexist, and speaking out against hostile treatment led to exclusion.

Yale was my consciousness-raising moment. Though I'd studied gender, class, and power at Washington University, I'd failed to grasp the level of disrespect that the "leaders of tomorrow" had for women. I'd thought that breaking these barriers and getting into institutions previously reserved for men was the end goal, but learned that sexism and classism were formidable challenges for students like me. I faced the truth that being wanted and desired as a marriage partner was very different from being accepted as an equal in the worlds of commerce, politics, and academia. I'd underestimated the level of disregard and even contempt that so many men had for us women. I'd confused being admitted to an elite school with being accepted by the elite. Policy changes, like admitting women, needed to be followed by institutional support and challenges to **patriarchal ideologies** that would take much longer to obtain.

The good news, however, was that we were fighting to be accepted, and those changes were on their way. But changing the culture at elite institutions would be much slower and more uneven than I ever would have imagined. It wasn't just my father, or his generation, that needed to revise their estimation of women. As I write this now, women all over the world are oppressed by men in institutions and countries with misogynist cultures. Here in the United States, racial, economic, and social injustice still limit the opportunities of women of color; poor women; lesbian, gay, bisexual, and trans women; and women with disabilities. Still, there has been progress. Yale's incoming class of undergraduates in 2023 is 50 percent female, and women make up more than 50 percent of the students in eleven of the fourteen professional school programs, including the law and medicine programs. Half of Yale's domestic students are non-white. Sexism isn't gone, and it needs to be addressed in conjunction with racism and other forms of inequality. Still, I celebrate the progress we've made.

KEY CONCEPTS

Patriarchal ideology — A way of thinking about the world that legitimizes a system of gender inequality where men have more access to power, wealth, and prestige than women have. Elements of patriarchal ideologies include the beliefs that men should be the head of the household and thus deserve higher wages and that women are naturally more nurturing than men and thus should spend more time at home caring for children (something they are expected to do out of love and not for pay).

Power elite — A label that sociologist C. Wright Mills coined for the group of powerful leaders who control the military, the government, the media, and the economy. These leaders tend to have interests that are interconnected and to share many social network ties.

Social control — All of the processes used in a society to try to get people to follow the norms of the dominant culture. These processes can include direct rewards and punishments (called positive and negative sanctions) but can also include the often-hidden lessons we learn in school and through the media about how we should behave and what we should think. For example, boys are sometimes ridiculed for writing poetry or studying dance.

DISCUSSION QUESTIONS

1. Have you witnessed the intersection of sexism and classism in your own life or community? If so, did one seem to take precedence over the other? Why?
2. What examples does Schwartz give to show that an ideology of "separate spheres" contributed to a difficult work environment at Yale? How does this ideology impact your own life for better or worse?
3. How did Yale as an institution ensure that a "glass escalator" was available to an elite group of men?
4. Does the "Geisha girl theory of co-education" ring true today? What remains the same and what's changed?

LEARN MORE

Domhoff, William G. 1983. *Who Rules America Now?* Hoboken, NJ: Wiley & Sons.

Friedan, Betty. *The Feminine Mystique*. 2013. 50th anniversary ed. New York: W. W. Norton & Company, 2013.

Gerson, Kathleen. 2011. *The Unfinished Revolution: Coming of Age in a New Era of Gender, Work and Family*. New York: Oxford University Press.

Gerth, H. H. *From Max Weber: Essays in Sociology*. Oxfordshire: Routledge, 1991.

Lever, Janet, and Pepper Schwartz. *Women at Yale: Liberating a College Campus*. Indianapolis: Bobbs-Merrill Co., 1971.

Yale College Class of 2023 First-Year Class Profile. https://admissions.yale .edu/sites/default/files/2023classprofileweb.pdf.

Yale Factsheet. This site is updated for each new calendar year. https://www .yale.edu/yale-factsheet.

Pepper Schwartz has devoted her life to furthering the fields of intimacy and sexuality. After achieving a BA and MA at Washington University, Schwartz went on to receive her PhD in sociology at Yale University in 1974. Schwartz has authored many academic and popular articles, as well as twenty-five books on the subjects of love, sexuality, and commitment. Two of them, *American Couples: Money, Work, and Sex* (William and Morrow, 1983) and *The Normal Bar: The Surprising Secrets of Happy Couples* (Harmony, 2014), were on the *New York Times* Best Sellers list. Schwartz is the former president of the Society for the Scientific Study of Sexualities and the Pacific Sociological Association. Currently, Schwartz serves as AARP's first Love & Relationship Expert & Ambassador and teaches at the University of Washington in Seattle. She appears as a relationship expert on the reality television show *Married at First Sight* and lives on a horse ranch outside Seattle.

Bad at Being a Boy

Tristan Bridges

I spent a portion of my senior year of high school hospitalized. I tried to take my own life multiple times. One of those times, I got caught. I hooked up a hose to the exhaust pipe of the car my parents had bought me and stuffed the other end in the window. I turned on the radio and fell asleep. I woke up on the street. I saw glass on the ground from the broken window where a man who'd seen my car got me out. As paramedics put me in the ambulance, I wanted to cry. "Oh no," I thought. "It didn't work."

Between us, I didn't identify as someone with suicidal tendencies. So, when I got to the hospital and was asked how often I'd tried to take my life, I was just as surprised as the doctor when I told him I had no idea. "A lot," I added. Hearing it out loud for the first time, I cried.

The first night, they made me sleep in the room right next to the doctors' station, its windows netted with chicken-wire glass. It had a mattress and blanket and a water bottle. The next night, I got a room on the hall. Little things about the hospital reminded me where I was. The door in the hallway was locked, but my room could not be locked. My bathroom didn't lock, either. There were no hangers in my closet, and the hooks gave way with any significant weight. My shower didn't have a curtain, and the towels were too small to wrap around your body. I wasn't allowed a razor or nail clippers. Alone in that bathroom, embarrassed by the sparse hairs on my face, I tried to pinch hairs out one by one.

The furniture was affixed to the floor, including the lamp by my bedside. My window was locked. I was checked on periodically throughout the night, often waking to the click of my door. It was weird, creepy and comforting at the same time—creepy because I realized they didn't trust me to take care of myself, comforting because I didn't either.

At my first group meeting, I found that some of the other patients were there for similar reasons as me. A couple boys were there because they'd been violent toward other people. At my first lunch, a young Black girl who was thin in a scary way started talking to me before she sat down. "Okay, new boy," she said. "You know why I'm here. Why are you here?" She ate a blueberry yogurt using animal crackers as spoons and told me she struggled to find food that she felt comfortable eating.

My first friend on the hall was another boy, a couple of years younger than me with short, curly hair and smooth light-brown skin. He hugged me sweetly after the first group meeting when I shared why I had been admitted. He didn't have much hair on his arms, which made it easier to see a collection of the tiny dotted scars that accompany wounds that have to be sutured closed. He'd been admitted for similar reasons as me. During free time, we found each other to play board games, talk while walking up and down the halls, or just sit together. A few days after we got close, we found ourselves on different schedules. I asked about him, and one of the doctors said, "This is hard, Tristan. But sometimes, kids share the scary stuff with each other, and we really need you to be sharing that stuff with us."

At that point, it became my personal goal to get out quickly. I've always been a bit of a nerd, so, even though I'd tried to kill myself a week prior, I was terrified of falling behind in school. I think my parents asked my older sister to get my schoolwork from my teachers, and it was dropped off at the hospital. Looking back, this seems a silly concern. I now make sense of it by realizing that I was trying to pretend it hadn't happened and move on.

The first time I asked a doctor when I could get out of the hospital, I explained that I felt safe and ready. "Then what was *that*?" he asked, referring to the reason I'd been brought to the hospital. "That was . . . ," I hesitated, "selfish." I hung my head and looked down at the floor, feeling ashamed and mumbling something about being "bad." "Bad?" he asked. Sort of laughing, I said, "I'm bad at being a boy." He said something like "What does that even mean?"

I wasn't questioning my **gender identity**. I just had a sense that I didn't cut the mustard as a human, and somehow understood that this was a gendered failure. Looking back now, I realize my shame and insecurity were connected to what I perceived as my failures with masculinity. As a scholar of gender, I now know that my struggle is actually incredibly common. I often felt ill-equipped and always felt uncomfortable with the status games boys (and men) play to enact masculinity in interactions with each other. They left me feeling empty. The constant teasing and competition that characterizes lots of young people's experience with masculinity was demoralizing and painful. Designed to demonstrate dominance, masculine rituals and behavior made me feel dominated, defeated, and often invisible.

I tried to kill myself because I struggled with depression. I still struggle with it. But my feelings about myself were and are integrally related to gender. There's a gender gap in suicide. It's not that boys try to kill themselves more than girls. They don't. Girls and boys attempt suicide at similar rates. Those identifying as trans or outside the binary are even more at risk. But, compared to girls, boys rely on much more fatal methods when trying to kill themselves. That's where the gender gap comes from. It's not *what* they are doing; it's *how*. Gender is something accomplished in everyday life. It's something we *do*. But it's a performance many are so accustomed to undertaking that we fail to recognize it as a performance at all. And when I tried to kill myself, I was doing gender, too.

My feelings about not measuring up as a human and not deserving to live were gendered. I don't have a recollection of deciding to study masculinity because it was something I felt particularly "bad at" growing up. But as far back as I can remember, masculinity was always something I felt I never fully understood. While I have friends of all genders, I've learned that I'm least comfortable in groups of only cisgender men. In high school, I think I thought this meant something was wrong with me. But I've come to see this as a resource rather than a flaw.

I don't remember the rest of that conversation when I first asked to go home. I just remember feeling awkward and not wanting to share things that felt really personal with the doctor, who I didn't know very well.

I don't want to kill myself anymore. But I still feel lucky to be alive.

I'm a cisgender man and have always identified with the gender assigned to me at birth. But I'm also a middle child, sandwiched between two sisters. And I grew up immersed in girl culture.

Masculinity is something I have always held at arm's length; I now realize it's always been something I've studied in one way or another.

As a boy, I studied it because I always felt like it came so much easier to other boys. When I tried on masculinity, I felt like it didn't fit right, and it made me self-conscious. It felt like coming to school dressed in a new style and hoping your friends don't notice or comment, but knowing that someone is going to say, "Um . . . Tristan . . . What are you wearing?" I have a vivid memory of coming home my first week in high school, pulling a chair up to a full-length mirror in my older sister's room, and looking at how I sat in it. I had been teased by a boy for sitting "like a girl." I tried to laugh while others laughed at me.

While growing up, my closest friends were mostly boys, but I also hung out with my sisters a lot. In one picture, I'm smooshed between my two sisters in the backyard, all three of us wearing "girls'" one-piece bathing suits. In our family photo album, my dad scrawled a little note next to it that reads "My son, the gender scholar." My sisters and I also dressed up like ballerinas. I desperately wanted to be just like my big sister, and wearing leotards wasn't policed by my parents. Femininity and girl culture saturated our house, and girl culture still feels more comfortable to me.

Now I study gender, sexual identity, and inequality. Most of my research deals with issues of masculinity. I study what men think it means to "be a man," how people enact masculinity, the different kinds of masculinities they enact, and how all these various gender projects are connected with enduring systems of inequality that shape all our lives. My journey to sociology is informed by my early childhood experiences and the feeling that somehow I was failing at being a boy.

If I could go back and comfort myself when I wanted to end my life, I would tell that younger version of me about the oppressive power of **hegemonic masculinity**. Years later, reading Raewyn Connell's work on the topic gave me a theoretical framework for all my research. But her theory and concept have also helped me put my own pain in perspective. When scholars study hegemonic masculinity, they are examining **gendered ideologies** that work to legitimate inequality both among men and between men and women. Understanding certain gender relations as "hegemonic" means that ordinary people often willingly consent to and uphold ideologies and ideals that sometimes work to their individual and collective disadvantage and in the interest of gender inequality as a system. When we judge ourselves by hegemonic ideals associated with masculinity (or femininity), we're a part of this larger system. In other words, I would share with my younger self that my feelings of inadequacy and not measuring up arose from our culture's rigid notions of what it means to be a boy and a man—and that these cultural ideals of male domination are bad for everyone.

A body of work published in the early 1990s in sociology debated the extent to which hegemonic masculinity was actually achievable. My younger self might have found some comfort in this. Scholars were interested in whether or not someone could reasonably approximate the ideal in such a way as to be recognizably hegemonically masculine. Connell's definition of the concept suggests this is a fool's errand. Indeed, the antiwar activist, actor, and writer Norman Mailer once wrote, "Masculinity is not something *given* to you, but something you *gain*. And you gain it by winning small battles with honor." In other words, hegemonic masculinity might not actually be an achievable state of being. Indeed, as my own research has shown, what hegemonic masculinity might actually *look like* is, to Connell, much less important than what it *accomplishes*, in terms of upholding existing systems of power and inequality.

As a cultural ideal, hegemonic masculinity is not actually attainable and, as I came to realize in my own gender journey, wouldn't be worth attaining even if it were. But recognizing the ways it structures our lives, gets inside us, and shapes our understandings of ourselves and the world around us is something I'm dedicated to conveying to others.

Feminist change and gender equality are, like masculinity, moving targets. They involve continuous effort and demands for structural and institutional change. Being able to recognize some of my own struggles with gender within this larger struggle for equality has been personally healing. Sometimes sociology helps us understand that while we are each unique, we are also all connected to something much larger than ourselves, and our experiences are often part of larger patterns. My students sometimes find sociology challenging because it can feel as if it strips them of feeling the idiosyncrasies that make them who they are. For me, it helped me realize I wasn't alone. That feeling of connection continues to inspire my research and advocacy for feminist change and equality.

KEY CONCEPTS

Gendered ideology — Ways of thinking about the world that have embedded ideas about how gender is organized and what people are supposed to be like as a result of their gender. For example, gendered ideologies that support the dominant culture in the United States contain the belief that gender is a system of two options (femininity/masculinity, woman/man, girl/boy) that are naturally opposite to one another, where men are naturally more powerful.

Gender identity — The way people think of themselves in terms of categories like woman, man, genderqueer, transgender, and genderfluid. Gender identity is distinct from gender assignment (the categories we are placed into at or even before birth) or gender expression (the way we perform our genders). Here, Bridges is assigned male and identifies as a boy and then a man, but performs his gender in a way that is often more feminine than masculine, as evidenced by the stories about the bathing suit and the ballerina costumes.

Hegemonic masculinity — The way of being a man that is represented by the dominant culture ideal of manhood. There are many kinds of masculinity. This is just the one that is the most highly rewarded and works to legitimate inequality. As Bridges writes, "what hegemonic masculinity looks like is . . . much less important than what it accomplishes."

DISCUSSION QUESTIONS

1. Have you ever felt like you were "failing" at being your gender or at some other socially significant category that you were assigned to? When and how so?

2. How does hegemonic masculinity impact your life physically and emotionally?

3. What are some of the losses and wins that men and women would experience by dismantling hegemonic masculinity at a structural level? What about dismantling it in our individual lives and relationships?

4. Bridges talks about gender as something we perform in a variety of ways. How do you perform your own gender? What costumes, behaviors, and interaction rituals do you use in your performance?

5. Do you see similarities between this essay and Meadow's essay? If Meadow and Bridges were to have a conversation, what do you think they would say to one another?

LEARN MORE

Connell, R. W. *Masculinities*. 2nd ed. Oakland: University of California Press, 2005.

Messerschmidt, James W. *Hegemonic Masculinity: Formulation, Reformulation and Amplification*. Lanham, MD: Rowman & Littlefield Publishers, 2018.

Plante, Rebecca F., and Lis M. Maurer. *Doing Gender Diversity: Readings in Theory and Real World Experience*. Oxfordshire: Routledge, 2010.

The Representation Project. *The Mask You Live In*. Documentary, 2015.

Tristan Bridges is associate professor of sociology at the University of California, Santa Barbara, and a faculty affiliate with the Feminist Studies Department. He has published widely on shifts in the meanings of masculinity in contemporary US society and the diverse consequences associated with these transformations. As a part of this, he has studied communities of bodybuilders, feminist men's groups, fathers' rights activists, the enduring relationship between masculinity and sexual prejudice, American couples with "man caves" in their homes, gendered and sexual biases in Americans' search interest on Google.com, and the relationship between masculinity, guns, and mass shootings. His research appears in *Gender & Society*, *Signs*, *Body & Society*, *Sociological Perspectives*, *Sociology Compass*, *Contexts*, *Frontiers in Psychology*, and more. He also coedited *Exploring Masculinities: Identity, Inequality, Continuity, and Change* (Oxford University Press, 2016) and coauthored *A Kaleidoscope of Identities: Reflexivity, Routine, and the Fluidity of Sex, Gender, and Sexuality* (Rowman & Littlefield, 2022). He also serves as a coeditor of the interdisciplinary and international journal *Men and Masculinities*.

39

Big Dick at the Beach

C Ray Borck

"Let's swim out to the buoy," she says to me.

We're sitting side by side on our towels in the sand, eating bodega sandwiches and drinking neon Gatorade in big summer gulps. A bright Tuesday morning, we've stolen the day and each other.

Plumb Beach is located a quick swerve off the Belt Parkway—a series of connected highways that wrap around the bottom of Brooklyn and Queens, cinching the boroughs in from Jamaica Bay, an estuary that dances a slow sway of give and take with the North Atlantic Ocean. The beach is known for its erosion, litter, and illicit cruising scene. Easy to miss and nothing special, it tends to be sparsely populated.

We're out at the easternmost point—Point Breeze, duly named— where the horseshoe crabs mate on the shore each spring. Males use their boxing-glove-claw to clasp on to the female's carapace. Amplexed and bobbing in the shallow surf, they are natural animals, a contrast to my humanness and artificiality.

My **medicalized** transgender body has been made male via surgical and hormonal technologies. I can fuck, but I can't fertilize. Whatever reproductive capacities I had are all atrophied organs and scar tissue now. Still I watch the crabs, amazed by their biology, prehistoric and purposeful, hardheaded and dogged, lumbering millennia just for a chance at life, some kind of tragicomedy.

I look up from my book. Lisa Jean, wearing a modest floral one-piece and gas station aviator sunglasses, presses the cove of her hand into her brow, a visor. Around her wrist, a thick knot of gold bracelets, handed down through generations of Bronx Italian women, every style of link. Her silver hair is wild in the scant winds, sunlight glinting everywhere, abundant and free.

Our vista is a clean robin's eggshell sky, backgrounding a Battleship board of lazy boats bathing about the harbor. A steady whir of traffic crosses over Marine Parkway Bridge above us. There's no one around.

"Okay," I agree, but she has already taken her head start. Constitutionally competitive, she turns everything into a race. I watch her strong shoulders work, rotating her arms, a windmill with a lot of splash.

She gets to the buoy first, grabbing on to it as she looks back at me with a big smile. "I beat you."

"I love you too," I say, pretending to have misheard her.

"I SAID, I BEAT YOU."

"I SAID, I LOVE YOU."

She rolls her eyes as I lag up to her, hooking my feet around her hips. I pull her in, kissing her smile.

At the surface of the water, infinite solar reflections dance laterally out from us—an amaranthine gang of ephemeral aquatic paparazzi. We are the stars.

Loving Lisa Jean is extravagant, an excess that precedes and produces us rather than the other way around. A quantum certainty, it is impossible not to do.

Our legs kick and slip against each other, seaweed soft. She tugs at my waistband, pulling me to her. Reaching into my shorts, she slides her fingers inside me. A reflex, my shoulders bow into her. Clung together, we buck in the break. I hold on to her as my breath gets up to gallop.

Relieved of our urgencies, we swim to shore, slow and sure. Walking toward our towels, I notice someone crouching in the dunes. He is peering out, leering at us.

Lisa Jean tenses beside me, prey spotting her predator.

I feel like he's been watching us for a while. Considering his optics, I imagine him imagining us as heterosexual intercourse, a contrast to our queerer submarine inversions.

"Ew, he's jacking off," she whispers into my shoulder. "We have to go."

Down the beach, the man hovers above the ground in a broken plank, one elbow jammed in the sand as he kickstands his body, his other hand pumping his dick, white swim trunks a taut band around his thighs.

Embarrassing, I think to myself. I get to fuck her while this loser hides in the bushes, wanking at my girl.

I luxuriate languidly in the possession of the symbolic phallus, its cultural supremacy, the delicious, easy entitlement of it. I should be ashamed of myself, but I'm not—I'm having too much fun being a man (hetero and white, too—exponential shortcuts, long jumps, and high fives). Every ten days, I inject testosterone into my belly for the exact purpose of looking like someone who has a respectable Caucasian penis.

To Lisa Jean, I insist, "He's harmless." I'm not going to let this creep ruin our beach day.

She stands, wrapped in her towel, shoes in one hand. "I want to go. We have to go."

I'm still sitting on my towel, looking up at her petulantly. "Why? I won't let anything happen to you."

She squints at me, indignant, then walks past me, a single dyke march down the beach toward the parking lot.

The masturbator scurries into the brush, a large rodent.

See, there he goes, I think to myself, still under the impression I'm right. I don't understand why we have to leave or why she's so pissed. She's being dramatic, I think. But she's meters away now and moving fast, so I gather my things up and jog after her to catch up.

By the time I get to her, she's radiating rage.

"Why are you so mad?" I ask.

"Let me give you a clue," she says, then continues like she's already rehearsed. "When someone is masturbating at your girlfriend, and she says she needs to leave, you just do it. You don't argue with her. You don't tell her *he's harmless* or promise paternalistic protection. You don't tell her *nothing bad is going to happen*. Something bad is already happening, you dumbfuck. When someone is jacking off at your girlfriend, you get her the fuck out of there as fast as you can." A moment passes before she adds, "What the fuck, C Ray?"

Listening to her, I see that what she says is reasonable. I try to demonstrate that I'm taking her seriously by not responding too reactively. "You're right," I say, wondering how long it will take me to churn this humility back into swagger.

"I know I'm right."

Walking together in the hard part of the sand where the tide licks our feet in slow, easy rhythms, I feel simultaneously guilty and defensive, a combination that results in my unfortunate pouting expression. I'm still clinging to the idea that she might be overreacting.

I run around inside my brain looking for something reassuring to say but come up empty. This happens during fights with Lisa Jean because she is so much smarter than I am. Half the time I just stumble around the dark alleyways of our arguments, struggling to strike a tone that comes across as sensible and confident, relying on whatever tidbit I most recently read after having googled *How to have Big Dick Energy* yet again.

"GOD," she exclaims, impatience meeting disgust. I am reminded of the joke where I respond, *Yes?* but save it for another time.

A few different versions of myself are starting to argue with each other at the aspirationally horizontalist consciousness-raising group endlessly holding court in my mind.

"I'm so fucking pissed at you," she says.

"Tell me why."

"Because, C Ray, how do you think you would feel if you were me in that situation?" An actively weathering bloom of vocal sound that had been integral to her anger is being replaced by the mossiness of quiet curiosity that grows a layer under conditions of genuine hurt.

I say it slowly back to myself in my head: *If I had been you.* This had not occurred to me. I was too busy basking in the pleasure of being me in the situation. Prompted now, memories unfold in me, a suitcase-worth of angry origami. What is it like to be a woman on the beach as some dude jacks off, lazily using your body to coax his arousal along? I have been in similar situations. We all have. I mean, all women have.

I do then remember what it felt like—the quickening, a chain-link fence emergent from my dewy grasses, growing up around my solar plexus, every time some guy pulled his dick out at me. No fight, just flight. *I want to go. We have to go.* The ghost of nonconsensual sexualization swells a sickening reminder in my gut. The bird of my past flaps for somewhere to land.

I pursued and purchased **sex reassignment** not in small part due to my inability to tolerate experiences like the one I had just minutes ago asked Lisa Jean to endure. Sure, I felt and feel like a man, wanted to become a man, live as a man (whatever any of that means). But I also gave up on womanhood (whatever that is). I threw in the towel. I couldn't do it anymore. Compulsory feminization was unbearable for me, exactly because of guys like the one just jacking off, *because of guys like the guy I have become, am.*

Back in her car, Lisa Jean is driving jerky and mad. "I fucking hate trans men," she says.

"I know," I say, trying to stay above personalizing such a comment. *What the fuck does that have to do with me?* I want to ask, but don't.

"You all transition thinking it's this radical thing to do, then you become men in the world. You think because you used to be women, you somehow remember what it's like to be a woman, but you don't remember. And the longer since your transition, the more you forget. Eventually you are just like any other man, only worse, because at least cis men were taught how to take care of women."

Ouch.

"And then! You're the one who gets to look down at your feet, sulking, and I'm the one who has to take care of Your Fucking Feelings. It's incredible, truly."

"You're righ—"

"—*Of course I'm right.*"

*

Sociologist R. W. Connell coined the term hegemonic masculinity to name and describe the type of masculinity that is socially constructed as most legitimate by the dominant culture. Hegemonic masculinity is a form of gender power that inoculates its possessors from vulnerability and harm, and all but ensures their dominance in any given social situation.

I was a feminist, sociologist, and gender studies professor long before I decided to transition. As my experience on the beach shows, having a robust critique of hegemonic masculinity, toxic masculinity, and male privilege doesn't ensure that a man (me, in this case) will behave ethically. **Normative gender scripts** work through us even when we know better.

A triptych of the male gaze: becoming a man, becoming a partner, becoming a dick at the beach. Finding myself in possession of this lens, I learn how it blurs my capacity for other types of vision and witnessing.

Who's right? Who's wrong? Who decides? These are ethical questions.

In a culture so focused on individualism and personal identity, it has become fashionable to imagine that gender as a social construction is not so powerful at all. Such imaginative revisioning and refashioning invites individuals to cast off their genders, as if such projects were inherently desirable or liberatory. It is tempting to take comfort in such depoliticization.

Yet our genders are not only our own. Gender is also something we negotiate with others in social contexts. Our genders become meaningful when someone else finds us intelligible (or not). And the relationship between having a body and having a gender is clumsy, even when it appears graceful. We don't have perfect control over our genders or our bodies, and we are never perfect political agents. Our embodied selves are always repeating the past into the present, in search of livable futures. We reproduce the world even as we seek to change it. This terrain is a fertile site for ethical growth.

Becoming is an emergent state, and my becoming a man has involved an ongoing negotiation with my memories of masculinity and femininity in history, representation, and lived experience. Gender— with its intersubjective, interactional implications—is an occasion for engagement with such emergences (and emergencies).

Lisa Jean was right. And I have the opportunity to be a better man each time I am wrong.

KEY CONCEPTS

Medicalization — The process of taking a characteristic, behavior, or process and turning it into an illness or a treatment. The disease model of addiction is one example. Addiction used to be understood as a moral failing but was medicalized and is now seen as an illness. Here, gender identity is medicalized through the processes surrounding diagnosis and treatment related to gender transitions.

Normative gender scripts — Socially approved patterns of behavior and interaction associated with gender roles. For example, there is a common pattern among women of vocalizing statements to sound like questions, which can be attributed to a normative gender script that, in this instance, women are socially rewarded for following. It is important to note that, like actors, people are capable of improvising and modifying scripts, though they risk a backlash for doing so. This is one of the ways social change occurs!

Sex reassignment — Often referred to as gender affirmation surgery, this term generally refers to the surgical and other medical processes of altering one's body to align with one's gender identity. You might encounter terms like "top surgery," which refers to mastectomy to remove breast tissue, or "bottom surgery," which involves transforming the genital organs. People make a variety of choices about how much to alter their bodies to align with their identities. Some nonsurgical options might include the use of hormone treatments, voice coaching, or the use of drugs to delay or block puberty. A number of states have banned gender-affirming care, especially for young people.

DISCUSSION QUESTIONS

1. How does your gender shape the way you interact with others?
2. In what ways do you follow or break gender rules? Does following (or breaking) gender rules ever cause conflict with others?
3. What do you think of Borck's initial reaction to his girlfriend when she insisted on leaving the beach? Would you have reacted similarly?

LEARN MORE

Connell, R. W. *Masculinities*. 2nd ed. Oakland: University of California Press, 2005.

Kimmel, Michael. *Guyland: The Perilous World Where Boys Become Men*. New York: Harper Perennial, 2018.

Pascoe, C. J. *Dude, You're a Fag: Masculinity and Sexuality in High School*. 2nd ed. Berkeley: University of California Press, 2011.

Pascoe, C. J., and Tristan Bridges. *Exploring Masculinities: Identity, Inequality, Continuity, and Change*. Oxford: Oxford University Press, 2015.

C Ray Borck is a writer, teacher, and sociologist living in Brooklyn with his family. He is associate professor of sociology and gender and women's studies at Borough of Manhattan Community College, City University of New York, and his published work has appeared in *Surveillance & Society*, *Transgender Studies Quarterly*, and *Qualitative Inquiry*. He is most curious about epistemology, identity, and subjectivity, and is currently working on a manuscript that blends autoethnography and literary realism to investigate various compulsory experiences of inequity that characterize modern childhood.

PART 8

Healing and Changing the World

There is always light,
If only we're brave enough to see it.
If only we're brave enough to be it.

Amanda Gorman

40

I Am Neo

Michael L. Walker

Movie magic is made when the elements of a film come together to evoke a feeling in us: fear, love, frustration, sexual arousal, anger, excitement. For instance, the original *Saw* movie opens with a man awakening underwater. He's in a tub. He stands in panic, trying to make sense of where he is in a dark room. In our rational minds, we know we are watching an actor on a movie set with microphones, writers, a director, and a slew of other people. But thanks to the magic of film, we suspend reality and watch the opening scene while gripped with anxiety and fear. That's the movie magic we demand, but there is another kind of magic at work in film, sociological magic—the ability to view film and art through a sociological lens.

In fact, the power of sociology is that it isn't magic at all. Rather, it's a way of seeing and understanding. A sociological imagination helps us analyze who writes the code and how that code reinforces the status quo. For example, every element of film (and television, of course) is carefully chosen. A writer or a group of writers decide what the story will be: the themes, the characters, the setting, diction, and message. Decisions are made about wardrobe. The lighting in every scene is designed to misdirect, direct, or stimulate some set of emotions and thoughts. Actors are chosen thoughtfully. *Can we have a Black 007? Is Idris Elba the right fit?* Someone must decide the diction with which Transformers speak. *Should Optimus Prime speak like a Black American native to Los Angeles?* The sociology in film is hiding as background code—the patterns of social relations that make movie magic possible.

When movie magic is at its best, our whole selves are immersed within the **lifeworld** of the film we're watching. By applying a sociological lens, we see the background assumptions reflected in the choices directors and producers make. Just over six minutes into the film *Thor: The Dark World*, for example, we enter the third scene, set on a faraway planet called Vanaheim. It's an unremarkable battle scene in which the tide turns for the protagonists when Thor arrives at the 6:40 mark. We are then shown various protagonists winning their individual fights against baddies when, at the 7:08 mark, we are shown an Asian-looking protagonist. He's wielding a mace like nunchucks—swinging and catching it in an armpit before swinging it again—and his fighting style is . . . martial arts.

Keep in mind that there are no humans in this scene. There are no "Asians" or "Black people" or earthly living things. And, if you blink, you'll miss the alien Asian martial artist. That's how unimportant his character is to the film, yet his presence screams loudly at me, and it's because I know that someone involved in the production of *Thor: The Dark World* wanted to be sure that the Asian-looking alien fought in a style stereotypical for Asian people. Someone wanted to be sure that behavioral expectations matched up with racial stereotypes—even in a damned fantasy, folks are constrained by stereotypes. Sociology helps me see that even within movie magic and the suspension of reality, stereotypes are reinforced without making a clumsy statement like *Asians use martial arts when they fight.*

I've asked my students to watch that *Dark World* scene, and rarely do they identify what's problematic. This is a matter of training. Remember that scene in *The Matrix* where Neo finally starts to believe what he's been told by Morpheus, a trope African American helper character whose only job is to ensure a white savior does the saving? Neo is on the ground after being shot several times by an agent, but after a magical kiss from Trinity—in another overused motif, a woman's love is supernatural—he is able to stand and stop bullets. We are then shown the Matrix the way Neo sees it, as columns of green code against a black background instead of the virtual reality that the Matrix renders for humans. I like to think of Neo's ability to see Matrix programming code as a metaphor for the *seeing* that sociology trains into us. In my experience, once that seeing is turned on, it cannot be turned off.

And even if I enjoy movies as much as the next person—perhaps more than most, I am able to see that the *Avatar* movies include a hefty amount of sociological significance. In them, modernity is represented by unidimensional white military and capitalist organizations driven to control and extract resources from a distant planet occupied by the

Na'vi, themselves a bundle of stereotypes: they use primitive weapons, they're barely clothed, they seem part human and part beast when they growl or grunt in anger, and they're connected to their land and each other in ways diametric to the values of eurocentrism. And I cannot unsee how inhabiting the literal bodies of Na'vi is an extreme power dynamic, a form of resource extraction, and a kind of social puppetry between superordinate and subordinate social actors examined in studies of racism, gender relations, labor studies, and punishment in prisons and jails.

As you might guess, pointing out the sociological codes in movies, television, and music can be annoying to others. Early in my graduate career, I often felt compelled to comment to my neighbor about how social exchange theory, status construction theory, or double consciousness explained why characters interacted the way they did. "The wife in this movie is hardly more than a prop. Look," I said, pointing. "She's only here as a motive for Denzel's character to display this incredible fatherly love."

"Why can't you just watch *John Q* without all those thoughts in your head?"

I've gotten a version of that question more times than I can remember, and the truth is, I *can't* shut off my sociological decoder—nor do I even want to. Once you see the underlying code, you can't pretend not to.

Indeed, I enjoy art more *because* I see sociological code shaping how it's made as well as what's included and excluded from the art we consume. And it's not just movies. I recently visited museums in Lisbon, Portugal, where an overwhelming number of exhibits told a religious story; more revealing, the history of colonialism was absent. Standing in a museum courtyard overlooking the ocean that birthed the Atlantic slave trade, I was angry.

The decision to ignore the brutal history of slavery reminded me of Joachim Savelsberg's work on **collective memory**. Savelsberg shows that a nation's **institutional response** to atrocities can shape national memory of what occurred and how people contend with such atrocities in the future. On the one hand, museum exhibits are highlighted moments of human events or creativity. On the other hand, curators decide what to include in their exhibits, a museum director decides what kind of story the museum will tell, and whatever narrative is constructed will necessarily reflect the sociopolitical context of the day.

So, when I strolled through Lisbon museums, I had one response to the art and another to the sociological accounts told and purposefully left untold.

Applying a sociological lens can make you angry or hurt, but I'm reminded of a life-changing conversation with my friend Damion—the first African American person I knew who was earning a doctorate in anything. It was the fall of 2000, about a month before I began my undergraduate career at the University of California–Riverside. We were discussing the significance of my being a first-generation African American student. I'd spent nearly as many years in foreign countries as I had stateside, and in all those places, my Blackness took a backseat to being an American. By focusing on lynching in American history, Damion explained to me in graphic terms just how much Blackness mattered in the United States.

I was horrified! Shaking my head, I looked at Damion as if seeing him for the first time. "How do you sleep at night knowing all this stuff?" I asked him.

In a classic Damion-esque way, he gave me an answer I could not have anticipated: "I sleep better *because* I know."

That is still one of the single most important things anyone has ever told me. Sleeping better *because* I know has guided me and never let me down.

I feel at peace—I sleep well at night—because seeing the code not only helps me understand myself but also gives me the power to analyze how institutions, structures, and ideologies support ways of thinking. The power of sociology lies in the decoding. We can all be Neo.

KEY CONCEPTS

Collective memory — The stories a group of people pass from generation to generation about their past. Compare the standard narratives taught in predominantly white elementary schools in the United States about the colonists to the narratives that might be passed from generation to generation among those whose ancestors were internally displaced or killed in the process of colonization.

Institutional response — The way that governments and large organizations treat historical events, particularly atrocities. You can see this play out in the United States in many ways, including in debates about historical monuments and statues, or about school curricula related to the enslavement of people or the colonization of lands.

Lifeworld — The shared sense of reality held by a group of people that creates a coherent way of experiencing the world. It is often used to refer to the shared background assumptions and meanings that make the world make sense. Here, becoming immersed in a movie universe illustrates the way that people can experience a lifeworld that isn't their own.

DISCUSSION QUESTIONS

1. How might Walker's essay and sociology in general change the way you view TV and movies?
2. Why does Walker claim that sociology helps him sleep better at night?
3. Becoming a sociological decoder doesn't only apply to art and film. What else might you be more aware of when you see the code? What have you noticed already?
4. Like society and social structures, computer code is constructed by people and can be changed by people. What code do you want to rewrite? What type of collaboration and/or organization do you need to rewrite the code you'd like to change?

LEARN MORE

Savelsberg, Joachim J., and Ryan D. King. *American Memories: Atrocities and the Law*. New York: Russell Sage Foundation, 2013.

Sutherland, Jean-Anne, and Kathryn Feltey. *Cinematic Sociology: Social Life in Film*. 2nd ed. Thousand Oaks, CA: Sage Publications, 2012.

Tolnay, Stewart E., and E. M. Beck. *A Festival of Violence: An Analysis of Southern Lynchings, 1882–1930*. Champaign: University of Illinois Press, 1995.

Michael L. Walker is the Beverly and Richard Fink Professor in Liberal Arts in the Department of Sociology at the University of Minnesota–Twin Cities. His broad research concerns stratification, social control, punishment, and social psychology, which he translates into studies of race relations, carceral patterns, identities, emotions, and time. He is the author of *Indefinite: Doing Time in Jail* (Oxford, 2022), which won the 2022 Charles H. Cooley Award for Best Recent Book from the Society for the Study of Symbolic Interaction, and the American Society of Criminology's 2018 Joan Petersilia Outstanding Article, "Race Making in a Penal Institution," published by the *American Journal of Sociology*.

41

Systemic Racism Is . . . You!

Eduardo Bonilla-Silva

After the brutal public execution of George Floyd, the term "systemic racism" became popular, but what does it mean? I believe most whites do not know the meaning of the term and, worse, do not understand its implications. For example, both Joe Biden and Kamala Harris have said the police have a systemic racism problem, but that most officers are not racist. The problem? Systemic racism is not about racists, but about racism, and racism includes both the rotten and the healthy apples in the societal orchard.

Systemic racism refers to the *collective* practices, behaviors, and beliefs geared toward maintaining whites' advantageous position at all levels in society. In the case of the police, the selection, training, and culture of officers engender practices that reinforce America's racial order. How do we know this? Because while most encounters between whites and the police tend to be safe, respectful, and pleasant, those involving people of color and the police involve suspicion, disrespect, and violence.

A few years ago, I was stopped by the police very close to my home. The officer took his time to approach my car, then banged on the side of it just like the Minneapolis officers did when they approached George Floyd. The officer proceeded to ask me inappropriate questions ("Where are you coming from? What were you doing?") and was quite terse. (Readers who think I am being hypersensitive and inappropriately attributing racial intent in this interaction should recognize that the typical opening request in a traffic stop is "License and registration, please," and that the exchange is usually respectful.) When he was done with this "routine" traffic stop, he lowered his head and asked my wife, a light-skinned Palestinian, "Ma'am, are *you* OK?"

What is the nature of contemporary systemic racism? As momentous as the Civil War and the Civil Rights movement were, to paraphrase Audre Lorde, they did not dismantle the house racism built. In the 1970s, Jim Crow was replaced by a "new racism," the post–Civil Rights–era institutional and seemingly nonracial practices that reproduce **white privilege**. Neighborhood segregation offers an example. The crude Jim Crow tactics of the past (such as bombs and housing covenants) have been largely replaced by the smiling discrimination of Realtors steering clients into different neighborhoods, loan officers offering people of color inferior products without their awareness, and whites avoiding, in clever ways, renting or selling properties to people of color. For example, in 1984, a landlord in liberal Madison, Wisconsin, used a seemingly nonracial strategy to dissuade me from renting an apartment. He told me that I had to pay him two months' rent in advance as well as put down a hefty security deposit. The man also made a point of letting me know he did not like tenants who played loud music or had parties all the time. Although I sensed his behavior was racially motivated, as a first-year graduate student, I did not have the knowledge, resources, and time to pursue legal action. Besides, as some fellow white students told me at the time, "But Eduardo, the landlord didn't call you any name, so how do you know this was a racist incident?" Ah, my dear white friends, when will you stop playing the "anything but racism" game?

People of color experience racist interactions in almost all areas of life. In many stores, for instance, we are followed in creative ways, killed with "politeness" (clerks ask us several times, "May I help you?"), or ignored altogether. I have experienced all of the above. A few years ago, for instance, I went to a JoS. A. Bank store in fancy Chapel Hill, North Carolina, to purchase winter gloves. Although my wife and I were the only clients in the store, the three clerks stayed in the back, where they were having an animated conversation. After about ten minutes, I realized I was not going to receive service and decided to leave. "But honey, don't you want to ask them about the gloves?" my wife asked. I raised my voice a bit, hoping the clerks would hear me, and said, "Why? They obviously do not wish to sell me anything."

As an Afro Latino, my phenotype and accent make me the perfect target for new racism as well as old-style discrimination. A few years ago, I made an appointment with a white psychologist at a Duke clinic. My doctor had recommended her highly after I mentioned I was angry all the time and a bit depressed. A few minutes into our first session, the psychologist stopped me and said, "You know, many foreigners use big words, and I think it is better if you guys use simpler words and speak in shorter sentences." Needless to say, that was our first and last meeting. Had she checked my file carefully, she would have known that I was a professor at Duke, born in Bellefonte, Pennsylvania, in the foreign nation called the United States! Instead, she read me through my looks and accent, and felt comfortable giving me her "words of wisdom" on how to become a successful "immigrant." Interestingly, a few days after my visit, she left a voicemail on my office phone urging me to come back. "I think I can help you," she said, but acknowledged she might have said something "problematic." I hope she reads this essay, as what she said was not problematic, but racist!

At the ideological level, systemic racism is organized around the notion of **colorblindness**. It is about whites proclaiming their racial innocence about their actions ("What did I do?") by using liberal tropes and arguments in a decontextualized and abstract manner. Colorblind racism is about plausible deniability and self-exoneration. It is talking about race without using the N-word. For example, a former colleague once told me I was paid more than him because of racial considerations. When I challenged his assessment and urged him to get an outside offer, something I had done a few years before, he told me, "I don't have what departments want." I replied, "Harvard, Yale, Columbia, and other places have mostly white professors, so you have the skill they seem to prefer." He smiled in a smug way and left.

In case you missed it, systemic racism is *you*—not you as an individual, but as a member of the racial group in charge. To extend what Marx said about capitalists to race, whites are personifications of the racial order and need not be evil to march to the tune of whiteness. Their normative practices are racialized and make up the structures of everyday life. Accordingly, systemic racism is not propelled by the actions of the Proud Boys, but by the behavior of nice whites enacting "white normativity." You, my dear white friend, by following the white script of life from birth to death, almost innocently support systemic racism.

Systemic racism is you taking upon yourself to discipline people of color in parks, restaurants, neighborhoods, stores, or jobs, and acting surprised when we check you. A few years ago, I was waiting in the coffee section at Southern Season, an upscale store in Chapel Hill. An older white woman joined me at the counter. When the clerk, who had seen me before, turned and asked, "Who's next?" the white woman began to order. This happens to us often enough that we joke about it: whites believe they have the right to be served before us. But that day, I decided not to let her get away with this small act of white supremacy. I interrupted, "I was here first and want a pound of double Dutch chocolate coffee and another of your dark-roasted Kenya." The woman, likely trained in the Jim Crow era, was livid, and the clerk was nervous. But I waited calmly, picked up my order, and stayed in the area to prevent them from having the chance to commiserate ("Can you believe this Black fellow? He's so rude!").

People of color also participate in systemic racism, but our participation is not symmetrical to yours. We have endured racial domination from slavery till today and fought it whenever possible. But I do not have a binary view of race (good people of color versus bad whites), so let me acknowledge that not all whites and Blacks are manufactured equally. For various reasons, in the process of **race-making**, fractures and variance occur. For example, the racial mixing that occurred in the United States created many people who fit the white designation who were not white by ancestry. Historically, this allowed some Blacks, Latinos, and Native Americans to "pass." Today, many phenotypically white-looking individuals pass incidentally—some unwittingly (like my wife in the incident I described) and some in a more conscious way.

And the variance can be enormous. For example, many elite free people of color during slavery became slaveholders, and some white people, such as John Brown, died fighting racism. These fractures and variance are still in place, as race-making is an imperfect and continuous process. However, systems of domination would not exist if ruptures in the subjectivity of racial actors impeded their reproduction. In general, once a system is in place, we all become habituated to its norms and take part in its collective practices. Thus, despite variance, the existing racial structures of life lead most whites to follow the path of least resistance. Karen, Todd, Megan, and Chad keep on trucking without thinking much about race. (White) life is good!

Systemic racism is you, white person reading this chapter and feeling enraged as you think, "I cannot believe this guy just called me racist! He doesn't know me. I'm a very good person." If this is your reaction, whiteness is still blinding you. Making a structural claim about the nature of racism that pivots to include actors in the racial structures of life is not calling anyone "racist." It is an effort to explain what makes systemic racism *systemic*; to account for how whites' *habit-uated* behaviors comprise the racial structures of everyday life.

If you are white, I urge you to work to become an anti-racist. While the racial liberal looks at herself and says, "I am a good person," the anti-racist seeks to advance racial justice. Don't attend a BLM rally, only to return later to "(white) life as usual" in your segregated community. You must do better, much better. For the beloved community MLK envisioned to have a chance, a significant number of retooled whites must join the struggle and shout with us, "No justice, no peace!"

KEY CONCEPTS

Colorblind racism — At the individual level, colorblind racism refers to the idea that if you "don't see race," you are not racist. In fact, if you live in a society characterized by systematic racial inequality and you claim not to see race, you are blind to the numerous ways that people of color experience racism on a daily basis. We are more likely to reproduce racism when we claim not to see race.

Race-making — Races are not biological realities; rather, they are socially constructed, reproduced, and challenged. This process is called race-making. Race-making occurs through language, inter-action, and policy. For example, the racial categories used in the US Census have changed over time, sometimes in response to ac-tivism. In 1930, the term "Negro" replaced the term "Black," but in 1970, the term "Black" was re-included in the Census in response to Black pride activism and the Civil Rights movement. Even earlier, in the 1890 Census, terms like "Octoroon" and "Quadroon" were used, based on white supremacist ideas about the proportion of "Black blood" a person might have.

White privilege — Privilege is an unearned advantage, and white priv-ilege is any unearned advantage a person gets because they are so-cially identified as white. For example, not having to think about your own race while shopping, driving, or renting an apartment is a white privilege.

DISCUSSION QUESTIONS

1. Throughout the essay, Bonilla-Silva speaks directly to "you." Did you recognize yourself or people you know anywhere in this essay?

If so, where? What effect did his use of "you" have on your reading the essay?

2. Were there specific moments in this essay that made you uncomfortable? Why? What is your reaction to that discomfort?

3. Why do you think it is so much easier to talk about individual acts of racism (committed by others, not by us) than to talk about systemic racism? Why does a focus on individual racism do less to advance the cause of justice and peace?

4. The author asks us to start making anti-racist changes to white life as usual and describes ways that he has intentionally disrupted racist moments in his life. What changes can you make to actively fight racism?

LEARN MORE

Alexander, Michelle. *The New Jim Crow: Mass Incarceration in the Age of Color-blindness*. With a new preface by the author. New York: New Press, 2020.

Kendi, Ibram X. *How To Be an Antiracist*. London: One World, 2019.

Oluo, Ijeoma. *So You Want to Talk About Race*. Cypress, CA: Seal Press, 2018.

Saad, Layla F. *Me and White Supremacy: Combat Racism, Change the World, and Become a Good Ancestor*. Naperville, IL: Sourcebooks, 2020.

Eduardo Bonilla-Silva is the James B. Duke Distinguished Professor of Sociology at Duke University. He received his BA in sociology with a minor in economics in 1984 from the Universidad de Puerto Rico, Río Piedras campus. He received his MA (1988) and PhD (1993) from the University of Wisconsin–Madison. He worked at the University of Michigan (1993–1998) and Texas A&M University (1998–2005) before joining Duke University in 2005. He gained visibility in the social sciences with his 1997 *American Sociological Review* article, "Rethinking Racism: Toward a Structural Interpretation," where he challenged analysts to study racial matters structurally rather than from the sterile prejudice perspective. His book *Racism Without Racists* (Rowman & Littlefield, 6th ed. in 2022) has become a classic in the field of sociology and is used widely by scholars in other fields as well. His book *White Logic, White Methods: Racism and Methodology* (Rowman & Littlefield, 2012, with Tukufu Zuberi) has helped reshape the conversation of how to measure the impact of racial stratification on various social outcomes. Bonilla-Silva has received many awards, most notably the W. E. B. Du

Bois Career of Distinguished Scholarship Award in 2021, which is given by the American Sociological Association to "scholars who have shown outstanding commitment to the profession of sociology and whose cumulative work has contributed in important ways to the advancement of the discipline." He served as president of the Southern Sociological Society and the American Sociological Association in 2017–2018.

42

Horseshoe Crab Lessons

Lisa Jean Moore

For the past eight years, I've taught at Bedford Hills Correctional Facility, a New York State maximum-security prison. With a capacity of 962 inmates, it is the largest women's prison in the state. At the BHCP, my students are predominantly poor African American and Latinx mothers. As a white woman and a middle-aged professor and mother, I've leveraged and interrogated my own identity positions—both distinct from and shared with those of my students—while teaching classes like Great Social Thinkers, Social Movements, Birth and Death, and Bioethics. We've shared stories of our children's milestones while simultaneously acknowledging our racial and economic differences; we've built trust over time. Success in the prison classroom, I have found, comes from taking risks with intimacy and being vulnerable in an extraordinarily regulated environment.

In the fall semester of 2018, I taught a course called Critical Animal Studies, in which we explored how humans and animals exist in our shared world. Together, we considered what forms of life get to qualify as human and thus worthy of civil rights and social power. Typically, I explained, we humans don't have the capacity to grasp how nonhuman animals are impacted, often negatively, in our everyday lives, just as most privileged people don't really consider the everyday lives of poor people. My students who are incarcerated identify with what it is to be treated as less than human from their experiences of "being put in a stall" or "let out to the yard." When we disqualify individuals from being human, we often tacitly and overtly give permission to exploit and torture them. Many students have shared with me how Black people, incarcerated people, and disabled people aren't treated as human beings. "I'm being treated like an animal in here," more than one has said. In the class, we explored other ways humans are treated like animals, such as ongoing racial bias in pain management, which leads Black people to be systematically undertreated for pain compared to white people.

One of the class's required readings was my book *Catch and Release: The Enduring, Yet Vulnerable, Horseshoe Crab*, an account of my three years of fieldwork observing horseshoe crabs and the scientists who study them on beaches in New York and Florida. In the book, I describe the pharmaceutical industry's routine practice of collecting horseshoe crab blood for biomedical tests aimed at ensuring injections are safe for humans. I call on readers to always think of ourselves as human in relation to other living beings. After all, we come to be *human* in an ongoing relationship with *nonhuman animals*—our companion species, the food we eat, the clothes we wear, the medicine we take, and the space we occupy.

This idea of exploring ourselves as interconnected to animals relates to the sociological ideas of status and **stratification**. We create a status, meaning a rank or position relative to other beings (usually just other humans). At the same time, we are stratifying ourselves and arranging systems of classification of categories. Statuses are layered on top of one another, with those at the top having the most access to power, prestige, freedom, resources, and privilege. In contemporary cultures, stratification is often hierarchical, with humans at the top and animals lower down. Humans are also further segmented based on categories such as race, class, and gender.

Becoming conscious of how our lives are made possible through collaboration with animals can be a big challenge for students, and I acknowledged the difficulty of simultaneously *being* in the moment while *knowing* we are sharing the earth with other living creatures. A footnote in my book draws on a scene in Thornton Wilder's play *Our Town* to illustrate this challenge of being and knowing. In the scene, the main character, Emily, is tormented by the challenges of fully being in her life while consciously absorbing all the mundane experiences of living her life as connected to others. Personally, I have had difficulty being in the moment at peak life events. For example, I have a hard time recalling my parents' fiftieth wedding anniversary because I was so swept up in the responsibilities of the party, even though I reminded myself on my way there to try to be present so I could enjoy the memories later.

That fall, during our class discussions of *Catch and Release*, it was difficult for me to quiet my internal dialogue of self-recrimination. Most of my students hadn't ever seen, and likely never would see, a horseshoe crab. Asking them to care about horseshoe crabs amid the circumstances of their imprisonment, their legal cases, the conditions of extreme surveillance, and the rituals of degradation seemed ludicrous. I found myself deep in a spiral of self-criticism for assigning a book I had written to students who are incarcerated. My instruction seemed to me a classic example of self-indulgent academic navel gazing and completely unrelated to the lives of my students. Hyperaware of my own privilege and flustered, I withdrew from myself. I saw myself as glaringly white, an entitled woman sociology professor, my cultural differences unrelatable to my students.

As I was taking myself through these paces, one of my students, Kiana, raised her hand. "I want to tell you something about this book," she said. "It's amazing to me that now I care about horseshoe crabs. I loved how you explained how hard it is when we get so wrapped up in being human that we don't consider other animals. And I really loved this footnote about *Our Town*." She described playing Emily in a performance of *Our Town* for families and guests at the prison. Wilder's description of the ephemeral nature of moments and consciousness created an epiphany for her and strengthened her conviction that we must care for horseshoe crabs.

Astonished, I started to cry. "Don't be starting that, Lisa Jean," Kiana laughed as her own tears fell.

Sitting back on the desk, I nodded my head at Kiana. "You know, I really didn't want to have to care about these animals," she continued. "I really didn't. But I see if I don't care about animals, then I'm just never going to really get it. The way we make these boxes to put living things into and then get to use them however we want. We take their blood and don't think about it. We don't care about them. And until we do, we can't really care about ourselves," she sighed.

Stratified statuses can prevent us from feeling solidarity with others outside our status. But Kiana was able to break through the hierarchy and see her shared struggle with a nonhuman animal. Thanks to her empathy and compassion for another being, she was able to question the **power structure** and **exploitation** of others. We both cried from the intensity of realizing how stratification has allowed horseshoe crabs to be tortured and incarcerated people to be mistreated.

Kiana's profound connection to the text and to Wilder's play in particular broke down my negative self-talk. I snapped out of it enough to facilitate a productive class discussion. I shared with the students how stratified rankings of human/nonhuman, Black/white, and rich/poor can give rise to structures—the prison industrial complex, the medical industrial complex, agribusiness—that reinforce these rankings while justifying the inhumane treatment of all life.

As I drove home, I played out the class in my head. I entered the classroom thinking about our differences and worrying they would make connection impossible. While there will always be an existential gap between my life and the students' lives, Kiana bridged that gap. The moment was beautiful, proving the lesson I was trying to teach through connection.

I learned that noticing the consciousness of nonhuman animals requires us to recognize and transcend stratification and status. In this transcendence, we can see our shared struggle, and perhaps lay bare the mechanisms of exploitation that maintain hierarchies across species.

KEY CONCEPTS

Exploitation — Exploitation means taking advantage of someone. If a person is paid less than the value of their work, they are being exploited. Consider that the people who make a product and thus produce the actual value for a company are often paid low wages, while the company's CEO might make many millions of dollars in a year, particularly when stock options are taken into account.

Power structure — Social systems have structures that determine who has power and who does not. In a prison, the corrections staff has significantly more power than those who are incarcerated. In a school, teachers have more power than students. A person's place in the power structure can be the result of many systemic factors and their own individual actions. The term can refer to the structure itself (e.g., the system of stratification) and to those with the most power.

Stratification — In its most basic sense, stratification refers to a system of layers; in societies, stratification means layers of inequality. For example, in the class system, layers might include the wealthy, the upper middle class, the middle middle class, the lower middle class, the working poor, and the underclass.

DISCUSSION QUESTIONS

1. Which nonhuman animals do you take for granted in your life? Which do you consider more carefully? What beliefs allow you to make those distinctions?
2. Moore points out that incarceration can be a dehumanizing experience. What beliefs does this dehumanization depend on? How does providing college education in prison work to rehumanize incarcerated students?
3. What lesson is Kiana able to grasp about human connectedness? Why is this such a profound moment for teacher and student?

LEARN MORE

Hoffman, Kelly, Sophie Trawalter, Jordan Axt, and M. Norman Oliver. "Racial Bias in Pain Assessment and Treatment Recommendations, and False Beliefs about Biological Differences between Blacks and Whites." *Proceedings of the National Academy of Sciences of the United States of America* 113, no. 16 (2016): 4296–4301.

Moore, Lisa Jean. *Catch and Release: The Enduring, Yet Vulnerable, Horseshoe Crab*. New York: NYU Press, 2017.

Szlekovics, Monica. "Cultivating Community: Grass Roots Organization Brought College to Bedford." *The Monitor*. Marymount Manhattan College, May 11, 2015.

Lisa Jean Moore is a medical sociologist and SUNY Distinguished Professor of Sociology and Gender Studies in the School of Natural and Social Sciences at Purchase College, SUNY. She is also an adjunct professor in the Bedford Hills College Program through Marymount College. Her books include an ethnography of honeybees, *Buzz: Urban Beekeeping and the Power of the Bee* (NYU Press, 2013), coauthored with Mary Kosut, and *Catch and Release: The Enduring, Yet Vulnerable, Horseshoe Crab* (NYU, 2018), which examines the interspecies relationships between humans and *Limulus polyphemus* (Atlantic horseshoe crabs). Most recently, Moore published *Our Transgenic Future: Spider Goats, Genetic Modification, and the Will to Change Nature* (NYU, 2022), which investigates the creation of spider goats, a genetically modified species that lactates spider silk protein. She lives in Brooklyn, New York, with her family.

43

When Ideology and Empathy Collide

R. Danielle Egan

My mother used to tell a story about me, and she recalled it often. As the story goes, when I was four or five years old, I would walk into my parents' darkened bedroom at naptime and approach my sleeping mother. Placing a fingertip to her eyelid, I would raise it gently and ask, "Are you dead?" My mother, disoriented, would answer, "No, Dani. I am just sleeping." It happened more than once, this searching I did for my mother during her afternoon nap, to see if she was still part of this world.

My mother would tell this story with laughter, but when I entered psychoanalysis, I came to understand that my childhood question was a way of verbalizing what she was struggling with at the time: Could she go on living? She never outwardly expressed to me that she was suicidal, but she struggled with depression and waves of suicidality throughout my childhood. Somehow this question of hers was transmitted to me, though she never meant to do so.

This transmission from person to person, often unwitting, occurs on conscious and unconscious levels. Parents intentionally teach children lessons they believe are important: respect your elders; look both ways before crossing the street; eat your vegetables; work hard in school. But they also transmit a lot of lessons unintentionally. When they show how tired and frustrated they are, they might accidentally convey how hard it is to be a parent. They might teach about substance use and mental illness unwittingly through their own experiences with those issues. They may even teach us about stigma and shame through their attempts to hide what they don't want others to know or their willingness to openly discuss what others won't.

As a sociologist and a psychoanalyst, I find all of this to be familiar territory. We learn culture through the process of socialization. Our parents are a key part of that process, as are our schools, media, peers, and religion. Sociologists point out the ways the **dominant culture** in a country—the one frequently transmitted through mass media, many schools, our political system, and often our families—teaches us many things that aren't true. For example, it teaches us that we rise or fall depending on our own personal merits: that if we work hard and develop our talents, we succeed; and if we're lazy, poor, or addicted to drugs, we fail—and it's our own fault. But sociology is full of research demonstrating that reality is a lot more complicated. There are many structural barriers to success even for those who work hard, particularly if they are starting out low on the socioeconomic ladder.

I have a great deal of empathy for my mother who, at twenty-four, was raising three children under five while managing the unbearable stress of urban poverty and a controlling husband. She was trying to negotiate the messages, feelings, and traumas of her own childhood with little or no support. So, you would think I would have been more understanding when my younger brothers, who grew up in the same household I did, ended up struggling with poverty, addiction, incarceration, and being unhoused.

But it hasn't been that easy.

Over the years, often in conversations with my mother, I have asked, how did things end up like this? How is it that I am here, and my brothers are in various precarious situations, struggling to survive? I am quite aware of how **structural inequality** functions and gets perpetuated. I have written and taught about the legacies and impacts of structural inequities and their racialized, gendered, and classed manifestations for over two decades. Nevertheless, whenever I voiced this question over the phone or in person, I wasn't thinking sociologically or empathetically. When I spoke of my brothers, I ranted. My question was fueled by frustration, anger, obstinacy, and judgmental righteousness. I worked hard while they chose drugs. I achieved, and they were lazy. I bought; they stole. I worked crappy, low-paying jobs until I finished school, so why couldn't they get it together? My question and its accompanying feelings were completely individualized, stripped of structure and an analysis of power, and absent any attention to how often my brothers asked for help in ways that I read as defiance. It is embarrassing to admit this, but it is true.

This is the power of **ideology**. This is the power of culture. My years of study and my understanding of data aside, when faced with my brothers' struggles, all my critical facilities were stripped away, giving way to the parroting of the stories our culture tells about drugs, homelessness, and poverty. It was not until I truly began to interrogate the contradictions between my own knee-jerk reactions and what I actually knew about structures of inequality, social determinants of health, and the ideology of capitalism, gender, poverty, and addiction that I could begin to unpack my own reactions and be with my brothers in a different way.

Culture, pain, and trauma are all transmitted from parent to child and from generation to generation. We can unlearn stories, but that doesn't erase them from our memories. A sociological lens can give us the tools we need to understand that feelings are complex, can be sources of powerful self-understanding, and are shaped by society. A sociological imagination offers the tools to untangle the impacts of ideology and make us more empathetic. It takes an intentional effort to remind ourselves of what we know to be true rather than being guided by false but powerful stories, but this is what we must do to see clearly and act compassionately, whether toward ourselves or those around us.

KEY CONCEPTS

Dominant culture — In any society made up of multiple cultural groups, the dominant culture is the culture of the group with the most power. In the United States, the dominant culture would be the culture of white upper-middle-class Protestants of northern European descent. Egan's feelings about her brother's struggles are shaped by the dominant culture idea that working hard is all it should take to get ahead.

Ideology — An ideology is a set of ideas and beliefs used to justify or explain political and economic systems. For example, the belief in meritocracy—the idea that people who work hard and live virtuous lives will get ahead and that those who don't get ahead have failed in some way—supports the economic system of capitalism by encouraging people to believe that inequality is a matter of personal achievement or failure rather than an outcome of the system itself.

Structural inequality — Structural inequality refers to differences between groups of people that are produced by social systems and institutions. For example, drug addiction will affect poorer people and richer people differently because they have differing access to high-quality healthcare and addiction treatment services, and because of their different likelihoods of being criminalized for drug use.

DISCUSSION QUESTIONS

1. Egan is embarrassed to reveal that she applied stereotypical thinking to her brothers' struggles even though, as a sociologist, she knew better. She attributes this stereotypical thinking to the power of ideology. What ideas do you sometimes hold on to even though you know they aren't accurate? Why do you think those specific ideas are so powerful?
2. Egan asserts that we transmit trauma and pain, just as we transmit culture from one generation to another. Can you identify examples of trauma or pain transmitted generationally by people you know or interact with regularly? How do those transmissions affect your relationships with those people?
3. How can empathy and ideology lead us to better or worse public policy decisions? When you think about politics, how do empathy and ideology influence your position on issues or candidates?

LEARN MORE

Clark, Candace. *Misery and Company: Sympathy in Everyday Life*. Chicago: University of Chicago Press, 1997.

Correspondents of the *New York Times*. *Class Matters*. New York: New York Times Co., 2005.

Lareau, Annette. *Unequal Childhoods: Class, Race, and Family Life*. Oakland: University of California Press, 2011.

MacLeod, Jay. *Ain't No Makin' It: Aspirations and Attainment in a Low-Income Neighborhood*. 3rd ed. New York: Routledge, 2009.

Piketty, Thomas. *Capital and Ideology*. Translated by Arthur Goldhammer. Cambridge, MA: Harvard University Press, 2020.

R. Danielle Egan is a feminist scholar, artist, and psychoanalyst. Egan has published widely and has exhibited paintings in juried shows. In all of her work, she attempts to deconstruct and understand the complex landscape of human emotions and the ways they can, at times, be a manifestation of ideology and, upon reflection, important sources of insight. Egan is the Fuller-Maathai Professor of Gender, Sexuality, and Intersectionality Studies at Connecticut College, where she currently serves as the dean of the faculty. She is also a psychoanalyst in private practice in Stonington, CT. Egan lives in Mystic, CT, with her parenting partner, two kids, and their pup.

44

Firefighting in Barcelona

Gerard Torrats-Espinosa

Becoming a firefighter in Barcelona changed my life and planted the seed of becoming a sociologist. Growing up, I was captivated by stories of the loyalty and self-sacrifice of men and women in uniform. During adolescence, I knew I wanted to become a public servant of some sort, but that path was unclear to me. My parents ran a bicycle shop in Ripoll, Spain, that had been passed down the generations on my dad's side since 1888. None of my family members or friends were motivated by a career in uniform.

I started college in Barcelona the day after the 9/11 attacks, and the Madrid terrorist bombings of March 2004 happened as I was approaching the end of my undergraduate studies in building engineering. These two events had a big impact on me and reinforced my aspiration of serving. After graduating college, I decided to enlist. I spent two years in a special operations team in the Spanish Army. We didn't deploy, but we trained in all elements and environments: parachuting, scuba diving, survival, and more. The bonds I formed with colleagues and officers are some of the strongest I can remember, and I maintain some of them today.

After my contract with the army ended, I sought to have more of an impact on the civilian population. Of all the options I considered, becoming a firefighter turned out to be the perfect fit. It allowed me to continue serving the public at the same time that I was applying technical expertise from my building engineering degree. Architects and engineers are very attractive to urban fire departments because of their knowledge of how buildings and structures behave under fire or potential collapse. So, in September 2007, I entered the firefighting academy.

Being a firefighter in a large city like Barcelona entails a wide range of tasks, from entering buildings engulfed in flames (less often than people think) to extricating passengers trapped in their cars after a crash to rescuing cats from trees (yes, I rescued cats, many times). In between these two extremes lies a large set of tasks that have a marked social and human component. Our certification as emergency medical technicians, combined with tools and skills that gave us rapid access to hard-to-reach spaces, made the fire department a versatile resource that the city used extensively in all sorts of situations. We were called to assist elderly people living alone, prevent suicide attempts, and intervene in domestic violence incidents. Serving the city and its most vulnerable populations in this capacity exposed me to a range of social problems and dynamics to which I had previously been oblivious.

During my first two years in the fire department, I didn't have time to make sense of the marked social aspect of my job. The adrenaline rush that we experienced multiple times a day when sliding down the pole and hopping on the roaring fire truck was not conducive to introspection. Back at the fire station, my time was absorbed with revising and preparing equipment, practicing with gear and internalizing rescue procedures, and dealing with the never-ending jokes and pranks of colleagues. The camaraderie and companionship that these moments created are what I miss the most from that job.

As time went by, I gained perspective and started to see the bigger picture. Suddenly, I became aware of patterns that had escaped me before. I noticed that we were called multiple times a day to the most disadvantaged neighborhoods of the city, but months would go by without any calls from the most affluent areas. This correspondence between the frequency of calls and neighborhood socioeconomic status was notable. Fires, falls by older adults, domestic violence, suicides, severe structural damage in buildings, and gas leaks showed predictable spatial and geographic patterns. Many years later, when I was in graduate school, this all clicked together when I read Robert J. Sampson's book *Great American City: Chicago and the Enduring Neighborhood Effect*. Sampson, a Harvard sociologist, has documented better than anyone how neighborhoods generate and reproduce all sorts of spatial patterns and interdependencies in outcomes such as crime, health problems, and poverty. What I saw as a firefighter made complete sense when viewed through the urban sociology frameworks I learned in graduate school.

Gradually, as a firefighter, I started to refine my sociological instincts without knowing it. I paid attention to the social context that surrounded emergencies and the people affected by them. After we put out a fire, we usually left a team at the site that could quickly respond if the fire resurfaced. If someone had committed suicide, we waited until the investigators and other authorities arrived to certify the death. While waiting, I observed how residents activated their networks in the aftermath of a tragedy. I was struck by how interpersonal ties and networks differed across disadvantaged and affluent neighborhoods. Residents of low-income neighborhoods had very dense and localized social ties. It was common for residents in those neighborhoods to know each other's names and occupations, and even to have each other's apartment keys. In contrast, residents in more affluent neighborhoods rarely knew their neighbors. Yet their weaker connections were more effective at solving problems in the aftermath of emergencies.

Here, too, the sociological theories I would later learn helped make sense of these observations. Sociologists refer to the **networks**, norms, and values that facilitate cooperation within groups as social capital. Just as individuals have social capital, so do communities. Personal networks are a key element of social capital. Mark Granovetter, one of the most influential sociologists of our times, studied the difference between what he called "strong" and "weak" interpersonal ties. In a 1973 study of how individuals changed jobs in a Boston suburb, Granovetter showed that most people found jobs through contacts they saw either rarely or occasionally, illustrating what he called "the strength of weak ties." This is precisely what I saw on the ground: neighbors in affluent areas rarely interacted, but they quickly mobilized resources in emergencies.

Personal networks were vital to some of the people we assisted. We were often called to check on an elderly person living alone whom neighbors suspected needed help. The neighbor who made the call usually met us in front of the building and explained why they had called. From that point onward, the story would evolve into one of two scenarios. Scenario A would be "We called because we haven't seen Maria from Apartment 7 for the past two days, which is very unusual. She is always running around talking to everyone, and we wonder if something happened to her." Scenario B would be "We called because there is a strong smell coming from Apartment 9. We don't know who lives there." We would then proceed to enter the apartment using our harnesses and climbing gear, descending from the window or balcony from the apartment above. In Scenario A, we would find the person lying on the floor, perhaps with a broken hip or femur, but alive. She might have been on the floor for the two days the neighbors hadn't seen her around—cold, hungry, dehydrated. We would transport her to the hospital, and in a few days she would be back at her apartment.

Scenario B unfolded very differently. Upon entering the apartment, the smell the neighbors reported would become unbearable, sometimes to the point that we had to put on the mask and high-pressure tank we used to enter buildings on fire. We all knew what it was: a body in advanced stages of decomposition. Dealing with fatalities was the hardest part of the job. But finding someone who died alone, unnoticed, was even harder to take. I remember one old man who had become trapped when the newspapers, magazines, books, and other objects he had piled from floor to ceiling all through his apartment collapsed on top of him. We found him dead, buried under a pile of newspapers and books. After calls like this one, I couldn't avoid replaying the story of what I imagined had happened.

The social connections that surrounded the person in Scenario A saved her life. And the **social isolation** of the person in Scenario B prevented anyone from noticing his absence until it was too late. Years later, enrolled in a sociology PhD program, I read Eric Klinenberg's book *Heat Wave: A Social Autopsy of Disaster in Chicago*. In it, Klinenberg described how elderly residents who lived alone were least likely to survive the heat wave that hit Chicago in July 1995. While reading it, I was taken back to my years in the fire department, when I witnessed firsthand how social isolation led to the same fatal outcomes.

As time in the fire department went by, I felt the need to understand these social phenomena more deeply and started to read books on sociology and urban planning. I was fascinated by how social scientists studied cities, neighborhoods, and the social dynamics unfolding in them. The more I read, the more I wanted to learn. Eventually, I decided to go back to school. A fellowship from Spain allowed me to study public policy at the Harvard Kennedy School so I could serve the city of Barcelona as a policymaker and try to improve the conditions I'd seen as a firefighter. But in my first year, I took a sociology class on neighborhoods and inequality with Robert Sampson, and I was hooked. Sociology became the clearest framework for making sense of the experiences I had lived as a firefighter.

I now study **urban inequality**, stratification, and how neighborhoods and cities shape people's lives. Conducting social science research on pressing societal issues raises awareness and drives change—although much slower than one would hope. In a sense, this is also a form of public service. While my path to becoming a sociologist was somewhat unconventional, and my interest in the social sciences emerged late, I am proud of the steps I took to get there.

KEY CONCEPTS

Networks — The ties between individuals that connect like a web. We each have a network of friends and family members that make up strong ties of support and solidarity, as well as weaker ties with work and neighborhood acquaintances who can be a source of valuable information. Mark Granovetter's influential 1973 paper "The Strength of Weak Ties" offered the interesting discovery that most people get job opportunities through weak ties.

Social isolation — The state of being where a person does not have regular interactions with others and is not connected to a group or community. Torrats-Espinosa shows us in Scenario B how social isolation can be deadly.

Urban inequality — Urban inequality refers to inequalities between neighborhoods and classes of people in cities. Frequently, cities are divided into neighborhoods that are segregated by class, race, and ethnicity. Torrats-Espinosa points out that those inequalities are associated with different social network patterns and different life chances.

DISCUSSION QUESTIONS

1. What is your emotional reaction to the difference between Scenario A and Scenario B? Is one scenario more likely than the other to occur in your own neighborhood?
2. Torrats-Espinosa explains the difference between Scenario A and Scenario B as related to social organization. If we wanted to create the kind of social organization that prevents the isolation or disconnection of vulnerable people, do you think we need to focus on changing public policy, changing culture, or doing something altogether different?

3. Firefighting and emergency service offered Torrats-Espinosa a chance to see his city from a critical perspective—to observe the impacts of class inequality in ways he hadn't noticed before. This may seem surprising. What other jobs might offer unexpected windows into social life and social structure?

LEARN MORE

Granovetter, Mark. "The Strength of Weak Ties." *American Journal of Sociology* 78, no. 6 (1973): 1360–1380.

Klinenberg, Eric. *Heat Wave: A Social Autopsy of Disaster in Chicago*. Chicago: University of Chicago Press, 2003.

Sampson, R. J. *Great American City: Chicago and the Enduring Neighborhood Effect*. Chicago: University of Chicago Press, 2012.

Gerard Torrats-Espinosa is an assistant professor in sociology at Columbia University and a member of the Data Science Institute. He uses causal inference and machine learning methods to conduct research on urban inequality, violence, and public health. His work has been published in the *American Sociological Review*, *Child Development*, *Demography*, the *Journal of Urban Economics*, the *Proceedings of the National Academy of Sciences*, and *Social Science & Medicine*, among other peer-reviewed journals. Findings from his research have been featured in the *New York Times*, the *Washington Post*, and Bloomberg. He received his PhD in sociology from New York University in 2019, a master's in public policy from the Harvard Kennedy School of Government in 2014, and a BS in engineering from the Polytechnic University of Catalonia in 2004. Before graduate school, he was a firefighter in the Barcelona Fire Department.

Flying Trapeze

Elizabeth Anne Wood

The long metal ladder shakes as I climb. "Keep looking up," I tell my-self. I'm more nervous than I thought I'd be. I'd been looking forward to my first flying trapeze class with much more excitement than fear, but right now I'm afraid.

Hand over hand, one rung at a time, I climb. Is the platform twenty feet up? Thirty feet? Is it getting farther away as I climb? I try not to think about the distance.

"You can grab that," the coach says as my head pops up above the platform she's standing on and I run out of ladder. She points to a half-inch steel cable curved and bolted to the platform. It turns out to be sturdier than it looks. Gripping it, I force myself to let go of the ladder, first with one hand, then the other, as my feet scale the last couple of rungs and I step onto the platform.

"Nice socks," the coach, who I'll call Andy, says. "Come around to my side." She's cheerful, as if standing this high in the air on a tiny platform that feels quite crowded with two people on it is what she does every day for fun. And, in fact, it is. She's a couple of inches shorter than me and probably twenty-five years younger, with short, wavy red-brown hair and freckles. She wears a Trapeze School T-shirt, the sleeves rolled up over her shoulders, and green running shorts. Her arms and legs are lean. She exudes a kind of easy confidence that makes me feel like this terrifying thing I'm doing is really no big deal.

I look at the tiny amount of space between the handrail I'm holding and the edge of the platform. I take a deep breath and step around to her side of the platform before I thank her for the compliment. My socks have cat faces on them. I'm the queen of fun socks, which is handy, because it turns out you have to wear socks during a flying trapeze class. The attention to my socks should draw attention away from my anxiety, awkwardness, and nervousness. At least, that's what I hope.

"How do you feel?" asks Andy. My body is vibrating—shaking might be more accurate—and my heart is pounding. I feel slightly giddy, and I'm not sure whether I want to laugh or throw up. "It's scarier than I thought, but I'm excited," I tell her. "I told myself as long as I could climb the ladder, grab the bar, and jump off the platform, it would be a win. Everything else is extra." She tells me I'm going to do great.

Andy directs me to face the rail I'd used to finish my climb. I hold on to it with both hands as she removes my climbing lines and secures the flying lines to my harness. Then she tells me to keep my left hand on the rail and to stand with all ten toes over the edge of the platform. "Nice wide stance," she tells me. I want to giggle, but I don't, afraid that even that much movement will cause me to fall. But the humor breaks the tension in my body anyway and makes everything that comes next a little bit easier.

Andy is simultaneously holding the back of my harness and using a long metal hook to pull the trapeze bar toward me. She's behind me, so I can't see how she manages this. "Now, lean forward—push your hips forward—and grab the bar," she tells me. This is about as counterintuitive as it gets. My brain can't understand how I'm not just going to fall off, but my body listens, and I push my hips forward and lean out over the empty space to grab the bar with my right hand. I'd been warned it would be heavy. I'd been warned it would make me feel like I was being pulled off the platform. Both of these things turn out to be true.

"Now, left hand on the bar," Andy says. At this point, my brain is switched off, and I'm simply trusting that this woman—smaller than I am, but clearly stronger—is going to keep me from falling. I allow my left hand to release the rail and grab the trapeze. The only thing holding me to the platform is Andy, and somehow she keeps me where I need to be.

The next commands are "Ready" and "Hup." On "Ready," I am to bend my knees. On "Hup," I am to jump off the platform.

Andy calls down to Jess, the coach who is controlling my flying lines from the ground.

"Elizabeth coming with a knee hang!" she says. It's time.

"Ready," says Andy. My knees bend.

"Hup," says Andy.

I take a deep breath, and . . .

*

What am I doing up here, twenty-some feet above the ground, a fifty-year-old professor with short gray hair, flabby upper arms, the beginnings of a perimenopausal paunch, and an overdeveloped aversion to risk? What made me think I could fly on a trapeze in the first place? My only physical exercise comes from fast walking and occasional yoga. I'm no gymnast. I can't even do a pull-up.

The truth is that I need something to help me climb out of a years-long period of deep depression and anxiety connected to my work and my personal life, exacerbated by the pandemic and the state of my nation and the planet. I've been feeling burned out by teaching and chairing a department at an underfunded community college. It's been bad. There have been strings of days when I wake up feeling disappointed to still be on the planet and a lot of other days when I feel angry and helpless. On the better days, I simply feel numb.

As an idealistic twentysomething, I chose to devote my career to community college teaching because of my deeply held belief that everyone, regardless of resources, deserves access to a high-quality education. Now I feel despair when I look at the college's shrinking budget and the increasingly complex needs of our students, and I wonder how we can make things work. Meanwhile, a pandemic is ravaging the world, and people in nations like mine, where vaccines are plentiful, resist taking them, while people in other parts of the world can't get doses. The virus is especially vicious in the communities where our students live, yet vaccine resistance is strong in some of those towns and villages. Farther from home, fires are burning the western United States, while floods are inundating Western Europe. Climate refugees exist on every continent. I feel like the world is falling apart around me.

Yet on an individual level, I have much to be grateful for: my education, financial security, wonderful colleagues, and the many kinds of love that exist in my life. I have a great deal of privilege that comes from structures of inequality I need to help dismantle: capitalism (my financial security comes from a respectable salary and retirement funds invested in the stock market), racism (I'm white with light skin and routinely afforded white privilege), heterosexism (even though I'm queer, I'm married to a man and am often assumed to be straight—a double-edged sword, to be sure). I appear to have it all.

Given these advantages, why do I feel so hopeless and disconnected, like I don't really fit anywhere, and like nothing I do matters? Durkheim called this **anomie**. More than just an individual experience, anomie is a social condition that occurs at times when a society seems to be breaking down. The United States has demonstrated many elements of breakdown in the Internet Age. When large communities can form around the belief that the earth is flat or that vaccines contain tracking devices, and when large groups stage protests and counterprotests because there is no consensus on whose lives matter, it's safe to say that we are in a state where anomie might spread like mold.

If I'm feeling anomie, I'm probably not the only one. Ironically, though, I'm unlikely to feel connected to others who share my experience, as one outcome of anomie is a withdrawal of trust from basic social institutions. It's no accident that Durkheim found that societies with more anomie also had lower levels of **social solidarity** and higher levels of suicide, while societies that had greater levels of solidarity had less anomie and less suicide. Our societies can literally lead us into depression.

I also feel **alienated**, in the Marxist sense: the conditions of my work have separated me from the meaning and joy I used to find in doing it. Twenty years ago, it was easy to think the state valued public higher education, but its willingness to fund it has atrophied. To make up for this loss, administrations strive for greater efficiency, eliminating many elements of the "life of the mind" that draw so many of us to academic work and replacing it with "cogs in a wheel" approaches that rely too heavily on measurable outcomes and contingent, replaceable labor. Faculty like myself have to fight against the sense that we are interchangeable parts.

Most days, instead of fighting, I just want to put my head under the covers and hide.

After struggling with these feelings for a few years, I ultimately did seek therapy, and it is enormously useful. But to survive, I need more than therapy. Understanding sociological ideas like anomie and alienation helps me see that the depression and anxiety I'm feeling are not the fault of my brain itself, but rather are a product of my society. I need to get back to one of the most fundamental lessons of sociology, this discipline that has saved my life so many times. The lesson is that none of us exists alone. We can only learn what it means to be human in the context of societies and cultures, and when our societies and cultures fail us, we can work to change them.

I used to joke that if I could rename my Introduction to Sociology class, I would call it "No, it isn't all up to the individual," because students so often respond to questions about cultural and social influences on their lives by answering, "It's all up to the individual." The larger structures of our society may provide us with advantages or may betray us. The smaller structures of our lives may do the same. But even when we are being betrayed by the society or community or family around us, there are also networks of people, communities, and social structures that support us. It might be a gay bar on the outskirts of a largely conservative and homophobic town. It might be the chosen family that has your back when your family of origin turns you away. It might be the nonprofit organization that funds the childcare program that makes it possible for you to work, or the public library that provides free tutoring that helps you pass the math class you need to advance in school.

For me, it will be a flying trapeze class that helps me remember that there are people, organizations, and cultural practices that can support me and help me heal.

Even though I climb the ladder alone, I am protected by safety lines attached to a harness around my waist. Even though I'm the one who has to ultimately make the leap off the platform, there is a coach beside me and one below, guiding me and protecting me at each step.

And, of course, there is the net.

*

. . . I jump.

As I jump, I remember to listen. Caleb, the coach who gave us beginners our ground training at the start of class, told us that it would be hard to listen for commands while flying because the adrenaline rush would flood our brains, and the excitement might drown out our attention. He emphasized the difference between listening and thinking. "Don't think about what you're doing," he said. "Just do what you're told."

As a person who is routinely responsible for making decisions that affect dozens of faculty and hundreds of students, this comes as a relief. I don't want to think. I just want to do what I'm told.

I fall through the air, allowing gravity and momentum to move my body. The feeling is hard to describe. It's like the first big drop on a roller coaster, but without the roller coaster. It's what I imagine the freefall of a parachute jump to feel like, but suddenly I'm rising again, tracing an arc defined by the cables from which the trapeze hangs.

"Legs up," I hear from below me, just as I reach the top of my swing. This is Jess, who is controlling my flying lines and calling out my moves. Nearly weightless, I pull my legs to my chest and fold them over the bar. "Stay there," I hear from below. I obey. I can't imagine doing anything else. My body, hanging from the trapeze by hands and knees, is falling down to the bottom of the arc and then rising again back toward the platform.

"Hands off," I hear. I let go, letting my body unfold, arching my back and reaching my hands over and behind my head as I swing down and then up again on the opposite side of the arc. I reach that weightless moment again and then feel myself falling back down and then swinging up toward the platform. I am free and unworried, alive in my body and in awe of what is possible.

"Hands on the bar," calls the voice as I reach the top of the arc by the platform. I put my hands back on the bar. "Legs down," the voice calls, and I wiggle my legs over the bar and let them hang as I swing back the other way.

"Hup," calls the voice, and I let go of the bar and drop into the net without any concern about how far beneath me it is. It doesn't matter. I know that it is there, silently protecting me this whole time.

After the freedom of flying, I am surprised by how awkward my movements are as I crawl to the edge of the net, hang my torso over the edge, grab the handholds, and roll out.

"How do you feel?" asks Jess.

My legs are trembling. My hands are shaking. I can barely speak. My smile feels as wide as the arc of the trapeze. "Amazing," I tell her. "This is the best thing I could have ever done for myself."

And it is. This trapeze class has reminded me just how important it is to see that even when we are hurt by the world around us, the only way to find freedom is to find—or build—the structures and networks we need for liberation.

We build the ladders, platforms, and trapezes that carry us into the air. We find the people to hold our lines. We construct the harnesses that hold us and the nets that will catch us when we fall. And none of us does this alone.

KEY CONCEPTS

Alienation — In the Marxist sense, alienation is the experience of feeling separated from the product of your work, the process of your work, the people you work with, and even yourself. For example, a retail worker might feel alienated from the product of their work if they can't afford to buy the clothes they sell in their store. Wood reports feeling alienated from her relatively high-prestige job as a college professor because of the increased pressure to report on student learning rather than to focus on teaching, and because of the increased exploitation of part-time faculty.

Anomie — A concept coined by Emile Durkheim to describe the feeling that many people in rapidly changing societies (or societies with weak social solidarity) have when they feel as if the norms no longer apply or when they feel disconnected from the group.

Social solidarity — Social solidarity refers to strength in a society or group that comes from shared values and practices, or interdependence that binds people together. When communities are characterized by strong social solidarity, they are more likely to have social safety nets and mutual support networks.

DISCUSSION QUESTIONS

1. In what ways are alienation and anomie different from each other? How might each be connected to the experience of depression or anxiety?

2. Wood describes benefiting from systems of inequality that she wants to help dismantle. Do you have any conflicts like this? How do you deal with them?

3. Social structures can be oppressive, but they can also be liberating. Wood asserts that to find freedom, we have to build structures that liberate. What do you think such structures would look like at the community level? At the societal level?

4. Who are the people who hold your lines? What structures help you fly? What nets are there to catch you when you fall?

LEARN MORE

Durkheim, Emile. *On Suicide, with an Introduction by Richard Sennett*. London: Penguin Classics, 2006.

Gaines, Donna. *A Misfit's Manifesto: The Spiritual Journey of a Rock-and-Roll Heart*. New York: Villard Books. 2003.

Karp, David A. *Speaking of Sadness: Depression, Disconnection, and the Meanings of Illness*. Updated and expanded ed. New York: Oxford University Press, 2016.

Tucker, Robert C., ed. "The Economic and Philosophic Manuscripts of 1844 and *The Communist Manifesto*." In *The Marx-Engels Reader*, 2nd ed. New York: W. W. Norton, 1978.

Elizabeth Anne Wood is a SUNY Chancellor's award-winning professor of sociology at Nassau Community College, where she also served as acting dean of instruction. She is also a senior strategist for the Woodhull Freedom Foundation, a nonprofit dedicated to education and public advocacy in support of sexual freedom as a fundamental human right. She's been writing about sex and society since receiving her PhD in sociology from Brandeis University in 1999 for a study of gender, interaction, and power in strip clubs. Her scholarly work has been published in *Journal of Contemporary Ethnography* and *Feminism & Psychology*, and her commentary has been published in *Scientific American, HERS Magazine, Authority Magazine, Men's Health*, and *Elite Daily*. Her radio and podcast appearances include *Culture Shocks, Sex Out Loud, Our Better Half, Carnal Theory, LOA Today*, and *Peepshow Podcast*. Elizabeth's debut memoir, *Bound: A Daughter, a Domme and an End-of-Life Story* (She Writes Press, 2019), explores themes of sexuality, illness, aging, and the dysfunctions of the US healthcare system. When she isn't writing, teaching, or strategizing, you can catch her on the flying trapeze.

Acknowledgments

We'd like to express our heartfelt appreciation to Mollie McFee, our conscientious and gracious editor. We could always count on Mollie for thoughtful feedback and astute guidance.

A big thank-you to Katharine Donato, Amin Ghaziani, LaShawnDa Pittman, and Victoria Pitts-Taylor for their early endorsement of our central premise—that storytelling can be sociological—and for being constant sources of wisdom, support, and inspiration.

We so appreciate Katherine Shonk's superb editing skills; we were fortunate to have such a gifted writer and editor on our team. Also, our most ardent cheerleader, Ella Lindholm-Uzzi, offered a valuable Gen Z perspective on the essays.

Elizabeth would like to offer a special thank-you to Allan Rachlin, her first sociology professor, whose classes changed her life. She is also enormously grateful to her colleagues in the Department of Sociology, Anthropology, and Social Work and the Office of Academic Affairs at Nassau Community College for their encouragement of her work and their confidence in her abilities. Most importantly, she gives thanks to her partner, Will, and her friends and family (whether biological, legal, or chosen) for their deep and abiding love and support.

Marika thanks her mother, Marita, for always role-modeling intellectual passion and curiosity. And she sends a full-hearted shout-out to her husband, Ray, for his unwavering love and encouragement, and to their children—Ella, Jonas, Wini, Beck, and Sofia—who are proud of their mom but also keep things real with their honesty and humor.

Finally, we'd like to express our profound admiration for the sociologists who were willing to shed academic protocol and write their truth. Together, their stories offer revelation, strategies for healing, and the promise of social change—and for this, we are immeasurably grateful.

Index